KIRKUS REVIEWS says:

"This book will likely be red meat for a certain brand of American conservative"

THE

SUCCESSFUL

JIHAD

The Disuniting of the United States

by

P. S. NORAC

THE

SUCCESSFUL

JIHAD

The Disuniting of the United States

by

P. S. Norac

Copyright October 8, 2012

Published by P. S. Norac

www.psnorac.com

Printed by Create Space

jihad

[ji-**hahd**]

noun

any vigorous, emotional crusade for an idea or
principle

Origin:

1865–70; < Arabic *jihād* struggle, strife

Table of Contents

ABOUT THE AUTHORS

P. S. Norac is a husband and wife writing team. Paul and Sandra, having lived through the many changes that have taken place in the seven decades of their lifetime, although never having been politically active, became aware that the democracy and the comfort they had lived under was now being threatened. They began to question how this could have possibly happened and realized that they themselves had failed to live up to the requirements of democracy.

Democracy requires an educated, informed, involved populace. They have gone so far as to say that the populace should actively feel that they are the fourth branch of government: The Executive, Legislative, Judicial and "We the People". This is the point they hope this book will sound down into the hearts of its readers.

Inheriting a love for technical knowledge and application from his father and grandfather, Paul has worked in the technical fields including industrial electronics, radio control, refrigeration, and cryogenics. One of his hobbies was repairing televisions when they were constructed with vacuum tubes.

Paul says: "Having been brought up by my father who instructed me to not exalt any man, including myself, it was natural for me to not be impressed or intimidated by title or rank. Knowing that all men are equal, I felt qualified to challenge any reasoning, using the knowledge and experience of my life.

"Like Mark Twain, I spent decades describing myself as a misanthrope feeling that the history of humanity justified my feelings. There was just not that much good to be found in humanity.

"However, I have evolved: In traveling the United States and seeing people from all areas, I have come to realize that humanity is basically good. The major problem is that they fail to reach out beyond their small circle of life to address themselves to the larger social issues."

Sandra brings to the team literary composition from her love of literature and words inherited from her father who would study the dictionary for the pure pleasure of it.

Looking for a vehicle to generate reasoning, they have constructed these short stories, articles and commentaries to convey their concerns.

This volume is a compilation of new materials as well as previously published writings. They have drawn from a large variety of resources: Plato's *Republic*, Cicero's writings on Natural Law, Nietzsche's *The Will to Power*, Hitler's *Mein Kampf*, material on the Founding Fathers, as well as other sources including the Bible. Referencing the Bible is not to imply divinity; it is For Intellectual Value Only, thus the notation *FIVO* after scriptural references.

PROLOGUE

NEWS BULLETIN

A successful Jihadist attack has once again landed on American soil bringing tragedy and distress to American citizens; some live in fear that the towns their families have lived in for generations will become ghost towns with property values plummeting, wiping out much of their security.

These Jihadists have made it clear that their intent is to use the same methods to afflict anguish on all of America. In the past the Jihadist weapon of choice was to rain terror from the skies by hijacking airplanes. Today's Jihadists are hijacking the environmental movement, attacking the moral structure that has been a vital component of the American way of life, and using race as a divisive tool. By fabricating delusional lies they spread fear of a devastating future.

In 2007 Author James Lovelock predicted Global Warming Doom: "Billions of us will die...."

In 2008, in support of this "delusional lie", we were told that we would have to reduce our personal "carbon footprint"–a completely ridiculous concept– and that due to the necessity of regulations our personal electricity bills would skyrocket. This is the next attack by the Jihadists and it will be felt by all Americans. The claim is that the increased production of carbon dioxide due to industrialization is causing the atmosphere to warm to such a degree that James Lovelock felt compelled to write: "Billions of us will die..."

In 2010, P. S. Norac published the fact that there is not enough carbon dioxide in Earth's atmosphere to be a viable greenhouse gas. Please visit www.psnorac.com for details.

Then on April 24, 2012, James Lovelock reversed himself: "I was 'alarmist' about climate change and so was Al

Gore! The problem is we don't know what the climate is doing.'"

Nevertheless, at the time of this writing, the present administration has disregarded the democratic process that was instituted as a protection for the American people. Having failed legislatively to bring forward these regulations, it is presently using the EPA to enforce them.

To understand the mentality that is driving this Jihad let's look at the observation made by T.S. Elliot in *The Cocktail Party*, edited by London: Faber and Faber, 1974, page 111: "Half the harm that is done in this world is due to people who want to feel important. They don't mean to do harm— but the harm does not interest them. Or they do not see it, or they justify it because they are absorbed in the endless struggle to think well of themselves."

The activity of these Jihadists and the harm that it has brought is certainly liable for criminal action. If justice was the driving force, they should be punished and imprisoned. The harm the Jihadists and those who have been misled by them has brought to the Earth and its citizens makes Bernie Madoff look insignificant. However, understanding T.S. Elliot's sentiment, P.S. Norac chooses to view them as one would a demented uncle who nearly burned down our house.

As is the case with many demented people they find something to focus on that disturbs them. Due to their mental instabilities they begin to view this inconsequential observation as being a monumental threat.

In the sixties and early seventies this Jihadist movement influenced a contemptuous attitude toward the moral structure that existed then as well as focusing on capitalism and the United States as being evil. Although making some accurate observations to justify their hatred of capitalism and industry, they totally disregarded the advantages that have been produced: Individually, take away their cell phone, or some other equally modern necessity, and see if they can honestly deny capitalism's benefits. Capitalism and industry have brought more good to the world than any other form of society.

Barack Obama Sr. spent most of his life as an anti-colonialist. In Barack Obama Jr's. book *Dreams From My Father*, he displays the same anti-colonialism. Barack Obama Jr's. half-brother George makes the observation that of the countries that broke the shackles of colonialism, the countries that maintained the capitalistic structure have benefited and advanced their societies whereas the ones that rejected the capitalistic structure have suffered. The movie "2016: Obama's America" enlightens us to these facts.

We at P. S. Norac reference the saying often: Do not condemn eating when what you mean to condemn is gluttony. If you stand back and look at capitalism objectively you find that it moderates society, allowing individuals so inclined to socially advance themselves. This is something not possible under a Socialist/Communist society.

As people rise to the top, others benefit. A healthy redistribution of wealth results from individuals advancing themselves financially. This is true at all levels of capitalism: from the person running a small hot dog stand to the person running a large franchised chain of restaurants. This is the real wealth redistribution that has proven successful.

In accusing the United States of being evil, let's take a trip to Japan and remind its citizens that they were a conquered nation. Under the rules of war the United States would have had the right to govern and enslave them. Ask them if they can truly deny that the United States is a compassionate and caring nation in light of the fact that they did not enslave this conquered people but spent much effort, monetary and otherwise, to help them reestablish their own national sovereignty.

The Japanese recognized the benevolent nature of this democratic form of rule and have proved to be a strong ally and friend.

However, the conquered nation of Iraq, now freed from a brutal dictator, still views the United States with suspicion and contempt. One of the strong reasons for this is the Jihadist mentality quite similar to the one described above. Fostered by Islamic radicals or social radicals, the mentality is still the same: Hate built on unintelligent reasoning. Both are dangerous.

Take the social radicals and their reasoning. So eager to condemn capitalism and industry they blind themselves into believing absurdities: carbon dioxide is an effective greenhouse gas. So eager are they to support this greenhouse theory that they tried to use trees as evidence of global warming. Also absurd is the statement that they care for the American people while at the same time they are threatening to enforce regulations that even they say will cause personal electric bills to skyrocket. Can a family with a present electric bill of $150 to $200 a month afford to pay $500 to $600?

Passing legislation or regulation created by delusional fabrications that would cause all electric bills to skyrocket is the moral equivalent of dumping sand into the engine of our economy.

As you walk into a large grocery store or any large department store or a mall, observe the thousands of watts of power needed in the lighting alone to sustain these businesses and to light their parking lots in order to keep their customers safe. Now add to that the air conditioning, heating and refrigeration that are all high energy consumers. Consider the food processing plants with their large energy consumption; and the manufacturing plants with their huge demand for energy.

There is no facet of our economy that is not going to be affected by these rising electric costs. How will this additional cost be met? We the consumer – not only will we be paying more just to heat and cool our homes, but prices for food to feed our families and clothes to clothe our children are also going to rise dramatically.

To add insult to injury, all this is needless: constructed on fabricated lies.

We regularly hear Democrats say "I'm a Democrat, but I'm not that type of Democrat." Or a Liberal says, "I'm a Liberal, but I'm not that type of Liberal." This testifies that many people are recognizing the potential danger.

It is time for all people to intervene and not let these jihadists continue to carry out this attack on American soil. This must be addressed before it is too late. It is the responsibility of being a citizen.

The liberal movement in the 1960s brought forth such noble actions in defense of racial minorities. Where is the defense in behalf of the coal miners today who are losing their jobs needlessly because of regulations based on lies? Where is the defense of the American public whose financial security is being threatened?

Unfortunately, we Americans have proved to be negligent. The Indian Removal Act was passed and the American public said very little.

This is exactly what the Founding Fathers were afraid of: That the populace would not take the responsibility needed to support democracy. These facts are critical to the survival of our democracy.

INTRODUCTION

The Need to be Alert

Upon leaving Independence Hall after the Constitutional Convention in Philadelphia on September 18, 1787, Benjamin Franklin was asked by a lady, "Well, Doctor, what have we got a republic or a monarchy?" To which he responded, "A republic, madam - if you can keep it." Benjamin Franklin was very aware that it would be the responsibility of the populace to maintain this new democratic republic.

There is strong evidence that "we the people" have failed. We have failed to keep the power brokers and the politicians from bringing our country and our communities to near ruin. As an example, our communities that are now paying their fire department employees three times the average household income in their communities, allowing them to retire at 50 years of age and receiving extraordinarily high pensions. Thousands of coal miners are losing their jobs because of fabricated environmental concerns. These are only some of the threats to our democracy.

We should not kid ourselves: the cold war is not over: The Russians do not like us. The Chinese do not like us. Many Eastern regimes do not like us. Our demise would give them great satisfaction.

The United States has become unquestionably the most powerful nation on earth. However, let's not forget the lessons of history:

The city of ancient Babylon was also a very powerful nation. It was perceived to be unconquerable and infallible. Its gigantic walls extended out to encompass an area large enough that even if the city came under siege it could maintain itself indefinitely with its agriculture and other means of sustenance. Part of its fortification was the use of the mighty Euphrates River, which flowed beneath its walls. Relying on these walls, including the metal gates at the in-flow and out-flows deep in the Euphrates River, Babylon did not take the threat of the Persian army seriously. As a result, while the city was celebrating the feast of King Belshazzar, confident behind their perceived impenetrable walls and relying on the depth of the Euphrates to prevent any underwater entrance, they let their guard down and gave themselves up to the celebrations.

Undetected, upstream, Cyrus the Persian had the waters of the Euphrates diverted, causing the river to lower or dry up, draining away one of Babylon's vital defenses, allowing the Persian army to follow the riverbed. Marching unencumbered under the now ineffective metal gates, the Persians capture the outlying areas and eventually the inner city. History reveals that the Persians were unusually cruel to the captive Babylonians.

This is an example of people not properly perceiving the seriousness of some threats.

Arthur Neville Chamberlain, Prime Minister of the United Kingdom, tried to appease Hitler rather than identifying the seriousness of the threat. Osama Bin Laden openly declared war on capitalism and the United States. 9/11 demonstrates the need to take all threats seriously.

In 1969 the Weather Underground Organization was formed. Their mission was "to create a clandestine revolutionary party for the violent overthrow of the US government." (Wikipedia, Weather Underground)

An FBI agent successfully infiltrated the ranks of the Weather Underground and his report is chilling. When he asked what their goal was it was evident that they had no real plan except to overthrow the government. Further questioning resulted in a very disturbing response: they expected other countries, such as Vietnam or Russia, to take dominion over sections of the United States. But it didn't stop there. When asked what action would be taken if there was resistance the answer was: education compounds in the southwest to reeducate the populace with the new thinking. And finally, if the populace still didn't respond? They would have to be eliminated: Killed.

The estimate was that approximately 25,000,000 Americans would have to be killed.

We at P. S. Norac grew up in the '40s and '50s. We didn't realize that this type of hatred generated by the Weather Underground still existed until we heard the words expressed by a prominent minister: "G.D. America". Our investigation revealed that this hatred has grown like a toxic weed in some of our universities and churches.

Harvey C. Mansfield Jr., a Professor of Government at Harvard University, made the observation, in an interview with Peter Robinson on Uncommon Knowledge in September, 2010, that in the late sixties the New Left took over from Liberalism. During this "take over", the protesting youth took over the universities, pushing everybody to the New Left.

In the motivation of this New Left came a contempt for the United States, its industry, and capitalism. This helps us understand the following statement: In 1971, Eric Hoffer, an American social writer who was awarded the Presidential Medal of Freedom in February, 1983, wrote in *First Things, Last Things*, page 71: "Nowhere at present is there such a measureless loathing of their country by educated people as in America."

How much more applicable that statement is today! We at present hear reports of the Wall Street Occupiers saying that America is worse than Al Qaeda; and reports that some schools will not allow Lee Greenwood's song – "Proud to Be An American" -- to be sung. This reflects the attitude of the Weather Underground in their sentiment that the United

States government should be overthrown. Ask yourself: With the collapse of Democracy, *Where Would Liberty Live?*

The question is: How did this contempt for the United States and its people grow? History has testified that humanity's emotions can cause people to act in ways that negate all reason. Individuals seeking power have used this tactic to gain control. Hitler is said to have choreographed his gestures for the highest emotional impact. Charles Manson used an emotional appeal to develop a murderous contempt for the wealthy.

So it is with the radicals that started their quest in 1969: these Jihadists have used emotional hatred with surprising success to further their agenda to bring harm to the United States and drain away its defenses as the Persians did to Ancient Babylon. Let's not be ignorant of their intent. In a You Tube video entitled "Emergency: Warning to all U.S. Citizens" the Weather Underground is described as dedicated revolutionaries "working to exploit our weaknesses for the ultimate destruction of the United States system of government as we know it." As William Ayers, a leader of the Weather Underground, stated "Whatever it costs, whatever destructive activity we can do against the United States government the better." Although the Weather Underground no longer exists, technically, its presence is still felt as a shadow influence in many of our centers of higher learning.

Let's take time to review some of their attempts to bring harm to the United States.

Throughout the United States we have fisheries maintained to support the fish population and prevent the extinction of some species. And yet, on June 16, 2007, Western Farm Press reported: "Delta smelt shuts down major water supply: All it took was a sparse population of minnow-like smelt and two days for state and federal water contractors to turn off the drinking and irrigation water spigots for 25 million Californians and almost 1 million acres of farmland." Once when driving through this area I saw a sign from farmers stating that this type of regulation was causing the dust bowl conditions I was seeing. Can we say these radicals have not caused harm? What would your answer be if you were a resident of the area?

In 1973, Sandra and I had a small piece of land in southwestern New York which was surrounded by an oil lease where small contractors were pumping oil and delivering it to the local refinery. Those of us who lived through this era remember that 1973 was the year of the Oil Embargo by OPEC. To accommodate the need created by the oil embargo these small contractors began drilling more wells. There was such a sense of urgency and patriotism on the part of these lease operators knowing that their endeavors were contributing to the security of the country. They were putting in wells so fast it created a shortage of pipe to use for casings.

When the oil embargo ceased these contractors found themselves in a dilemma: the environmentalists, through the EPA, required that these contractors pour cement into these wells if they were not pumping regularly. Because oil was being received from OPEC there was no longer a market for the oil from these small wells. Following the regulations these now had to be filled with cement rendering them useless for any future production: all the investment, monetary and otherwise, was now obsolete. If the crisis were to return new wells would have to be drilled. It was the consensus of many that the environmental concerns could easily have been met without the destruction of these wells. Can we say that these racicals have not been successful in their Jihad?

Because of these environmental fabrications it makes it too expensive for these small oil-lease operators to make a profit. As a result, we get close to 40% of our oil from non-domestic sources. The money that Americans spend on foreign oil, if redirected to our domestic oil production, would contribute to half a trillion dollars circulating in our economy. Can you say that these Jihadists have not been successful?

Radicals have successfully used the environment as a tool for their Jihad against the United States and its people. Like the Islamic Jihadists they have become highly polarized, denying sound reasoning.

We have also had much "junk" science that has generated a great deal of fear and financial loss. As an example: In January, 2013, John Stossel ran a piece demonstrating how the news media have used this "junk" science to advantage themselves. The saying became quite common in news outlets: If it bleeds, it leads. They were using this type of sensationalism to keep their ratings up.

Don't get us wrong: The Love Canal was real. Rachel Carson's *Silent Spring* was real. These were sensational news events, but they were built on reality, not just a marketing technique to make money. It becomes very difficult for the public to differentiate between real science and "junk" science.

Let us repeat: Radicals have used the environment as a tool for their Jihad against the United States and its people. Like the Islamic Jihadists they have become highly polarized, denying sound reasoning.

The article, "'Ozone Hole' Hoax Was The Preview For 'Global Warming' Hoax", published by Tarpon's Swamp, states:

Dr. Wil Happer of Princeton wrote "The Montreal protocol to ban Freons was the warm-up exercise for the IPCC. Many current IPCC players gained fame then by stampeding the US Congress into supporting the Montreal protocol. They learned to use dramatized, phony scientific claims . . ."

The Ozone Hoax is a mere inconvenience in comparison to what is being played out on the world today. The environmental approach to ozone today is as weak as the reasoning on carbon dioxide: It doesn't take a great deal of intelligence or education to realize that those claiming carbon dioxide is an effective greenhouse gas are either fraudulent or ignorant.

We feel you will really enjoy the articles "It's Really Simple I" and "It's Really Simple II" published later in this book as well as on our website www.psnorac.com.

In line with our MO to write short stories to help people to reason, we have written the story of Joe Ellingworth, published later in this book, which we invite you to read. Also, the story of Bill Allen that demonstrates the poor reasoning of the greenhouse gas advocates: There are too many variables to use trees to determine temperature.

In our article *Intellectual Power*, published later in this book, we state that there are many highly educated individuals who cannot make application of the knowledge they have. In fact, they do not see things with a comprehensive mind. So it is understandable that they do not see the danger that depleting the atmosphere of necessary carbon dioxide poses, as Leighton Stewart testified before congress.

This same type of mentality, lacking comprehensiveness, also fails to set proper priorities when confronting responsibility. As an example, when given the responsibility of taking over a nation that is going through dramatic economic problems, rather than setting priories, these individuals energetically address themselves to their own agenda, trying to pass Cap and Trade legislation. This legislation did not pass because many of the legislators had doubts. However, restriction on carbon dioxide continues to be pursued. Coal fired plants are being shut down. Thousands of coal miners in West Virginia are now out of work. Can it honestly be said that these individuals are not bringing harm to the United States?

However this legislation should not even have become a priority. First of all because it is built on false science; but even if the science were true, the seriousness and the negative effects are decades away; the economy should have been the priority. If you found yourself overwhelmed in debt, you would address your means to the immediate bills that were threatening your financial security, not those that would come due decades later. It would be irresponsible to do otherwise. This only supports our statement of a lack of comprehensiveness.

There are thousands of miles of pipeline in the United States being run safely and effectively. And yet, the Jihadists, using again environmental concerns, have effectively blocked the Keystone Pipeline, denying Americans the benefit of these jobs. At the expense of being repetitive, this also results in economic harm to the United States.

THE INVASION OF THE SUPERCILIOUS

The dictionary describes the word "supercilious" as an adjective meaning "haughtily disdainful" or "contemptuous." The synonyms are "arrogant" and "scornful". Although the word "supercilious" is technically an adjective, in this article we have chosen to use it as a noun to identify the individual who so strongly manifests this trait he becomes the personification of the word.

The Supercilious view their lives as existing above the rim of humanity and the masses as vulgar. They are also plagued by a narrow bandwidth of reasoning that places themselves as the center of all things existing. They fortify themselves with a manic narcissism that creates a delusional view of the world and themselves as being important.

Throughout the history of the world the Supercilious have been a burden that humanity has endured. Many of them have succeeded in gaining influential positions, convincing themselves and others that they are a superior being having a higher intellect that entitles them. They don't even suspect that they are mentally deficient because of their narrow bandwidth of reasoning.

They maintain their esteemed position by attempting to keep the masses ignorant, as the ancient Babylonians have been recorded as doing. As a result they have adorned themselves with undue honor, convincing the masses of their right to this elite position.

This is reflected in the Biblical account of Jesus telling his disciples how difficult it would be for a rich man to enter the kingdom of heaven: Jesus said it would be easier for a camel to get through the eye of a needle than for a rich man to get into the kingdom of heaven. Hearing this the disciples exclaimed: Who then can be saved? (Matthew 19; Mark 10; Luke 18 – *FIVO*) It is quite evident that the Supercilious had convinced the masses of their superior being.

However, the masses have not always accepted these absurdities. As a result, folklore and stories have been told exposing this fallacy: Little Jack Horner, who stuck his thumb into his pie and pulled out a plumb exclaiming how great a feat this was, was merely a spoof on the Supercilious.

Again, on how the Supercilious were able to influence the masses into believing the absolute ridiculous, we have the story of The Emperor's New Clothes. It took the innocence of a child, not clouded by social priorities, to see the truth.

Enter Bill Grindle and his daughter, Chelsea, a 9th grader.

The Greenhouse Gas advocates were saying that the increased carbon dioxide generated by humans was causing global warming to such an extent that not only the polar bears, but all existence on earth, was being endangered unless something was done immediately to stop this. Yet, on the other hand were scientists saying the global warming trend we were seeing was a natural cycle, not due to man's influence.

Chelsea suggested doing a science project that would help her understand what was being reported in the news media. With her father's help she decided to do a visual comparison of the ratio of carbon dioxide to Earth's total atmosphere. But Chelsea took it one step further: how much of the increase in carbon dioxide that the Greenhouse Gas advocates were saying was causing this global warming was being generated by humans?

Quoting from the correspondence we received from her father, "We weighed how many grains of rice were in a gram then did the math. We went to Wal Mart and bought 8 kilos of rice. We came home and she weighed and measured out, believe it or not, 1,000,000 grains of rice" (representing Earth's atmosphere) "and put them in plastic sandwich bags. They covered the kitchen table. Then she coloured 350 of them with food coloring." (Representing the 350 ppmv of carbon dioxide in Earth's atmosphere.) "She coloured 1½ grains green to represent methane and I think half a grain to represent N20. She then found that about 4% of the 350 ppmv of CO2, caused by humans, was only 14 grains of rice. I had to drive her to school because she couldn't bring all that on the school bus. After her presentation, kids were coming up to her and saying 'that makes more sense', and 'what's the big deal about CO2'."

The facts that Chelsea presented should cause the world to demand an explanation. The Emperor's lack of clothes has been exposed, not by a scientist with a Ph.D., but by a curious 9th grader.

For decades now we have been deceived by the Supercilious whose bandwidth of thinking is so narrow that they would deceive themselves into believing that carbon dioxide is a viable greenhouse gas as well as that they could use trees to determine temperature. There are just too many variables.

The contempt for the United States and its people found fertile soil in the minds of the Supercilious. Thomas Sowell and others have been working for decades to try to make America aware of the danger. His book, *Intellectuals and Society*, and his comments about the intelligentsia, which he also refers to as the self-anointed, describes them as individuals who feel they have such superior intelligence that their reasoning should not be questioned or tested. Many of these are the same individuals that we call the Supercilious.

As previously mentioned, it was In the late sixties that the invasion of the Supercilious began. It invaded the centers of higher learning, indoctrinating and influencing the minds of the students. From this advantage point it soon invaded the media.

We find many individuals who openly say that they supported the activities of the New Left. As John Stossel said,

"I leaned to the left; that's how I got a job in the mainstream media, and then I was mugged by reality." Or as Charles Krauthammer said, "Charles Murray's book, *Losing Ground*, cured me of my Great Society liberalism."

Understanding that the Supercilious have a narrow bandwidth of reasoning is the only explanation of why they view carbon dioxide as a viable greenhouse gas or why they would try to use trees to determine temperature.

IT'S REALLY SIMPLE I

There is not enough carbon dioxide in Earth's atmosphere to be an effective greenhouse gas

In April of 2010 we published the fact that there is not enough carbon dioxide in Earth's atmosphere to be an effective greenhouse gas. We invited anyone to prove us wrong. No one has seriously taken the challenge.

Greenhouse gas advocates have influenced the world to invest massive amounts of money that has threatened the very economy of some countries. In view of the fact that we are being told that regulations need to be enforced, because of carbon dioxide, that will cause our electricity bills to skyrocket – it is estimated that the average family's electric bill will increase by thousands of dollars a year, all of us should demand that these advocates prove P. S. Norac, and all other challengers, wrong! The world deserves it. It is too serious to ignore. Since P. S. Norac describes himself as a simple, hard-iron guy, this should be an easy task.

However, the GHG advocates have successfully shut down all debate. As an example: Physicist Frederick Seitz supported the Global Warming Petition Project. Dr. Seitz was President of the US National Academy of Sciences and of Rockefeller University. He received the National Medal of Science, the Compton Award, the Franklin Medal, and numerous other awards, including honorary doctorates from 32 Universities around the world. There were 31,487 American scientists who signed this petition, including 9,029 with PhD's. These individuals, who were concerned enough to put their names on this petition perceived the science of the GHG advocates to be inaccurate and flawed. Their voice was stifled by the GHG advocates saying that these scientists did not have the proper credentials to address this issue. However, P. S. Norac says that the GHG advocates can be successfully challenged using simple high school science.

In P. S. Norac's story *LARRY*, President Slaughter's father told him, "There are just too damned many educated fools..." Sooner or later in your life you will be confronted with this type of person. They take you into the stratosphere with their lofty reasoning – until you confront them with a simple fact that shatters their delusional fabrication.

A good example of this is the highly educated individuals who present carbon dioxide as a viable greenhouse gas that they say is contributing to global warming. They reason that this can be proven by the width of tree rings, not taking into consideration this simple fact: carbon dioxide is a nutrient needed in photosynthesis, which is necessary to the natural growth of trees. The increase in carbon dioxide, as a nutrient, would in reality be more of a factor in tree growth than the increase in temperature.

The noted geologist, Leighton Steward, a one-time proponent that carbon dioxide was causing global warming, appeared before congress to testify to his concerns that cap and trade legislation could actually hurt the environment. His position was that more, not less, carbon dioxide, a vital nutrient in plant growth, was needed to sustain and expand plant growth. Thousands of studies have shown conclusively that enriching the air with carbon dioxide stimulates the growth and development of nearly all plants. His concerns can be further justified by the fact that carbon dioxide used in photosynthesis is the only way we humans get the oxygen we need.

P. S. Norac writes about the people who touch the earth. The hands-on workers of this world develop a physical awareness of dimension. As an example, in the story *COUSIN EDDY*, Evan was able to size up the field that he was plowing and determine that he could complete the plowing in that day. That was because he understood the language of dimension. Another example is the father of Darren, Darrell and Liberty in the story *WHERE WILL LIBERTY LIVE?*: He was a board sawyer who could look at a log and determine how many board feet of lumber it would produce.

It is understandable that an individual who has spent decades in application of physical dimensions would immediately see an incongruity in the statement that 387 ppm (387 parts per million) of carbon dioxide is having an effect on Earth's atmosphere. This is a 2583-to-1 ratio.

In *Cousin Eddy*, his father and he design a cube 14"x14"x14" in which they could create an atmosphere similar to that of Earth. Of the 2744 cubic inches in the cube's dimension, less that 1 cubic inch would represent carbon dioxide. Now let's understand dimension. In order for carbon dioxide in this cube to raise the entire cube's temperature by 1 calorie, it would have to have the capacity to gather and release 2743 calories of heat. Add to this the fact that carbon dioxide is a poor heat medium: This is a physical impossibility.

From our observations, GHG advocates, in their discussion of tree rings, have failed to reconcile the obvious fact that carbon dioxide is a nutrient needed in the growth of trees. Also, in our observations, they have failed to reconcile the dramatic ratio that exists between the amount of carbon dioxide in Earth's atmosphere compared with Earth's total atmosphere. In reading through their material, the only thing that comes close to an attempt to explain this ratio is when they address themselves to electromagnetic frequencies which we discuss in our story *COUSIN EDDY*. Due to the fact they deliberately falsified information about tree rings, which came to be called "Climate Gate", we have become confused as to whether their neglect to address these two vital issues is out of malice or their lack of soundness of mind.

In line with P. S. Norac's MO of telling short stories to create understanding, let me tell you about Joe Ellingworth:

Joe's company was relocating him to northern Maine. Joe and Jane, his wife, and two young daughters were eager to make this move. They had never lived in a community that had snow. However, they were concerned about being able to tolerate the extreme cold they had heard about. They certainly had been told about the cold.

Arriving in town late on Sunday, they called the potential landlord who owned the house they had located on the Internet. The house showed great potential from the pictures posted and they were excited to see if it met their expectations in reality. They requested a showing the next morning and arranged to meet the owner of the property at 10:30.

As they drove up the long tree-lined drive, the house appeared to support their hopes. They were a few minutes early so they proceeded to walk around the premises. Everything seemed to be positive. However, the owner was forty-five minutes late. They all agreed that things do happen so they moved forward.

The owner, a small, slim man, shook hands all around, introducing himself as Ansel Smith. Immediately they felt there was something strange about this individual. Some of his comments didn't border on reality. However, they continued to inspect the house, room by room, and everything was beautiful.

Joe asked Ansel, "How do you heat this place?"

"You don't have to worry about that," Ansel responded. "I provide all the heat."

"Well, that's very generous," Jane, the family bookkeeper, acknowledged.

Ansel walked into the kitchen, opened a drawer and pulled out a candle. Lighting it he said, "This is all you'll ever need." He motioned to the drawer full of candles. "If you run out I'll get you some more."

Jane looked at Joe. They knew they were "from away", but did they look that gullible?

Now this is an exaggerated example: however, it serves to demonstrate how gullible the greenhouse gas theorists think the public is. There isn't enough heat from that candle, or any number of candles in each room, to heat a house in a northern Maine winter – just as there isn't enough carbon dioxide in Earth's atmosphere to have a serious effect on Earth's temperature.

I am sure you, the reader, are able to understand the dimension between the candle, the size of the house and the ability to heat it. I am hoping that you will understand the dimension between the displacement of carbon dioxide in the atmosphere compared to Earth's entire atmosphere.

IT'S REALLY SIMPLE: There isn't enough carbon dioxide in Earth's atmosphere to be an effective Greenhouse Gas.

IT'S REALLY SIMPLE II

There are too many variables to use trees to determine temperature

We recently received a letter from Bill (last name withheld for privacy). While composing my response a storyline came into mind. As a result let me tell you about Bill Allen:

Bill's family had lived in America for centuries. His family settled here almost one hundred years before the United States was the United States. When the English came to Maine to harvest the virgin forests for needed lumber to build their ships, Bill Allen's family was part of the communities that came into existence to support this industry. It is said that the largest city in Maine, Portland, has one of its main thoroughfares named for this activity: Forest Avenue.

The Allen family fortunes increased from one generation to the next, from a log cabin to a large brick farmhouse. This is where Bill grew up. He inherited this beautiful brick farmhouse, as well as a large parcel of land with virgin timber that had never been cut. This parcel of land had been passed along for generations, untouched, viewed as security against the future possibility that the family would experience financial hard times. As the vicissitudes of life had been kind, the Allen family had never had to cash in this resource. From generation to generation the Allen men had viewed this possession with pride, grooming the trees to assure the best quality of lumber: as another might have pride in possessing, cherishing and caring for a highly valued diamond.

Bill was aging and he knew that his daughters, one a lawyer the other a doctor, did not have the same pride in the trees that he and his ancestors had. As a result he came to the decision to harvest these trees and have the gratification of understanding the true value of his long cherished and protected inheritance.

When the word got out about this virgin lumber being available, the lumber community was abuzz with anticipation about the quality of this timber. Bill was getting offers double and triple what he had originally expected. Then he got a strange call. Steve Watson inquired how old Bill imagined this timber to be. When Bill's answer was "hundreds of years old," Steve became very excited, exclaiming this was "perfect, just what we're looking for." Going on, Steve explained that he was a scientist and wanted to study the growth patterns of these trees. Arrangements were made for the two men to meet.

After the meeting, Bill walked into the house with a big smile on his face. His wife asked, rhetorically, "How did it go?" knowing from his expression that it had gone well. "Well, we're going to have enough firewood for the next few years," was the response.

"You're not going to turn those beautiful trees into firewood!" his wife exclaimed.

Bill grinned. "No, but as the trees are limbed, they'll cut the branches into firewood for us; and we're getting over three times what I had expected per board foot."

"Wow! They must have really wanted those trees."

"Actually they want to study the trees to determine what the temperature had been for the corresponding years," Bill explained. "When they explained what they were doing, I said that didn't make sense. But they were determined and at that price I had no reason to argue." Bill shrugged. "Just between you and me, they're going on a fool's errand."

"But, they must be highly educated to have that backing!" his wife protested.

"Yeah, educated fools," Bill grinned. "You remember about five years ago, that spring it was so cold the apple trees didn't blossom until about two weeks after their normal flowering time? Then the weather turned so hot and dry that we really didn't get much crop that year. Reason would say the trees didn't grow much that year. Even though the average temperature for the year might have been on the high side, the trees wouldn't show it. The temperature around trees is completely conditional to the weather. There is no way that trees can be used to determine temperature; there are just too many variables," Bill concluded.

It is very difficult to know these facts and understand that intelligent, educated people would not be capable of seeing this. In our article *INTELLECTUAL POWER* we bring out the fact that there are highly educated people who do not have a comprehensive mind and that are incapable of bringing a theory to its proper conclusion. In *COUSIN EDDY* we talked about his tendency to take off like a loose wheel, taking on a project with very little preparation and comprehension.

The question I have is: Are the greenhouse gas people being motivated and driven by the extreme left who have expressed their desire to bring harm to capitalism and industry? Or is it simply the lack of soundness of mind? Clearly their advancing the need for further regulation that will cause our electric bills to skyrocket demonstrates a lack of sensitivity for the common man's ability to meet his family budget.

BLIND HATRED

In Helena, Montana I met a black gentleman. We started talking as we sat at the lunch counter. I'm a big man but he was bigger. I asked if he had played any sports. He said he'd played a little football in college. Our conversation drifted from subject to subject. He related to me an experience he had with law enforcement; it was quite negative. Our conversation had been friendly so I felt comfortable asking him if he thought it was racial profiling. He answered quite emphatically, "No, the guy was just an a..hole!" It made me stop and think: How many times is it interpreted as racial profiling when in fact the individual was just not a nice person.

Then he went on: "I can tell you about racial profiling. I was ten years old and lived in Watts when the riots broke out. It was a scary time. When things settled down my family decided to move from that area. We moved to a small town a ways north of Los Angeles. It was a white community; they were kind and friendly and we were happy there. I had many white friends in school. I was truly a minority; the only black kid on the football team. I was big enough to be a presence and was treated with respect; not exalted nor diminished.

"I graduated from high school and had a few semesters in college; as a result I've only gone back to that town occasionally. In the interim something has happened there. On one visit I remember going into a store which I had frequented a lot and knew the owner on a first name basis. He had always encouraged me in my football efforts. He loved football.

"As I walked in the clerk looked at me; I didn't feel the same friendliness I was used to, I felt I was being viewed with suspicion. It made me a little uncomfortable. Then the owner came in from the back room and came toward me, 'Lee, how are you doing? I haven't seen you in a long time.' We shook hands and I felt the old friendship. I returned the gesture and asked how he was doing. He was reluctant. 'Well, things have changed dramatically since you moved away. A lot of people have moved in. It has changed the neighborhood. I've been robbed five times in the last few years. Some of these people are dangerous.' He concluded, 'I'm seriously thinking of closing.'

"What I found out was that a lot of the blacks had moved from Los Angeles into the area. They brought with them their prostitutes, their drugs and their gangs. I realized the racial profiling that I was seeing was not a product of racial hate but a product of racial fear and a protection mechanism. But I knew the people of this community and the old timers treated me the same friendly way they always had."

The truth is, there is racial profiling. But take away the drugs and the violence and the profiling nearly disappears. I have talked to a lot of black men who have lived in highly integrated areas who will testify to the multiracial friendships they have had. It appears to me the strongest source of racial hate comes from individuals who want to use race to disunite "we the people".

Another time in Laredo, Texas I met a Mexican man and as is my nature I generated a conversation. He related to me a number of experiences of his life. He talked about his father, a migrant worker, who had been injured on the job.

The doctor that they were dealing with seemed very cool and indifferent. They felt because of racial prejudice on the doctor's part they were not receiving the attention they needed. They questioned that racial profiling was involved. As time developed and things did not seem to advance to their comfort, they were getting more and more upset.

Then one day they received a letter from an organization that would give them the needed help. The reason this organization was getting in touch with them was because their doctor had taken the time to write an appealing letter on their behalf. How grateful they were for that doctor's concern when, with time, their father was able to walk again.

He commented that from that experience he had learned to wait and not to jump to the conclusion that racial prejudice was involved. Sometimes it is just circumstances.

Arthur Ashe, a prominent black athlete, when viewing the violence that erupted after the Rodney King decision, wrote in his book *Days of Grace*, "I felt sick. That's not us, I thought. That's just not us. It was as if spirits from another planet had come to earth and invaded black bodies. We were once a people of dignity and morality; we wanted the world to be fair to us, and we tried, on the whole, to be fair to the world. Now I was looking at the new order, which is based squarely on revenge, not justice, with morality discarded. Instead of settling on what is right, or just, or moral, the idea is to get even."

The riots that took place in Watts after the Rodney King decision were not spontaneous acts. As in the case of the Weather Underground there are people who are sponsoring hatred against the United States and its people, making their allegations from a racial point of view. Their Jihad was successful in bringing forth the Watts riots.

Their reasoning is as unsound as the Islamic Jihadists and the social Jihadists, trying to paint the American people as racist. The truth is the majority of the American people are too busy investing in their own little circle of life to expend their energy on racial hate.

The central theme of these Jihadists is that white people are evil. They point to the evils of the past to accuse the innocent of today who had no involvement in those evils. To take one segment of the history of one race while neglecting to look at the other races strongly supports the blindness of their hate.

Should the world hate black people because of the genocide carried on by the black men of Africa? Should the world hate the Spanish people because of the evil leveled against Montezuma? Should the world hate the Germans because of Hitler? Should the world hate the Italians because of Mussolini? Should the world hate the Chinese because of Chairman Mao?

To level such hatred against an innocent people is the product of an evil mind and should be recognized as such. There is no justification for bringing retribution to the Chinese people because of Chairman Mao; there is no justification for bringing retribution to the Italian people because of Mussolini; there is no justification for bringing retribution to the German people because of Hitler; there is no justification for bringing retribution against the Spanish people because of the past evil against Montezuma; there is no justification for bringing retribution to black people for the genocide committed by the black men of Africa.

These Jihadists fabricate a malicious doctrine saying that the Bible supports such actions. Using Biblical examples of collective responsibility, they teach the justification of holding any group or collective responsible, disregarding the innocent within these groups.

However, the Christian doctrine is far from that: It clearly states that each man is judged according to his own actions and not his associations. (Revelation 20:12-13 – *FIVO*)

A prominent minister of this theology whose church was in Chicago preached this hate and retribution. Is it any surprise that the black communities of Chicago have the highest black on black murder rate in the whole country? Hatred generates hatred.

COUSIN EDDY TAKES ON GREENHOUSE GASES

I, Paul, intended to inundate you, the reader, with technical data to counteract some of the claims made by the greenhouse gas advocates. (For good technical information click on "Middlebury" in our Greenhouse Gas discussion at www.psnorac.com) My partner, Sandra, pointed out that this might overshadow the critical and vital argument of the carbon dioxide ratio which must be addressed.

In line with our MO we decided to tell the story how Cousin Eddy, whom we introduced in the article *Intellectual Power* at www.psnorac.com, turned his attention to greenhouse gases. Here we will use common sense facts available to all our readers to expose the scam that is being imposed on the entire world.

COUSIN EDDY

TAKES ON

GREENHOUSE GASES

Part I
&
Part II

By

P. S. Norac

Part I

BBRRRNNNG-Rrrrrrap-Rrrrrap-BBRRRNNNNGG-Rrrrrap-Rrrrrap. Eddy was in the tool shed trying to start the chain saw. The door opened and his father walked in.

"What are you doing, Eddy?"

"I'm going to cut down the old oak and measure the tree rings," Eddy responded as he reached to pull the recoil cord again.

"What old oak?"

"The one that sits on the edge of the lawn. We could use the firewood, right?"

"You can't cut that tree, Eddy. My great-great- great-grandfather planted that tree. It's the last of five that he planted at the birth of each of his children. It has great sentimental value for me; I'd like to keep it alive as long as I can." His father paused. "You could find one about the same age in the woodlot. I'll give you a hand if you want. I was going to start cutting firewood for next winter, anyway. How about if we hitch the trailer to the tractor and go up to the woodlot and see what we can find?"

His father nodded toward the chain saw that Eddy was still holding. "You'll have to put fuel in that; I ran it empty last time I used it. Now, tell me about these tree rings?"

Eddy explained, enthusiastically, "Well, the increase of carbon dioxide due to industrialization is causing a greenhouse effect and is raising the temperature of the earth. Scientists say the warming of the atmosphere has caused an increased growth in the size of trees resulting in wider tree rings for those periods."

"I don't know, Eddy. This doesn't make sense." His father was silent as he pondered Eddy's comment. "Let's see if I have this right. You are saying that the earth's temperature has increased and we should see this in the width of the tree rings. I think the first question I have is: Is there any scientific data showing the affects temperature has on a tree's growth? Is there a range of temperatures in which a tree would gain its maximum growth? Are there other factors involved that need to be addressed? In order for tree rings to be an evidence of the temperature of the atmosphere of the globe you would have to remove all the variables that exist in the area of the tree you select to use in this research."

After a moment his father went on, "Let's be honest. This is not practical. It lacks intellectual integrity. The temperature of the air around any selected tree is conditional to the weather systems that exist. Weather patterns have been thought to be cyclical and if this were the case it would immediately negate tree rings as a statement of global temperature.

"Now, Eddy, they are saying that the increase in carbon dioxide is causing global warming resulting in additional growth in trees. Have you taken into consideration that carbon dioxide is one of the nutrients needed in photosynthesis that does contribute to tree growth? Carbon can be as much as 20% of a tree's mass which would mean that the additional carbon in the air could be what's contributing to tree growth and not temperature.

"Honestly, Eddy, using tree rings to establish atmospheric temperature is not very scientific; actually quite juvenile, in my opinion."

"But," Eddy protested, "Some of the top scientists are saying this. They are respected all over the world."

"I hate to tell you this, Eddy, but if you have enough money you can always find a bird that will sing the tune you want to hear."

"But, Dad, there are a lot of people that believe these scientists." Eddy still wasn't convinced.

"Yes, and at one time the majority of the population believed that the world was flat. That didn't make it accurate, did it?"

"Well, we know that *now*. But people aren't that gullible today."

"I don't know, Eddy," his father reasoned, "humanity has always been easily drawn along. That's the reason why the story of the Emperor's New Clothes was contrived. Also, we can't forget that there were a lot of intelligent people in Jonestown who drank the 'kool aid'."

Eddy reached into his back pocket and pulled out an article he had been reading and started reading it out loud: he thought his father would appreciate the technical content. After two or three paragraphs he looked up at his father. He knew that look: he'd seen it many times just before his father would say, "You're missing something, Eddy."

Eddy paused. "I know. I know. If they can't dazzle you with their brilliance they'll baffle you with their 'bull'," he intoned.

To his surprise his father said, "No, I wasn't thinking that. But that's a good point. But what you have here is bovine diarrhea."

Eddy and his father had a good relationship. They were both technocrats, they loved technical information. One of the flaws in their relationship, although both considered it minor, did crop up occasionally: Eddy had the habit of taking off like a loose wheel, making decisions on the slightest of information.

"Well, the four corners?" Eddy asked.

The four corners was an illustration that Eddy's father used frequently. It originated from a conversation that his father had with a Native American Apache woman. Her 91 year old grandmother had illustrated to her that life was like a series of squares and when dealing with a problem you had to understand what was in the four corners of that square before comprehending what was in the middle. Even though initially Eddy resented his father bringing up *the four corners*, he now had come to appreciate the meaning behind the term. So, he started to mull through his mind the facts he already knew in the way his father had trained him to approach a subject.

"Well," Eddy said, "we are really talking about heat transfer. That's what I would put in the first corner. Heat transfer specialists, AC and heat, would begin by calculating the volume of BTUs needed to accomplish a given project." Eddy went on, "But in this case the heat measurement would probably be in calories."

Eddy's father was pleased. He felt he had been successful in teaching his son how to be more analytical.

"In the next corner," Eddy continued, "we'd have to gather the facts of how many calories of heat so-called greenhouse gases can absorb and give back."

Eddy's father was enthusiastic. "Yes, Eddy, consider the ratio that you just read: 387 ppm of carbon dioxide in comparison to the rest of the atmosphere." Eddy's father was really getting into this. He walked to the workbench and began shuffling things around looking for something. Finding what he was looking for, he picked up a small hand held calculator and punched in a few numbers. "That's a 2583-to-1 ratio. That would imply that the greenhouse gases would need a high level of activity absorbing and releasing heat. That sounds pretty questionable to me."

Eddy said, slowly, "Yeah, I'm starting to see what you mean."

"Greenhouse gas is still just a theory; it hasn't been proven," Eddy's father observed. "I think I'd put that into the third corner."

"Yes, and when it comes to theories," Eddy added, "remember what Thomas Jefferson said? 'The moment a person forms a theory his imagination sees in every object only the traits that favor the theory.' Thus one might be blinded by one's own enthusiasm," Eddy concluded.

His father smiled. "And Einstein is attributed to saying: 'If the facts don't fit the theory, change the facts.' That implies that some of the facts could have been tampered with."

"Yeah," Eddy said thoughtfully. "I guess the fourth corner would be how it relates to me and my belief system and how I would use the information."

"I think we're ready to look over that article, now, and see why I felt some of the information was 'bull'." Eddy's father reached for the paper in Eddy's hand and began to scan the page. Locating what he was looking for, he read:

"'It is not possible to state that a certain gas causes an exact percentage of the greenhouse effect. This is because some of the gases absorb and emit radiation at the same frequencies as others, so that the total greenhouse effect is not simply the sum of the influence of each gas.'"

Eddy identified what his father was finding questionable. He burst out, "Why are they talking about frequencies?" He and his father were licensed ham radio operators and very familiar with electromagnetic waves. "It is the calories of heat that are absorbed and given back that need to be considered. Frequencies are not even relevant."

"Yes, although it is very interesting that certain molecules are susceptible to certain frequencies," his father interjected, "the bottom line is how many calories of heat are going to affect the atmosphere."

His father then reread the statement: "'It is not possible to state that a certain gas causes an exact percentage of the greenhouse effect.'" He shook his head. "Where's their thinking? It is no wonder they can't come to a conclusion. They've gone back to looking at tree rings. The real consideration must be how many calories of heat can be absorbed and radiated back into the atmosphere from each of the greenhouse gases. And there is really no reason why this study can't be done. It wouldn't cost millions of dollars like the research on tree rings did. I bet you and I could come up with a way of checking these gases, Eddy."

"I bet we could!" Eddy paused, contemplating. "We'd have to come up with a way to create an atmosphere identical to what we have on Earth in which the sun could have a reaction on the molecules." He and his father both knew they were contemplating some type of glass containment.

"We would have to build a glass cube. That way we could have absolute measurements," Eddy's father commented. Taking the calculator again he punched in some numbers. "If we made this glass cube, representing the earth's atmosphere, 14 inches x 14 inches x 14 inches, the amount of carbon dioxide would be right around one cubic inch, according to the article. We'll have to refine this, but this is the basic idea."

Eddy was catching on. He and his father really did work well together once they got going. "Then we could create an atmosphere in the cube identical to what we have on Earth, subject it to sunlight, and measure the response."

"We'd have to install a port by which we could evacuate the air and introduce gases in their proper proportion." Eddy's father continued. "We'd have to be able to measure the temperature of this atmosphere as well."

"We would need to connect a water column gauge in order to measure the pressure inside the cube," Eddy contributed.

His father interjected, "This would have to be a mechanical water column gauge to avoid any contamination."

Eddy and his father looked at each other, pleased with their idea.

"We could use this cube to test for gases independently, too," Eddy enthused. "This way we could determine how many calories of heat each one of the gases independently absorbs."

"That's far different than their statement that you couldn't determine the proportion that each gas contributed," Eddy's father said with amusement, gesturing with the article he was holding. Eddy nodded in support as his father continued, "After letting the cube collect heat from the sun we would have to put it into a measured container of water and extract and measure the calories."

Eddy picked up his father's line of reasoning: "One calorie of heat is what is required to raise one gram of water one degree Celsius. That should be easy to test with our experiment."

[This is just a brief outline but it serves to refute the statement that it is impossible to determine the exact quantities of each gas's contribution. For more information please send inquiry to Paul@psnorac.com and title inquiry "Glass Cube Experiment".]

Eddy said, "I wonder why they said it was impossible to determine each gas's contribution?"

"Well, as you get older you become a little more cynical," Eddy's father said. "It took me until I was in my early 30's before realizing that not everyone wanted to do what was right. There are some people who conduct their lives with malice and deception.

"By placing that statement in this article it might have been an attempt to derail people from looking into a very important factor, and that is the ratio that exists between the greenhouse gases and the rest of the atmosphere. Dealing with this ratio and presenting it the way they have obscures the fact of their proclamation that it is the increase of slightly over a hundred parts per million of carbon dioxide that has caused the greenhouse effect. This is a mere one per-cent of one per-cent increase. How could such an insignificant amount produce the dramatic effect that they proclaim? This is a proclamation that the atmosphere is so fine-tuned and ecologically sensitive that a ratio of such insignificance would have an effect. This does deny common sense.

"The other thing that bothers me," Eddy's father went on, "is that the political proponents of Cap and Trade have as their supporter's individuals who feel that there was some justification in the attack of 9/11 on the World Trade Center. The Jihadists' attack on the World Trade Center was their statement of opposition to industry and trade. The question is: Is Cap and Trade just an additional attack on the World Trade Center? Any responsible politician voting on Cap and Trade has the responsibility to make sure the greenhouse gas effect is the real thing. This means addressing with certainty the ratio factor: that it could be physically possible that something of such insignificant dimension is in reality having an effect. They really need to ask themselves if they are being influenced by people with Jihadist thinking. For once in their careers, politicians should study the facts and read the bill."

"You're right, Dad," Eddy agreed. "They have to establish the facts so that they are not acting on a mere theory."

"Well, Eddy, I think I'm going to cut some firewood today. Would you like to help me?" His father handed the article back to Eddy.

Eddy threw the paper on the work bench. "Sure. Let's go."

Part II

Leaving the tool shed, Eddy and his father returned to the house. They dumped bottles of water and beverages into the Coleman cooler and filled it with ice. Then, going back to the tool shed they collected the chainsaws, fuel can, axes, and splitting mauls, etc., stowing these on the back of the trailer. Hitching the trailer to the tractor they went to the woodlot.

They had located a fairly large oak and commenced to size it up. Eddy had watched his father and grandfather and was becoming quite knowledgeable. He observed, "I think it has to fall down into that gulley that way," he motioned with his arm.

His father studied it for a minute. "Do you think the wind might work against us trying to go in that direction?"

Eddy agreed that was a factor that needed to be addressed. Sensing the wind, "From what I feel, probably we should aim for just a little left of that gulley."

Eddy's father concurred with this conclusion. They began to prepare the tree, notching it to influence it to fall in the direction chosen. Beginning to make the cut, they noticed that the wind had shifted a little. Being concerned of what affect this might have, they proceeded cutting until they felt it was safe to insert a wedge. Then taking the sledge hammer, they drove the wedge home and the great oak fell to the ground, pretty much on target.

As they looked at the stump, Eddy's father ran his thumb across the tree rings; Eddy knew what he was thinking before he verbalized: "I still think that using tree rings to try to determine atmospheric temperature is not very scientific."

Eddy mimicked his father's gesture. "I think you're right," he nodded.

In short order they had limbed the tree with the chainsaws, cut it into stove lengths, and began splitting their firewood. They enjoyed splitting red oak; it split so clean and easily.

Eddy's father took off his cap and wiped the sweat from his brow. Walking over to the cooler, he took out two ice cold sodas. Eddy paused, watching his father. "Want one?" his father held out a can.

"Yeah, I guess I could use one," Eddy reached for the beverage.

"You know, Eddy, you're really a good kid . . . easy going. That must come from your mother: she's really a much milder personality than I am. I hate to admit it but when I was your age I gave my father a pretty rough time." Regret touched his father's voice. Eddy glanced up at his father's face. There was something in his tone he hadn't heard before. They had a good relationship, all in all, but his father hadn't talked much about the past. That had always been his mom's and Grampa's role.

"You see back then a new social value system was coming into play." His dad went on in a pensive voice. "It attacked the value system that had existed for generations, stressing that it was burdensome and unnecessary. It led young people to believe that their parents were misguided and slaves to a capitalist system that was driven by greed. Young people were encouraged to resist all authority and to challenge the establishment."

His father motioned to a log. "Let's sit down a minute. We're not in any hurry."

Emily and Evan Emerson, Eddy's mom and dad, had been discussing together with great concern the political events taking place in the country. Realizing these events would affect the whole American way of life, with the strongest impact on their children's generation, they felt the need to share their concerns with their kids. They had always encouraged their offspring to be participant thinkers. Others often expressed surprise at the maturity the Emerson children displayed. The children seemed to appreciate the intellectual respect and made an effort to be worthy of it.

The setting and the moment combined with the feeling of camaraderie between them made this seem to be the appropriate time for a father to share his concerns.

"One of the songs that came out of that movement was 'The Dawning of the Age of Aquarius,'" Evan continued once they were settled. "Astrologically, the lyrics of this song are inaccurate; however, the intent was to demonstrate that this new movement was an age of peace. This theme was supported when the 'Flower Children' made the scene. These were generally individuals who resisted responsibility and believed that everyone could do as they pleased with no restrictions.

"I bought into this hook, line, and sinker, but nothing like Jimmy did." Evan's voice held a note of sadness. "My best friend, Jimmy Holbrook, lived in the farm next door, as you probably already know. That's where your grandparents live now. Jimmy grew up on that farm pretty much the way I grew up here. With this new social value system, we both got feeling that farm boys were really abused: they worked way too hard. This new value system preached that working hard for self advancement was a futility and that no one should have to work hard.

"When Jimmy and I viewed our friends in school whose fathers' worked in factories, we realized they didn't have to get up at 4:00 o'clock in the morning and milk the cows and do other farm chores before going to school. We felt this was a gross injustice and I began to think that farming was the worst occupation that one could have." Evan grinned, deprecatingly, "I've grown up some since then but at that time I concluded that my father occupied his life with too much hard work for the questionable return he received and I felt I could do better."

Eddy turned his head to look at his father. "Yeah, you love farming now, don't you?"

"Yes, I really do, but that has a lot to do with your mother, you know," Evan's voice reflected the affection he felt for Eddy's mother. "Which reminds me, she'll be here before we know it. We'd better get the fire going."

It had come to be a family tradition that when Eddy and his father went to the woodlot to cut firewood, Emily and the girls, Edith, Evelyn, and Ellen, would come later for a cookout. Evan began gathering some stones for fire containment while Eddy went to get some seasoned wood from last year's cutting.

When the fire had stabilized the two men sat back down on the log. Eddy gazed into the fire as he asked, as though the conversation hadn't been interrupted, "What did you say to Grampa?"

"As I approached my senior year of high school, I decided that I was going to break free from this life of farming. Even though the farm had been in our family for generations, I wasn't going to buy into it. I was reluctant to approach Grampa, though. It took me months to prepare myself for the confrontation. When I finally went to talk to him, I had in my hand a copy of Thoreau's *Walden Pond*.

"I had marked the passage where Thoreau talked about spending a lifetime pushing the family barn. I hoped my father would understand what this meant: Thoreau was pointing out that parents often dictate what their children would do for a lifetime, and drew sympathy that this was unfair. Even though having a well-established farm with a well-built barn would be an advantage for the son, it might not be what the son wanted to do or what would bring him the greatest pleasure."

.   .   .   .

The day came when I mustered my courage and approached Dad. I pointed out that he worked very hard and individuals working in factories downtown made as much money as he made with much less effort and involvement. Then I brought out about pushing a barn from Walden Pond.

He looked the passage over and to my surprise commented, "There's a good chance you are right, son. But you have to take into consideration a very vital part of working for someone else: basically you are selling yourself as a slave to do as he wills. Now, your mother has said a number of times that I'm too contrary and stubborn to work for someone else. She's probably right. But, I like farming. I know you've looked at this and the hard work that you've done, and I do want to say you have worked hard. But I want you to appreciate the values you've received from this hard work.

"Before you were old enough and big enough to make a good contribution to the farm you had a little pony called Barney. Now let me ask you, how many kids in the school you went to had ponies?"

"Well, Jimmy had a pony," I said after some thought.

"That's pretty much it, though, wasn't it, you and Jimmy?"

"Yeah," I reluctantly admitted.

"Now remember the days when you and Jimmy went riding on your ponies. Did you enjoy that?"

I had to admit that was special. Then Dad said, "And when you got a little older you had a trail bike, both you and Jimmy. You were free to ride it anywhere on our land; that was miles of trails. You didn't have to ask anyone for permission. This was our land. The boys from town who had trail bikes had to get permission to ride on these trails. But this was your land. Didn't this make you feel good?"

Again, I had to admit it did.

"And in winter you had snow mobiles. Now you have to admit that with all the hard work, there were some rewards. Now you have a pickup truck you take to school and use as your own and you fill it up from the fuel tank here on the farm. Yes, you work hard. And to say that you were equitably paid could be questionable. And admittedly I felt that the equity was that you were investing in your future here on the farm. Now I see things might not be the way that I perceived it. But I have to say, in all honesty, I did you no harm. The hard work's been good for you."

. . . .

Eddy's father said, "I have to admit that Grampa's reasoning gave me doubts, however, my nature similar to his, contrary and stubborn, won out and I continued on my path of freeing myself from the farm. After graduation Jimmy and I ended up in college together. Jimmy really bought into this sense of being free of responsibilities. He started neglecting his studies. When I confronted him with it he would comment, 'Take it easy. You're up tight. You've got to learn how to mellow out.' Jimmy's solution to mellowing out came to be smoking a joint.

"Yeah, Grampa called Jimmy a dippy, hippy," Eddy commented.

"Yes," Eddy's father said, "Jimmy's life was sad. He dropped out of college and basically wasted his life.

"I continued in college and met a lovely young lady that was in my Business Administration class. She was different than the other girls. She seemed to be by herself, not a part of any group, certainly not a groupie. Her participation in class impressed me. I could see that she was really intelligent."

. . . .

One day as I entered the cafeteria I noticed her sitting alone, the girl from my Business Administration class. I couldn't help but think how pretty she was and yet she seemed to be very modest. She didn't flaunt her looks like some of the other girls. I liked that. There were other places I could have sat but I asked if I could share her table and she said "Sure," very matter-of-factly, moving her tray to give me room to put mine down. We began to talk about the class we shared, and as the conversation continued our observations and statements seemed to be in sync.

"Where are you from?" Emily asked. I told her that I'd grown up on a Midwest farm. At the mention of the farm her eyes lightened right up. "Evan, you grew up on a farm?" she proclaimed. "You're one of the luckiest people in the world!"

I looked at her to see if she was joking, but she was dead serious. "The fields and the animals; all that space . . . Oh, you were so lucky!" she repeated.

Our conversation up to this point had been intellectually pleasant but now she was excited. Her excitement about her fantasy about farms brought out a certain pride that I hadn't even been aware I had. All of a sudden I found myself supporting her fantasy, relating all the positive experiences, telling her that I was only nine or ten when my dad got me a pony.

"You had a pony? Oh, my, I always wanted a pony." Her eyes sparkled. "Your dad must have really loved you."

Suddenly I saw my father in a completely different light. It was as if I was seeing him through her eyes. She said, "Tell me about your pony. What were the things you did with him?"

"Well," I answered lamely, "I rode him."

"No, you did more than that. Tell me how you felt when you rode him."

Memory flooded back and I recalled long days when Jimmy and I would spend all day on the trails of the farm, stopping to eat the picnic lunch we had packed and drinking from the ice cold springs that dotted the farm. Once started, I couldn't seem to stop. Her responses just kept me remembering one episode after another. Finally, I realized I had been doing most of the talking and a little embarrassed, I smiled sheepishly, "My, I don't know where that came from!"

"Oh, don't apologize . . . I love hearing it."

"You do?" I still couldn't believe she was not putting me on, but there was only genuineness in her voice. I felt good inside. Was it my audience . . . or my memories that I had pushed to the back of my mind: probably a combination of the two. "I guess I like talking about it. Makes me appreciate what I had."

. . . .

"I remember a statement that I heard a number of years ago: Two men looked out from prison bars: one saw the mud; one saw the stars." Eddy's father turned to smile at him. "I guess I was inclined to see the negative side of life and the beautiful thing was your mother saw the stars. I hope, Eddy, you'll find someone who complements your life as well as your mother has complemented mine. In my world her optimism is absolutely beautiful."

Eddy's mother had shared so many of these things with him in private moments as he was growing up. But it was reassuring to hear it from his father.

.   .   .   .

"What about you?" I asked her.

"Oh, I don't have much to say," she responded. "I haven't had much of a life." After a moment she continued, "My father died in an accident when I was very young. My mom was a single parent. She worked hard but wasn't well paid so we lived in subsidized housing when I was in grade school. The conditions were not very good. The neighborhood had its pimps and its prostitutes along with the drug dealers. Mom was very concerned I'd get caught up in that and head in the wrong direction.

"But she continued to work to support us. Some of the other kids in the projects would ask me why Mom went to work because their mothers didn't. We talked about it and Mom explained that it was very vital that you work and support yourself to the best of your ability. She emphasized this was a social responsibility that everyone should accept. Trying to carry this responsibility to the best of her ability gave her a freedom from the despair that seemed to permeate the neighborhood.

"I understood this with more clarity when I heard the song by Johnny Cash, The Man in Black: 'I wear the black for the poor and beaten down, living in the hopeless hungry side of town.' When she wasn't working she devoted all her time to me The theme song of our life was You and Me against the World. I remember her rocking me in an old rocker she had purchased from a thrift store before I was born, singing that song. I almost always repeated the last words, 'I love you Mommy' when she finished." Her eyes were moist with the memory.

"The other thing that my mother did to reassure me that this life that was surrounding us was not what she would have chosen for me," Emily went on, "was to tell me about her life growing up on a farm. She would reflect on the hard work but did not view it as a burden. She would tell me about driving the tractor while her brother and cousins would load the wagon with bales of hay; working with her mother in the vegetable garden; the canning, which seemed to her to be hundreds of jars of vegetables and fruit; preparing meat, beef and pork, for the freezer and sharing that sense of accomplishment when everything was secure for the next year. She wished that I could have that type of life instead of growing up in the projects. This helped me to break free from the hopelessness of the projects.

"When I was sixteen, Mom was recognized for her abilities at work and received a promotion to a managerial position. This enabled us to move into better housing. This move was a breakthrough, confirming my mother's teaching not to give in to hopelessness. But basically, I grew up in the projects."

It finally fell into place and I knew she honestly felt what her mother had told her. "You know, I guess you are right. I was lucky to grow up on the farm."

. . . .

"From then on your mother and I were constant companions." Evan grinned. Eddy grinned in response when he heard his father's next comment. "Most of the time I worked hard at behaving myself but occasionally my contrary stubbornness would show up and we would have an argument. Finally she came up with a statement that would prove me wrong. In line with my contrary stubborn nature I would come up with some demented argument so that I wouldn't have to admit it. Your mother would smile sweetly and say, 'You're wrong.' I was left speechless, with no defense. How many times I remembered my mother doing this with my father and I understood that look of affection. I realized that this woman was too valuable not to have as my wife.

"On one occasion when she smiled and said 'You're wrong' I looked at her and said 'Will you marry me?' Still a little bit upset with my stubbornness, she was caught off guard. She was not prepared for that statement and looked startled. After stumbling for words and pausing for a moment, she realized I was serious. Looking at me with that smile she reserved just for me, she said, 'I think I have to. I might be the only woman that could love you.' I grinned, 'You're probably right.'"

"Listen, Dad," Eddy exclaimed, turning his head. "That sounds like Old John!" Old John was one of the original tractors that the Emerson farm had; these old John Deere tractors had a unique sound of their own. Anyone who had ever heard it would always recognize it.

Evan tilted his head toward the sound. "I wonder why she's bringing Old John?"

Within moments they could hear the sound of Old John cresting the hill. To their surprise on the wagon were Eddy's three sisters and two other figures. It took but a few seconds for them to recognize Sarah, Emily's mother, and Alan, her husband.

Looking at Eddy, his father grinned. "I know why she brought Old John. Gramma Sarah had always bragged how proud she was to be one of the few girls able to start a John Deere with fly-wheel start. I remember the day I showed your mother the combination that required. She was excited and was determined to join her mother in being one of the few women to master the art of starting a fly-wheel start. Knowing your mother, she had to show off to her mother!"

Old John came to a gentle stop. As Emily turned off the ignition the unique sound of the John Deere was silent. Into the silence came the enthusiastic sound of the three girls all talking at once to bring Eddy and their father up to speed on Gramma Sarah and Alan's surprise visit.

Evan hugged all around. He squeezed Emily, playfully, "Hey, were your ears burning? We were just talking about you. I was about to tell Eddy about the first time I met your mother." Evan put his arm around Sarah's shoulders, "Remember that old pickup we showed up in that weekend?"

"I sure do," Sarah laughed, putting her arm around Evan's waist. "It sure was noisy."

Evan grinned sheepishly, wondering if he should explain about the headers and the cherry bomb mufflers that created a minimal back pressure on the exhaust enhancing the power, but he thought twice about it and decided not to go there. But defensively he looked down at his mother-in-law, "Emily assured me that you liked pickups and that it was a natural part of being a farm girl."

"She's right," Sarah hugged her daughter, "pickups and farming go together as natural as breathing."

"I have to admit I was a little nervous about that old truck but you really made me feel welcome." Evan grinned, "In my judgment you tried so hard it almost had the opposite effect."

"I was afraid I'd gone overboard a little," Sarah smiled, reaching to give Evan another hug. "But looking back, I think we've done all right."

"I concur with enthusiasm," Evan returned her hug.

"But then it was time to meet your folks, Evan," Emily picked up the story. "Then I was the one having the jitters."

"You did at that, Emily," Evan said. "I got an entirely different picture of you that weekend . . . only endeared you to me more."

Eddy and his sisters laughed as Emily blushed, remembering. "I was so nervous about meeting your folks."

She turned to the kids, "Your father had told me so much about the farm and I felt inadequate. Even though Gramma had told me all about her life on the farm, I was sure there would be factors that I wouldn't understand and might embarrass myself. Then we drove into the yard and I saw that large brick farmhouse. I couldn't help remember my mother," Emily smiled at her mother, "being so proud to have grown up in one of the architectural masterpieces of the day."

"Those old farmhouses really were masterpieces," Sarah affirmed. "I remember my father and brothers bragging about how the old house was built. It was double-brick with an air space between the two brick walls with pilasters every 12 feet. My brother estimated that it would have had an insulation R-factor of about 12 to 14. This made the old house warm in the winter and cool in the summer." She paused, nostalgically. "I just loved it."

Evan said, "That's just the way our house is built."

"That's the reason I love it so," Emily said softly. "After all of you and Evan's family, the old house is my most prized possession."

Ellen, with her eight-year-old precociousness, said, "When are we going to eat?"

Everyone laughed. "O.K. we can take a hint," Gramma Sarah said. "Ellen's hungry everyone. Let's bring out the food." The buzz of activity filled the camp as the womenfolk set up the picnic, directing the men who had been designated as chefs du jour.

· · · ·

There was an unusual moment of silence after the picnic had been cleared away; Eddy threw a fresh piece of wood on the fire and plopped down on the blanket beside Ellen, affectionately tugging on a pigtail. "Dad was telling me before you guys got here about how he and Mom got together and how she convinced him that farm life was good." Eddy glanced at his grandmother. "I guess you convinced Mom, huh, Gramma Sarah?"

"I guess I did," Sarah smiled at Emily. "I do think farm life is good for children. It teaches them responsibility."

Evan chimed in, "You know, with the movement of the sixties came the message that responsibility was an affliction being put on us by the government and our parents. I bought into that for awhile. But, looking back, I can see that farming helped me understand responsibility. I had always resented the work on the farm, and as I told Eddy this morning, I was not as easy going as he is. My father would assign me a chore to do and I would do it, reluctantly, seeking anything to shirk the responsibility. Any excuse was justifiable in my eyes. Then, I remember the day that I had a breakthrough.

"My dad had leased some land off the Higley Road a few miles from here. He wanted me to get the fields plowed and ready for planting. Each day Mom would pack me a lunch and I would go to a field and work the whole day.

"One day the tractor was running good and I was feeling good. Looking back over what I had plowed a sense of accomplishment seemed to fill me and I was proud of the work I had done. I only had a little bit more to finish and the Higley fields would be all plowed. My nature had been up to that time that I had done my day's work and I'd go home and finish it tomorrow. Surely Dad wouldn't be upset if I went home at quitting time. But that day I had the desire to finish the plowing. I continued.

"It took a little longer than I had estimated and the sun was beginning to set just as I plowed the last furrow. I looked up the road and saw Dad coming in the pickup truck. I was curious why he would be checking up on me. When he got out of the truck there was a look of concern on his face. I realized I had missed supper, which rarely happened. He explained that Mom was worried about me so he had come to make sure I was alright. I saw him looking over the finished field. 'What do you think, Dad?' I asked.

"'That's a man-sized job done, Evan,' he said.

"Dad didn't give compliments lightly. It made me feel special. 'I'm sorry I made you guys worry, but I just wanted to see it finished.' This was when I had a breakthrough about responsibility. It was a vital part of life. It was not an affliction. It just had to be. From that time on I was able to take on responsibility without feeling resentful. This has been a blessing. I've never forgotten that day."

Sarah said softly: "Do you know a good portion of people never learn that lesson?"

"Dad told me to take the pickup back to the house" Evan continued, "and he'd bring the tractor. 'You must be hungry,' he said. When I got home Mom took a plate of food out of the oven where she was keeping it warm for me. I didn't waste too much time washing up that night. I was starved. I don't think I ever appreciated a meal more."

Edith said, "That reminds me of the song, *You're the Reason God Made Oklahoma*. The lyric says, 'All the cowboys down on the Sunset Strip wish they could be like you.' I think what she was saying is that these 'synthetic cowboys' would want to have the character of the Oklahoma farm boy she had left behind. According to the song, he could put in 10 hours on a John Deere tractor, reflecting how farm boys carry responsibility. Many of them have learned Dad's lesson of carrying responsibility with ease." She glanced over at her father who gave her a supportive smile.

Alan joined the conversation. "I was reading P. S. Norac and he says, 'You can't have true freedom without responsibility.' When you take on responsibility you can free yourself from many anguishing situations."

"I think I'm a good example of that," Evelyn piped up, with a grimace. "I haven't done my homework yet this weekend and now I've got to stay up late tonight or get up early in the morning and finish it before going to school. Wish I'd got it done Friday night."

Emily spoke up, "I empathize, Evelyn, I had to learn that lesson, too, didn't I, Mom?" Sarah nodded knowingly. "But," Emily went on, directing the conversation into deeper waters, "By acting responsibly you can avoid a lot of problems: for example, we know how AIDS is spread now so we know how to act responsibly and be free of that devastation."

Ellen interjected in her 8 year-old voice, "If you act responsibly you will be free of an unwanted pregnancy."

A small stunned silence swept the group at such wisdom from a child, causing Ellen to duck her head in embarrassment.

"No, Ellen," Evan spoke quickly into the silence. "That is a very responsible lesson to learn. That's very mature."

Ellen beamed, her embarrassment gone by her father's reassurance.

Evan continued, "I think it's sad that so many young people do not develop a sense of responsibility without going through dramatically hard lessons. The therapy applied to combat drug addiction is centered on the need for being responsible. How much kinder it would have been if they had been taught this lesson while still children and been free of the suffering that drug addiction brings."

"Yes," Emily responded. "The old Chinese proverb says: 'Give a man a fish and you feed him for a day. Teach a man to fish and you feed him for a lifetime.' If you teach your children how to handle responsibility it will serve them for a lifetime."

Sarah nodded. "A sense of responsibility supports virtue and virtue comforts and reassures us; adding to the strength of our moral character."

Evan commented, "This is far different from the movement of the sixties that promoted that responsibility was an affliction. It's shameful that many of the entertainers of this world promote the thought that responsible people are being duped."

"There is another freedom that responsibility brings." Alan paused before saying, "It requires the recognition that responsibility can bring carnal pleasure. This pleasure is not provocative such as eating chocolate or a feeling of felicity; it's more like the comfort of a warm bed. Many people will never understand this freedom or this joy but it is demonstrated in individuals who devote their lives to worthy causes. An example of this is Audrey Hepburn who, although a beloved and honored movie star, was proudest of her work as a devoted humanitarian. She didn't view this as a burden or an affliction, but as a privilege.

"The question is how do we understand this as being freedom?" Alan looked around the group. When no one responded he continued, "I picture it as being free from yourself; free from the tendency that demands that you put yourself first. Once you reach this freedom you can take on dramatic responsibilities or projects. Look at Mother Teresa. She gave up a comfortable life to serve the poor in the slums of Calcutta, India. There are many examples of persons who have been able to put self aside and devote their lives to the care of others.

"This selfless sense of responsibility does have its own reward. This is not easily understood, however, by self-inclined individuals. Consider parents who have born to them a child with disabilities. This responsibility produces a complete transformation of the way they think and live their lives. Starting with a modest acceptance of these unexpected circumstances they find this to be a life transforming experience."

As Alan paused, gathering his thoughts, Edith said soberly, "I was with Gramma and Grampa at Jessie Whitney's funeral." For Alan's benefit, she explained, "Jessie was born with MD, that's Muscular dystrophy," she glanced at Alan who nodded that he understood. "Jessie was in my class. No one expected that he would live even to start school, but he made it into seventh grade. When Gramma and Grampa and I walked up to Jessie's parents Grampa said, 'You did a good job.' They said, 'Yes, we did. Thank you. But Jessie was not a burden, he was a blessing.' 'I know that,' Grampa said, 'perhaps only people who have gone through what you have can truly understand.' Jessie's father said, 'I appreciate your understanding. Thank you.'"

"That's exactly what I was saying, Edith." Alan leaned across and squeezed her hand. "You are a very perceptive young lady."

Edith, looking over at her mother, saw Emily's eyes were moist. But the pride on her face filled Edith with a warm glow.

"The actions that commenced in the sixties," Alan ventured, "were not all bad. I remember when Franklin McCain, Joseph McNeil, Ezell Blair, Jr., and David Richmond sat at that Woolworth's lunch counter. It was February 1, 1960 and segregation hadn't begun to loosen yet in the south, especially there in Greensboro, North Carolina, and these four young men were all black.

"This was unheard of, a black person sitting at a whites-only lunch counter and expecting service: which of course they didn't receive, even though others, whites, were served food and beverages. An elderly white lady had come in for a coffee and doughnut. She looked at McCain in a way that he interpreted as suspicious and disdainful.

"However, when she got up to leave she walked behind him and put her hands on his and McNeil's shoulders, commenting, 'Boys, I am so proud of you. I only regret you didn't do this 10 years ago.'" Alan cleared his throat that had suddenly gone husky with emotion. "I was proud of them, too." Alan cleared his throat again.

"This action created great awareness throughout the country. I was a sophomore in college at the time," Alan remembered. "There was a great stimulus in the student body where I was that something needed to be done. I joined a group that became active in the Civil Rights Movement. I participated in some of the marches and demonstrations side by side with many black students. I also joined the Freedom Rides sponsored by CORE, Congress of Racial Equality, and SNCC, Students Nonviolent Coordinating Committee, which finally proved successful in ending segregation on Interstate bus routes.

"I ended up being one of the Freedom Riders who spent the night in Birmingham, Alabama, May, 19, 1961. When we drove into Birmingham, the bus was harassed by a white mob. We couldn't continue the ride because the driver was so frightened he refused to go any further.

"In the depot, I sat down beside a young sophomore from another college. She and I had talked on the bus and, surrounded by so many strangers, felt a familiarity because of that. We tried to get some sleep but I was way too uptight. She finally fell asleep and when her head slid onto my shoulder I didn't move away but felt good that I could support her so she could get some rest. When she woke up she was emphatically apologetic, reassuring me that she hadn't meant anything by it. That's when we exchanged names: her name was Beverly Schultz. I didn't realize then that she would later become my wife and together we would build a sizable business.

"The next morning, May 20th, we continued on our way. President Kennedy's administration had insisted that Greyhound provide a driver and Governor Patterson reluctantly promised protection from the mobs and snipers on the road between Birmingham and Montgomery. Knowing the potential danger, we commenced our ride. To reduce the success of any sniper activity the bus driver maintained a speed of 90 miles per hour. When we reached the Montgomery city limits the highway patrol abandoned us.

"At the bus station on South Court Street a white mob awaited. The white Freedom Riders were targeted for brutal beatings. As we tried to get away I was following Beverly when I saw a large white man swinging a pipe aimed at her head. I automatically raised my arm in defense and the blow fractured my elbow." Alan raised his left arm to demonstrate the restriction he still had. He smiled reminiscently, "I always teased her that she married me out of gratitude for saving her life. She knew I was teasing, because we really loved each other."

Eyes turned to Gramma Sarah to see how she was handling this revelation of the past. She was smiling at Alan with tenderness and all realized the mature love that Sarah and Alan shared, their past contributing to who they were now, together.

Alan said, "This is part of the reason that I have been in support of the Liberal cause."

"Well, Emily and I have also been in support of the Liberal agenda, in particular the Civil Rights Movement," Evan interjected, "especially when we studied how difficult it was for Presidents Kennedy and Johnson to get the Civil Rights legislation passed."

"There was a common saying in that time period that liberal legislation was being buried in the House Rules Committee: 'Held up in Rules' became the death sentence for much liberal legislation," Emily interrupted. "The House Rules Committee was chaired by Howard W. Smith, a 24-year-political veteran when he inherited that position by the age-old, iron-clad law of seniority. Smith was a dyed-in-the-wool Southern Democratic conservative. He used his position as chair to simply not schedule a hearing on a bill that he didn't like."

Evan broke in with a big grin. "I read how President Kennedy, Vice-President Johnson, and Sam Rayburn, Speaker of the House, manipulated to add three more members, liberals, to the House Rules Committee. It was touch-and-go but the vote passed by five votes, 217 for and 212 against. History reveals that votes were switching even during roll call. The conservative strangle hold was diminished and Liberal legislation began to flow, and Howard Smith himself lost in the 1966 Democratic primary due to Reapportionment, resulting from the Supreme Court's 'one person, one vote' earlier decision."

Emily spoke, "Yes, Evan and I were strong advocates of the Liberal cause for many years, and viewed conservatives as mean-spirited in trying to suppress human rights. Even though we still have a ways to go, we have made progress."

Evelyn looked from her grandmother to Alan and when she spoke her voice was hesitant as though unsure if she should be going where she was going. "I'm sorry, I don't mean to seem precocious or insensitive, and by all means tell me . . . but . . . what happened with your business? And could I ask about Beverly?"

Sarah put her hand on Alan's arm. He looked up into her face as his hand covered hers. He kept his hand on Sarah's as he turned to answer Evelyn, "Well, Beverly was special."

"Yes, she was," Sarah said softly.

Alan squeezed her hand gently, in appreciation for her support, knowing that Sarah understood that Beverly had been the love of his youth, that incomparable first love that comes only once, but no threat to the love that he and Sarah shared.

"Beverly and I got married right out of college. We both had good jobs. However, we were subjected to the wrangling, politics, and posturing that go on in corporate life.

"Then one day Beverly got a call from her father: 'I have a chance to sell the bakeries,' he told her. 'I wanted to run it by you before I make the final decision. Your mother and I have talked it over and it's time to slow down.'

"Beverly asked if there was anything wrong, were they sick. He assured her it was nothing like that, but it was a pretty impressive offer and he felt obligated to at least consider it.

"Beverly had been proud of her folks for having built up a neighborhood landmark from the small business they had inherited from her grandparents. She had fond memories of summers working in that original small establishment, and then the excitement as her folks expanded, adding five other storefront-style bakeries around the city.

"'Talk it over with Alan and let us know what you think,' her father said before ending the call.

"That was a bombshell we hadn't expected to face," Alan said. "As it happened, Beverly and I had been talking about where our life was going and we had to admit that we enjoyed being DINKs – dual income no kids. However, we also knew that we both wanted a family and had been discussing how and where we wanted to bring up our children. Beverly's memories of her happy childhood and the bakeries started to make inroads on our conversation. Beverly pointed out that her folks had not made anywhere near the income that the two of us were making and yet our sentiments seemed to disregard that as a viable factor in this decision. Neither of us needed materialistic recognition. Running our own business would afford us the time for parenting which had been presenting us consternation in relation to our present situation.

"Within a year we had sold our home and were moving 'back home' -- for Beverly, anyway. Her folks worked intrusively hard to make me comfortable. It didn't take long. I enjoyed the physical hard work and the techniques that they had developed through the years to produce a respected, quality product. Beverly was naturally industrious and she found she enjoyed and was good at marketing. She immediately started a distribution of our products to other stores. We had many regular customers throughout the surrounding urban and suburban areas.

"We were really doing well and we considered it the right time to start our family. We found this older home with several bedrooms and lots of land which seemed to fit into that plan. As with all of Beverly's endeavors she approached motherhood full steam ahead, and within six years we had our three girls.

"When our oldest, Peggy, was two and we were expecting Carey an opportunity presented itself. Through the years Beverly's folks had established a good relationship with the local bank. The megabanks hadn't come into our area yet; this type of relationship was commonplace. The day came when Stephen Holmes, the president, stopped by the bakery and said he had something he wanted to talk with us about. We immediately wondered if there was something wrong with our banking affairs, but Beverly was so on top of our finances we weren't really worried. Beverly invited him back to the office while I got us some doughnuts and coffee, still wondering what this was about.

"Stephen started the conversation strangely, 'There's something I want to share with you, but I must ask you to keep it under your hat for awhile. Foster Bakeries is going bankrupt, the numbers can't be denied. They owe our bank millions of dollars. Their company is highly unionized. These contracts are killing the company; it's only a matter of time. Foster as well as the bank has been looking for someone to take over the business and keep it running. Each time we've got a prospective buyer these union contracts have put an end to negotiations. It looks like the business will have to be dismantled, sold in pieces; most of the equipment will probably go for scrap metal price. However, some of that equipment would fit into your operation. I wanted to make you aware of this to see how we could turn this into an advantageous opportunity for all concerned.'

"To make a long story short," Alan interrupted himself, "It worked out that Beverly and I absorbed the Foster operation into the Schultz operation, effectively getting rid of the union. It was a tough go, but Beverly got us contracts with grocery chains which eventually brought our operation up to full speed, 24/7. Admittedly the bank was very instrumental in securing some of these contracts. However, the Schultz name and reputation opened a lot of doors as well.

"It seems surreal, that one moment when Stephen Holmes walked into our small bakery and changed our life's direction so profoundly. We ended up purchasing other operations, similar to the Foster Bakeries, expanding the Schultz Bakeries into a multimillion dollar operation. Then our lives turned upside down," Alan paused.

The others waited while he collected himself.

"Beverly hadn't been feeling well. She kept ignoring it, thinking she was just feeling her age. But, finally she decided to go to the doctor. When she came back she had a very drawn, unnatural look on her face. 'I've got to have tests tomorrow. They think I might have ovarian cancer.' I couldn't accept that. But she said softly, 'These things happen to others. Why should we be exempt?' Through the whole ordeal it was Beverly who gave me the strength to move on. The tests proved positive. They did a complete hysterectomy, but as is so often the case with this disease, it had spread. Her condition was terminal.

"During the last days of her life I couldn't leave her. She pretended to be annoyed by the constant attention, but I knew she would have done the same if the tables had been turned. She knew I was doing it out of devotion, and never failed to appreciate my being there. It was hard on the girls, but she prepared them. Of course it was hardest on Amy. She was just 16 when Beverly lost her fight." Alan's eyes were filled with tears and his voice gruff with emotion.

Everyone shared his sadness.

Alan struggled on, "With Beverly gone running Schultz Bakery just wasn't the same and I think it started to show."

Sarah patted Alan's hand. "I remember that. I was working in the North Avenue factory when Beverly passed away. She was a wonderful person. I had worked my way up to being one of the managers; it was Beverly who had recognized my potential. We all missed her."

"While Beverly was alive running the operation was exciting, but with her gone it became a burden," Alan took up the story. "The girls and I sat down and talked about the future. None of them were really interested in running Schultz Bakery. My oldest daughter had a career planned in dentistry which she was excited about it. My second daughter had been well aware of how hard her mother had worked running the operation and she wasn't ready for that, commenting that she really didn't want to push 'Walden's Barn'. Amy, at sixteen, didn't feel she was old enough to make that decision and had no problem if I decided to sell. So, I pursued that. It wasn't as hard as I had imagined. Beverly and I had apparently done everything right and anyone who was interested would have no trouble finding investors.

"Then I found out how unjust the American tax system is. Everything that Beverly and I had worked for and owned was now subject to massive taxes. We had imagined that the value of our hard work would be passed on to our children. This was far from reality. After consulting with some of the best tax lawyers, my daughters and I still ended up giving over fifty percent of what we had worked so hard for to the government. It wouldn't have been so hard if I had been assured that the government would spend the money as discreetly as Beverly and I would have."

Sarah broke in, "I agree with Alan. There is so much waste in our tax money. It is no wonder that so many try to avoid paying taxes."

"A few years after Beverly died my daughters decided I should be moving on with life. Amy was going to start college and she didn't want me to be alone. They all started suggesting that I start dating again," Alan had to smile at the memory. "I agreed, so they began introducing me to prospective marriage candidates. Some of these were debutantes of society, which I must admit I was the least attracted to.

"Finally, I began to think seriously about finding a partner for the autumn of my life. I remembered that Beverly had introduced me to one of our managers," Alan paused and looked fondly at Sarah, "Sarah. Beverly and Sarah had been very compatible and had got along well in their business endeavors. I recalled Beverly's enthusiasm about Sarah. I began to wonder how I could get in touch with her, or if I should get in touch with her. It took me a few weeks to get my courage up and then I decided to call the factory and ask for her, hoping she was still working there."

"Yes," Sarah laughed, "that was a shock. I couldn't understand when I went to the phone why my old employer was calling me. Then, after a few uncomfortable sentences, it just seemed natural to talk with Alan. And . . . here we are."

Impulsively, Ellen jumped up and ran to her grandmother. Hugging both Sarah and Alan she exclaimed in her eight-year-old manner, "Oh, we are so glad you both are here."

The sun was low in the western sky and the day was cooling rapidly. By silent consent all began to gather the camp stools and other picnic gear to load onto Old John's trailer. Eddy and his father, joined by Alan, loaded the cut wood onto the other trailer.

Sarah, with a grin, walked over to Old John, assured herself that the tractor was in neutral, turned the ignition and set the choke and gave the fly-wheel a spin: 'Putt-putt . . . Putt-putt'. She immediately adjusted the choke and the familiar sound of the John Deere filled the early twilight. A chorus of applause sounded, and Sarah bowed, acknowledging the admiration. Gesturing to Emily to indicate 'it's all yours now', she climbed onto the trailer with the three girls. Alan jumped up beside her, squeezed her knee with a communication of pride, and the procession started homeward.

Through the light beams from the two tractors, the farmhouse came into view. Viewing the old house Emily was filled with a sense of pride. Looking at her mother she saw the same sentiment of pride mingled with affection reflected in her eyes. Both women recognized the value that such a building had for the frontier woman who, having supported her husband in all the pragmatic needs to provide a livelihood and security for their family, finally saw the fruits of her desires and needs being met: this architectural masterpiece, the accumulated progression from the years their forebears had begun in a sod hut . . . each generation advancing forward to this accomplishment.

It being late, the decision was made to unload the trailers in the morning. Evelyn ran upstairs to do her homework. Emily encouraged Ellen, as the youngest, to get ready for bed. Edith decided a shower sounded good and disappeared upstairs. The day had been exhausting, physically and emotionally, for adults as well as young people, and within a short time the lights were out.

.   .   .   .

The day was just breaking. The aroma of coffee awakened Emily. She slipped out of bed without waking Evan. She wasn't surprised to see her mother in the kitchen getting reacquainted with the ancient wood stove. She glanced at the new electric stove and then at her mother's face. "I had to prove to myself that I could still regulate and cook on an old wood stove," Sarah said in response to her daughter's look. "I've got biscuits in the oven, almost ready to come out," she bent to take a peek and closed the latch on the black door. "Not quite . . . couple of more minutes. This wood is perfect!" Sarah praised.

Emily smiled, "Evan and his father take great pride in having the right type of wood for the kitchen stove, well-seasoned and cut and split to the right size. Evan's mother really has that stove down to a science. She's taught me a lot." Emily held her hands over the stove feeling the radiant heat, comforting on this chilly morning. "You seem to be doing pretty good with it, too."

Sarah's smile shone with pride. "Some things you never forget, I guess." She reached for a holder and took out a cookie sheet of golden biscuits. Carefully she placed them in the basket she had prepared with a clean dish towel, wrapping the edges to hold in the warmth and keep the biscuits moist.

On the back of the stove was a gently boiling pot of eggs. On the front burner a large cast iron skillet gave off the delicious aroma of sizzling bacon.

Emily said, turning to leave the kitchen, "Mom, you seem to have everything under control here. I guess I'll get in a shower before the gang wakes up."

Half an hour later when Emily came back into the kitchen she was met with a happy buzz of morning interaction as the family put the last touches of breakfast on the table. Ellen exclaimed, "Here's Mom. Can we eat now?"

"I'm sorry to keep you waiting," Emily hugged her youngest child. "I thought everyone would be a little slow after our workday yesterday." She sat down at one end of the table as Evan pulled his chair out and sat down at the other. The rest of the family took the remaining seats and the meal began. Conversation was scarce for the space of time it took for everyone to get served. Then the usual questions were asked about school and the day's activities.

Glancing up at the kitchen clock Eddy said, "Hey, we better get going or we'll be late. Are you girls ready?" Evelyn and Edith scattered in all directions, gathering up their backpacks and all the paraphernalia teenage girls needed for a Monday morning. With last minute hugs and reassurance that Sarah and Alan would be there when they got home, the three oldest children left the kitchen and soon was heard the roar of the pickup.

Alan glanced at Evan and exchanged male appreciation for the sound. Turning to Ellen, Evan said, "How about you, half-pint? Are you ready for the bus?"

"Don't call me half-pint," Ellen protested good-naturedly.

"Come on, little one," Emily said, pushing her chair back. "I'll walk out with you and get the newspaper." Turning to the other adults, she said, "I'll be right back. Evan, could you see if there's more coffee? I could use another cup."

"Stay where you are, Evan," Sarah motioned, rising, "I'll put on another pot."

By the time Emily returned with the paper Sarah was pouring steaming coffee. She filled Emily's cup as Emily sat down and out of habit opened the paper to see what the stock market was doing.

Evan explained, "She's very good at that. Emily's become an expert on commodities. That's enabled us to know what crops to plant and in what quantities. At first my father was skeptical but he decided to trust her and it has paid off big time. This year we'll plant 6000 acres."

Sarah's eyes widened in surprise, "I had no idea you were that big!"

"Yes," Evan said, "that's the way the market's going, get big or get out. We decided we loved farming enough to learn how to play the game. The men we have working for us are all from farm families. They're good men. They're very supportive." He smiled at Emily proudly, "Emily's education has really paid off. She has excellent business savvy. You know the money's made in the paperwork."

"Do you do it all yourself, dear?" Sarah asked.

"No, I have a couple of girls who come in two days a week each to help with payroll and filing, etc. I'd be going crazy without them."

"Do you plant all one crop?" Alan asked.

"That could be a little risky," Emily answered. "We like to diversify: corn, wheat, sugar beets and some of the other grains. We watch the stock market and make adjustments with that in view."

"That's impressive," Alan nodded with admiration.

Evan said, "Emily insists on a family garden as well. The kids are expected to do their share." He looked over at Sarah, "I think she gets this from you, Sarah." Then after a pause, "But my folks always had a family garden, too."

Sarah said, "You know, I remember being a young girl and the sense of accomplishment when each stage of the crop cycle was finished: preparing the ground, planting, cultivating, and harvesting. Then came the canning, freezing, and preparing the meats." Her eyes glowed, "My, that brings back fond memories."

"Would you like to see our operation?" Emily asked Sarah and Alan.

"Just waiting for you to ask," Alan said, rising from the table. "Let's clean this off first, though."

"Thanks," Emily said, "we'll just put the dishes in the sink. I'll load the dishwasher when we get back. Some different than when you were young, Mom."

"Oh, yes. I've done my share of washing dishes," Sarah laughed.

The group filed out to the family sedan, the two men in front, the ladies in back. Coming to the end of the drive they turned right, bringing the farmhouse into the direct view of where Emily and Sarah were sitting. Sarah sensed and understood the pride that Emily felt for the old house. She reached over and squeezed Emily's hand, understanding clear between them, without the need for words.

Momentarily they came in view of a field that stretched out endlessly toward the horizon. Near the edge of the road one of the farm workers drove a large farm tractor, preparing the ground for planting corn. "That's Frank Johnson there. He's a real nice family guy," Evan pointed out. "Loves farming," he added. "He has strong mechanical skills and during the off season he keeps busy working in our fabricating-repair shop. Think I'll stop and see how it's going."

Emily chimed in, "Yes, I'd like to know how he thinks the soil looks." Emily had a keen interest in making sure the fields had the proper nutrition for the various crops.

As the group approached, the man on the tractor brought it to a stop and waved. He climbed down as they neared. Evan took the initiative, introducing Frank to Alan and Sarah. Frank nodded in recognition and then turned to Emily who had bent to grab a fistful of the prepared soil.

"This looks good, Frank. What do you think?"

"I think we've done well in bringing this soil up to our standards," Frank answered, appreciating Emily's involvement in soil quality.

"Seems like farming has become very scientific," Sarah said.

"It really has," Frank agreed. "Emily has taught us a lot. She's a good example of a contemporary farmer," he grinned.

"Thank goodness for the Internet," Emily retorted. "I've learned so much and have been able to stay up to date on the latest research and techniques."

"The results testify that it has worked," Evan said proudly, looking at his wife. "She's the farmer in the family."

Emily didn't protest with false modesty. She acknowledged that she had found her calling when they took over the farm.

Evan clapped Frank on the shoulder. "We'll let you get back to work."

Frank climbed up on the tractor and as the four others reached the car they heard the tractor come to life as the engine engaged, taking up the burden at hand. Evan glanced back, identifying from the sound that it was running well.

The next few hours were spent viewing the remaining fields in their various stages of cultivation.

"So you have a fabricating and repair shop?" Alan inquired.

"Yes, we do repairs for the local farmers, and naturally for ourselves. Would you like to see it?"

"That would be great," Alan answered.

"We also do some fabricating and specialty engineering," Evan said modestly. He turned the car in the direction of the shop.

Emily said with a smile, "Some?" She looked at Sarah and Alan. "Evan and his father are natural mechanical engineers. This is his passion. At times when he's involved in a project he practically lives in the shop."

"Some of these farmers have good ideas," Evan said. "However, we did get in trouble when some of these ideas were improvements and add-ons to the green/John Deere designs and red/International Harvester designs."

"But after discussions, Green and Red concluded that we weren't much of a threat," Emily laughed, remembering. "It was settled that we had improved their designs; they even adapted some of our ideas."

"My father never had a chance for an education in mechanical engineering like I did," Evan commented, "yet he's a natural. Most likely that's why I had such an interest in it. I didn't tell you everything about that day I had a breakthrough on responsibility. You see, my dad and I had just finished putting together a pickup truck that my grandfather had. My grandfather had worn the engine out and it needed to be rebuilt, but we decided we'd go to the local junk yard to see if we could find a good used engine to put into it. As we wandered around the yard we couldn't find a good engine for a 1953 Ford pickup. This is when the naturalness of a mechanical challenge was demonstrated to me by my father. He said, 'Well, maybe we can make one of these other engines fit.'

"I looked at him inquisitively. He saw my puzzled look and said, 'Some of these newer engines are really better engines. Those old Flathead engines have had their day.'

"I asked, 'Do you think we could do that?'

"'Oh, yeah,' he said unexcitedly, 'with a little bit of time and ingenuity, there's not much we can't do.' His confidence was empowering.

"As he was speaking, a car that had been totaled was being hauled into the salvage area. It was a Chevy convertible. It had been quite a car and drew my interest. Surprisingly my father recognized that I was interested in that car so he didn't hinder me when I walked closer to get a better look. My father followed. I pried the hood open and there was a 409 cubic inch V-8 with a four-barrel carburetor. This engine had quite a reputation, but I wasn't sure that my father knew that. I looked at my father as if to ask if this engine would do.

"He walked up to the car, stuck his head through the broken driver's window, and looked at the speedometer. Straightening up he said, 'That should be a pretty good engine. It only has 30,000 miles on it.'

"Do you think we could make that fit into the old Ford?" I asked with anticipation.

"Dad looked the engine over. 'It might take a shoe horn but I think we can make it work.'

"I was excited. I wish I appreciated my father then as much as I do now.

"During the next few months my father and I found time to get the old truck running. Just the week before the day I talked about as having a breakthrough on responsibility we had it licensed and on the road.

"Some of the driving force behind getting the field done that day was hopefully to have time to drive my pickup truck. I had spent the day imagining taking the old pickup down to the local Dairy Queen where Claudette Coultier worked. I felt she might be impressed by my truck and be willing to go out with me. I had typical teenage hormones and Claudette really moved my chemistry.

"As I had expected, Dad appreciated the hard work I had done and instructed me to take a couple of free days to enjoy the summer. When I got to the Dairy Queen, Claudette hadn't come in to work yet. I sat in the old truck and waited. It wasn't long before a nice Ford convertible drove in. It was David Douglass. His father owned a local factory in town and had bought David this convertible. My stomach sank when I saw Claudette sitting in the seat beside him. He opened the door and stepped out; she slid out under the steering wheel, and reached up to kiss him lightly on the cheek before going in to work her shift.

"I looked at the convertible." Evan grinned. "Then I looked at my '53 Ford pickup. I glanced over at the passenger seat where I had placed a pillow to fill the gap where the mice had pulled the cotton batting away to build their nests. I had to accept reality. There was no chance she was going to be impressed by my pickup. A little bit upset is really an understatement of how I felt; I started the old Ford. I guess you could hear the wheels spinning and dirt flying as I left the yard."

Emily laughed as she explained, "That's the old pickup we came in to visit you, Mom."

"But that was a nice looking old truck," Sarah protested.

"Well, from the time since showing off for Claudette to the time you saw it, I had put a good paint job on it and had done a lot of dressing up," Evan explained. Turning to Alan he said, "I also put on headers with a minimal back pressure exhaust system with stacks behind the cab."

"Yeah, minimal back pressure exhaust . . . that was noisy," Emily interjected. "The entire campus knew Evan as the guy with the truck."

"The first time Emily and I talked she made that statement: 'Yeah, you're the guy with the truck.' I thought the interest was going to be dead before it began." Evan said sheepishly.

"Well, Mom had told me that farm boys liked machinery," Emily smiled. "I guess I was a little prepared that if I had an interest in a farm boy I would have to accept this fact." Emily looked at Evan with a twinkle in her eye. "I remember when the Dean called you into his office because there had been complaints that the windows in the classrooms rattled when you left campus."

Evan smiled, unapologetically. He really had loved that truck. "I toned it down after that," he laughed ". . . some."

"I'm surprised that your father would let you have something that powerful," Sarah said.

"Ditto," Emily said.

"However," Evan interjected, "when we got it running my father pointed out that the speedometer only went up to 80 miles an hour. If I drove it any faster and ruined the speedometer he'd take the keys away. There's a story about that, too.

"One cold morning the speedometer was making an awful noise and reading all over the place and I was afraid it was going to break and Dad would take the truck away from me. That evening when I got home I was eager to explain what had happened that morning. He never said a word, but after supper he said, 'Let's go take a look at that truck of yours.'

"He had me jack it up and put it on stands and instructed me to pull the speedometer cable off the transmission. At the same time he removed the cable from the speedometer. He pulled the cable out and it was a mess. He told me to clean the cable and went out to get a little diesel fuel and poured it into the speedometer housing. Taking an air gun he blew air down into the housing and it was surprising the amount of debris that came out. We lubricated the cable and reassembled it. That was the last time it gave me any problems.

"As I reflect back I really had a special dad, even though he could be cantankerous and difficult."

Stopping the car in front of the large Butler building, the four went into the shop. The sounds of activity: grinder's grinding, lathes turning, impact wrenches assembling and disassembling equipment, assailed their ears.

Evan led the way and Alan was impressed with the size of the operation and the potential this represented. Evan's father approached and recognizing Sarah gave her an affectionate hug. Sarah turned to introduce Alan to Sam who shook his hand firmly.

"You have quite an operation here," Alan said.

"Yes," Sam acknowledged. "Evan's put a lot of work into it. I've helped some. It hasn't been easy."

Emily couldn't help but feel grateful that Sam was giving such credit to Evan. She knew that the father and son relationship had been tested through the years.

Evan, with gratitude, said, "It couldn't have been done without Dad's help."

Looking at her watch, Emily announced, "Wow! I hadn't realized it was so late. The kids will be home from school in a few minutes. I hate to cut this short, but I think we better get back to the house."

. . . .

As they walked into the house, the aroma of the chicken they had put in the slow-cooker that morning greeted them. Sarah started peeling potatoes as Emily took out a quart of corn canned last fall and reached into the cupboard for the stuffing mix.

The guys asked if they could help. Emily directed to Evan, "If you want to load the dishwasher that would sure help."

"Sure I can do that," he said walking over to the sink full of dishes.

Alan sat down at the kitchen table, feeling useless, but not uncomfortable. "You two have really done well, between farming and the shop."

"It hasn't always been easy," Emily said. "Surprisingly when the farming was slow the shop filled in, and vice versa, sometimes the farming had to carry the load. There were years when our employees made more than we did. Those years we really appreciated the farm's bounty, the vegetable garden, the beef and the pork, you know what I mean."

Sarah commented, "That's pretty much the way I remember farming. It is hard work but we had a certain amount of security as far as where our next meal would come from."

"Yes," Emily said, "but now both the farming and the shop seem to be holding their own. Hopefully we're pretty well established."

Alan said, "Beverly and I had some of those years running the bakery when the employees made more than we did. Very few people understand the challenges of running a small business; they only see the gross capital that you bring in without viewing the expenses. Most would not believe that you could gross nearly a half-million dollars and yet your personal income would be less than your employees."

Emily was eager to explain to Alan the events leading up to the present. "You know when Evan left the farm as a teenager he wanted nothing to do with farming. It is surprising how life can change on you."

Evan chimed in, "Yeah, I really don't mind farming: but I have to admit I still don't want to milk cows. But, it was the farm that opened the door and has allowed me to do the work that I really enjoy."

"When Evan and I got out of college," Emily continued, "I got a job that was supported by my education in Business Administration and Evan went to work as a mechanical engineer. We were doing real well. We eventually bought a nice little home and were living the life-style of most college graduates. Evan was very successful in his career; he was really good at mechanical engineering and excelled above the other engineers hired around the same time. However, he was not always happy and often came home stressed out. He found it difficult to deal with the politics and kissing up that seemed to be required for advancement."

Evan chipped in, "Yes, I remember my dad saying that when working for someone else you are selling yourself as a slave. That's what it began to feel like."

Emily now continued, "For some strange reason I started wanting a baby. Perhaps my biological clock kicked in early. We talked about it . . ."

"And talked about it," Evan broke in.

"And I explained," Emily went on as if she hadn't been interrupted, "that I could keep on working: a lot of women do. This was out of Evan's comfort zone and image of motherhood. He had a fixed picture that mothers should be a constant presence in the life of their children: his mother was.

"We finally came to a comfortable understanding that we could, with a little discipline, get by on Evan's paycheck and still enjoy a family. Thrift had always been a hallmark of Sam, Evan's father, and we were willing to apply it to our life. However, I had not grown up with abundance and knew what making-do meant, so we didn't anticipate any real difficulty.

Two months before Eddy was born I gave my resignation and became a stay at home expectant mother. Eddy was a big baby, especially for the first, and it was a relief to not have to go to work every day.

"Shortly after I resigned my job the atmosphere changed where Evan was working. There had been an opening for a chief mechanical engineer in one of the departments and it seemed that the entire factory took it for granted that Evan would be moving up to that position since he had proved himself well beyond the others. The additional income would have helped offset the loss of my income and we were feeling optimistic about the future. Evan and I were very disappointed when Don Smith, a master kiss-up, received the promotion instead. Then things became more difficult when Don Smith, aware that Evan should really have had the position, tried to fit Evan under his thumb. Evan was really unhappy and under the circumstances we didn't have many options."

She heard the pickup come into the yard and knew the older kids were home. Good, the girls could help setting the table so dinner would be on time.

"To be continued," she smiled at Evan as the kids invaded the kitchen.

. . . .

The meal was a comfortable setting for sharing personal experiences, and all participated, even Ellen who contributed the story of Boots, the family cat, who had turned out to more than justify her existence by being a good mouser. When the main meal was cleared away they moved into the living room where Sarah and Emily brought in dessert: coffee, milk and cookies.

Due to Evan and Emily's encouraging their kids to join in adult conversations to expose them to what their future as the next generation would be, it was natural for the young people to stay when the conversation turned toward these topics. Alan and Sarah turned to Evan and Emily with nods of acknowledgment when the kids joined in with intelligent comments. It pleased Evan and Emily to see how the kids, from Eddy to Ellen, took an interest in the values they held as well as their heritage which had formed these values.

"Alan, I never finished telling you how Evan and I ended up on the farm," Emily broke in when there was a lull in the conversation.

"Oh, I love this story," Ellen exclaimed with the anticipation of hearing a favorite family narrative. Snuggling against her mother, Ellen commanded with enthusiasm, "Tell Alan, Mom."

Emily squeezed her youngest child and laughed softly, "O.K., Ellen. I'll pick up where we left off before you kids got home."

"Dad says none of this could have happened if it hadn't been for Grampa," Eddy interrupted.

"You're right, Eddy," Emily acknowledged. "Grampa and Gramma Jane always hoped that your dad would come back and run the farm. I don't know if Evan was even aware of it," she glanced at her husband, who smiled with a small shrug.

"No," Evan admitted. "I had been pretty adamant about how I felt about the farm." There was a long pause. "Never say never," he smiled apologetically. "Life has a way of changing our values and our best laid plans." He nodded at his wife who picked up the story.

"Sam continued to run the farm," Emily said to Alan. "He's thrifty and a good manager."

"Yes," Evan broke in, "I use to resent my father's thrftiness. But I have to admit without his thrift much of this would not exist." He waved his hand to encompass the stately home they lived in and the lands that went with it. "In the early years of my parent's marriage my father bought my mother a Mercedes Diesel car. My mother had objected that she didn't need anything that elegant, that a regular sedan would have served her well. But Dad said, 'We'll get our money's worth out of it.' He knew the integrity with which these vehicles were built and fully intended to run the Mercedes for decades." Evan grinned. "Which he did . . . sometimes to my teen-age discomfort.

"The year came when the farm had a really profitable year. I talked with Dad and encouraged him to buy Mom a new car. He answered, 'What's wrong with the one she has?' Well, I said, it's getting pretty old. She even has to use glow-plugs to get it started in the winter. 'Yeah,' my dad said, 'She's quite a lady, isn't she. She understands that old car's temperament better than anyone else.' How could I argue with that? Secretly I was pretty proud of Mom for being able to manage that old car. I knew my friends' moms would be at a loss how to do that."

110

Emily nodded in remembrance, "Yes, it was his thrift that enabled your folks to buy the farm next door when it became available."

Evan said, "Yeah, that's kind of sad the way that all came about. That was the old Holbrook place. John and Patty had inherited it from his folks. They had a son named Jimmy whom I grew up with. We were close. When John had a heart attack my father took over running both farms. These two men were like brothers. There was really nothing else my father could have done. He was compelled to do all he could to help John."

"What about Jimmy?" Edith asked. "Couldn't he have come back to help run the farm?"

"No," Evan said slowly. "Jimmy had died of a drug overdose. I don't think his folks ever recovered from that." Evan was quiet for a moment. Everyone sat respectfully, waiting for him to go on.

"When it became evident that John would never recover enough to be able to run the farm, my father made him an offer to buy the farm and to run it while John and Patty stayed there as long as they wanted. It didn't need to be publicly known that John was not the owner. The transition was made and everyone felt it was a fair and equitable transaction, both men feeling they had given something special to a good friend.

"A few years later, John died, and Patty couldn't stand the emptiness so she moved in with her widowed sister in Florida. Dad continued to increase the value of the two farms and rented out the Holbrook house."

"After Eddy was born," Emily took up the story smiling at her son, "it was time to bring him here to let his grandparents appreciate him." Eddy squirmed a little.

"We didn't know what Gramma Jane had in mind when we planned this visit. She and Sam had talked extensively about their dream that Evan would come back to run the farm. The farm had grown by this time and it was getting a little hard for Sam, who was beginning to show some age, to handle it all. They had considered hiring a manager. They knew it might be unreasonable to expect Evan to take a 50 per cent cut in pay to manage the farm . . . but Gramma Jane couldn't help but hope. She started to think of what other enticements might be given to encourage Evan to come back.

"She presented the argument that he would have free housing: Sam thinking that she was referring to the Holbrook farmhouse which was a fine building. He was startled when Gramma Jane said, 'You know how Emily loves this old brick farmhouse.' Sam was stunned. 'You'd give up your home?' He now understood how badly his wife wanted to fulfill this dream. 'The Holbrook house is much smaller and will be easier for me to take care of. I know we'll need to make some repairs, but it shouldn't take that much.' Grampa could see that she had really thought this out. 'Well, it might be. But you wait for me to bring up the subject.' He knew how impulsive Jane could be.

"When your father and I got here," Emily spoke to the four young people who were hanging on her words although they had heard the story many times, "your grandmother's love for your father and me radiated like the warmth of the spring sun. It was so comforting. I felt so at ease it was natural to reciprocate. I still do. Gramma Jane is so special to me."

Sarah looked at her daughter, comforted that Emily had such a friend; not threatened in the least.

Evan broke in softly, "After all the anguish we had suffered from the downturn at my job, it was comforting." He smiled fondly at Emily, "And you two women . . . Dad and I didn't know what to make of it!"

Emily broke out laughing. "Your father for once was speechless. After all the baby talk and catching up, all of a sudden I was telling Gramma Jane all about Evan's job and the disappointments we had undergone. I noticed that Jane kept looking over at Sam. Finally, he nodded and said with a shrug, 'Go ahead. I'm afraid you'll explode if you don't.' Jane excitedly explained what she and Sam had talked about.

"I didn't dare look at Evan for fear he would see how badly I wanted what his folks were offering, but when Gramma Jane said that we would have the old brick farmhouse my bubble burst. 'Oh, Jane, we couldn't do that . . . this is your home. I know how much you love it.'

"I had no more than got the protest out when Gramma Jane said, 'Now you listen to me. This house is meant for children. It's getting too big for Sam and me. We just rattle around here. The Holbrook house is much smaller. No, I really want Eddy to grow up here,' she pressed her cheek to Eddy's little face. 'And all the other children you have. I'm ready to be a grandmother living just down the road where they can come visit whenever they want or whenever they're driving you crazy and you need a few minutes of peace.'

"Oh she knew she had me," Emily paused. "When I looked at Evan and Sam they knew, too."

Evan took up the narrative: "Dad said, 'You can't fight these two women, son, but I want you to take a few days and seriously consider what we're offering. This is a big decision and we'll have a lot to talk about.'"

Evan glanced at Emily who was smiling at him tenderly, "Dad didn't know but I think Emily did that the weight of the world lifted off my shoulders right here in this room. Later when Emily and I were alone, she said that she could drive the same car for decades and be content, especially if she had such a fine home; she pressed the point by saying that we could grow all our own food, pointing out that my folks had always cone that. When she asked me what I thought, I said, 'I've done a lot of growing up since I left here. I now appreciate that my dad wasn't some evil taskmaster, but just a dad who wanted his son to be responsible.'

"I didn't tell Dad for a couple of days, but I knew this was going to be our future."

Evelyn took advantage of a pause in her parents' story to comment: "Gramma and Grampa told us all about the Emerson family. She brought out the old family album and showed us pictures of way, way back."

"They were dressed funny in some of those pictures," Ellen giggled.

Edith chimed in, "Yes, Gramma and Grampa's great grandparents, the first Emerson's, lived in a sod hut! We studied about those in history class at school. Gramma asked

114

us girls how we would feel living way back then, having to help build a sod hut and then trying to make it livable."

"I'm sorry," Evelyn said, "but I'm glad I live now. I don't know if I could have cut it back then. I know Gramma Jane impressed on us that it was because of the hardiness and hard work of these women that we have what we have now. I appreciate all of that; I'm just glad I was born today when life isn't quite so physical . . . Sorry." She shrugged deprecatingly.

"Grampa said those women were a special breed." Eddy smiled remembering his grandfather's next comment: "'Ayah, they knew how to deal equally with diamonds and dirt.'"

Sarah spoke, smiling, as the others turned to her. "Yes, those frontier women put their dreams aside for the advancement of the family welfare: each generation contributing to the advancement from that original sod hut, to a small wood-framed house, to this beautiful brick farmhouse." She continued, "I grew up on a farm, I was proud to be a farm girl. I understood what the heritage was and the genes I inherited from these extraordinary women."

Emily smiled teasingly at her mother, "That's why you take pride in being able to start a fly-wheel-start John Deere."

"Ayah, you're right."

"Me, too," Emily said softly. "Tell us about the farm you grew up on, Mom."

Sarah sat in thought for a moment. She felt Alan's hand cover hers and glanced up to find his look of encouragement.

Some of her memories were painful. "Well, I grew up in a nice big brick farmhouse similar to this. My brothers and I had an ideal life. Until that terrible call came late one night. Our mother and father had been killed in an accident caused by a drunk driver. My oldest brother, Sean, was only 18. I was 14 and Dickie was 16.

"Sean wanted to maintain the farm. The three of us were all in agreement, but we didn't get any support from others. With the inheritance tax hanging over our heads, we made the decision to sell the farm.

"My, how I miss that farmhouse," Sarah said softly. "My father had taken such pride in the quality of its construction. In the extreme summer heat he always mentioned how nice and cool it was coming in from the hot fields. In the winter, coming in from tending the animals in the cold barn, he'd say how good it was to have such a welcoming warm home to come into.

"My father was from an industrious farming family. Industriousness was indoctrinated into us kids from a young age. History shows that industriousness was a critical and unique part of American history. Thomas Jefferson admonished his oldest daughter that she had the responsibility to instruct her sister, the youngest Jefferson daughter, on being industrious. He was also concerned that Americans would send their children to Europe to be educated, being afraid that these children would pick up the non-industrious attitude of some Europeans and thus compromise American values. Benjamin Franklin and many of our Founding Fathers promoted industriousness as a vital part of this new nation.

"P. S. Norac writes that humanity has a tendency to go to extremes. He also wrote that freedom dictates that a person should have the right to work as hard as he wants or as little as he needs, provided his choice does not infringe on others.

"In our family, Grampa Charles, my father's father, was highly driven and industrious. Grampa George, my mother's father, was not as driven. Grampa Charles had a really successful farm while Grampa George's farm was comfortable but more average. Yet, both of them met all their responsibilities. In my mind this is an example of P. S. Norac's statement: Grampa Charles worked as hard as he wanted, with no criticism, and Grampa George worked as hard as he needed, with no criticism. It would have been wrong to force either one into a different way of life.

"Coming from different backgrounds, my mother's and father's, my brothers and I feel we have developed a better balance."

"Industriousness served our nation well," Alan commented, "but with the Industrial Revolution it possibly moved the social uniform to an imbalance: perhaps too much emphasis being put on industry and industriousness. Even today people who are not industrious are viewed as losers, not quite fitting the social uniform.

"To understand how industrialization can be viewed as a negative influence let's take for example a young man who attended Evergreen Park Community High School in Chicago, Illinois.

"In 1958 he was accepted into Harvard at the age of 16, graduating in 1962. In 1967 he became an assistant professor of mathematics, the youngest professor ever hired at the University of California at Berkeley. Uncomfortable with the pressure of the industrial/academia world in which he found himself, in 1973 he moved to a remote self-built cabin in Lincoln, Montana to live a simple life.

"There his life was sustained by doing as little as he needed, basically living off the land: he had made a study on edible natural food that could be found around his cabin. Basically he had the right to live this way. He was not a burden to anyone. Many might be confused that an individual with such intellectual capacity would choose this type of life. Applying the rules of the social uniform, he would certainly appear to be out of step with the world. The question is: Has the world become out of balance?

"In 1983 he felt the world was crowding in on his seclusion and after reading books such as the works of Jacques Ellul, a French Philosopher whose main concern was that the world was moving toward technological tyranny, he was known to say that he had lost hope of any reform and saw violent collapse as the only way to bring down the techno-industrial system which he felt was threatening human freedom.

"He began a campaign of sabotage and bombings, killing three people and injuring twenty-three others. You may have already identified him as Ted Kaczynski, the Unabomber.

"So when Sarah said she and her brothers got a better balance, this is what came to my mind. Listening to Sarah helps me understand that the social uniform should not be designed in such a way that it forces all individuals, irregardless of their inherent nature, into the highest level of industry. Individuals should be allowed to work as little as they need," Alan concluded.

Edith asked, "He was in Harvard at 16 years of age? That's how old I am. How could he be emotionally prepared for the demands put on him in that setting? I know I wouldn't have been. I still need my family." She glanced around the group, remembering how homesick she got sometimes just on a sleepover with friends.

"If he wasn't emotionally mature enough," Evan answered, "it is possible that the industrial/academic world might be held partly responsible for his conduct. In a mechanical world, individualism, with its needs, can be ignored."

"I think I understand where they were coming from," Evelyn commented, "when they spoke about technological tyranny. I admit I don't have it all in place, but this is what I see. When the United States moved from an agricultural society to an industrial society, those who had enjoyed the choice of working as hard as they wanted or as much as they needed on the farms found that choice taken away from them.

"When you go to work for someone else they have the right to demand the highest level of your physical ability and productivity. This could easily be in conflict with your nature, as reflected in the song by Johnny Cash, *Oney*: 'Always got somebody looking down his neck, trying to get more out of 'em than he really ought to have to put in.'"

"Yes, my dad said when you go to work for someone else you're selling yourself as a slave," Evan said. "When my dad was growing up he had a friend named Arthur Moore.

When farming made dramatic changes in productivity and crop yield, the nature of farming was get big or don't bother. Art moved in a different direction. They sold most of their land to the expanding farmers and kept approximately a hundred acres. They then concentrated in getting all their needs of food and shelter off the land even going to the level of shingling the r roof with shingles made from their own cedar trees.

"They use to say the only food they bought at the grocery store was milk, butter, flour and salt. To cover their other needs they ran a sugar bush operation, kept bees, and had a vegetable stand where they sold the surplus crops they grew along with their own homemade maple syrup and honey. Arthur's income was actually below the poverty line - although they never applied for government assistance - and yet he lived better than a lot of his neighbors, even being able to buy a brand new car with cash.

"His wife and daughters were very well dressed. One day when my dad stopped by the vegetable stand, he asked Arthur, 'How are you doing?' gesturing to all the produce on display. Arthur answered, 'Well, I'm doing very well. It's not how much money you make it is how you spend it. I've taught my girls to be intelligent in the way they spend their money.' Arthur is a good example of freedom and not being enslaved to materialism."

"When my mother got married," Sarah said, "she was somewhat intimidated by the amount of nice things that my father's family had acquired. Along with industriousness Grampa Charles' family had been indoctrinated with thrift and the most effective way of spending money. This was difficult for her to adjust to and often she viewed my father's attitude as stingy and miserly."

Evan broke in, "That's pretty much the relationship my mother and father had. Dad had been indoctrinated with such a level of thrift that my mother found it hard to understand at times. But I think she grew to appreciate, from the nicer things she had, that thrift does have its value." Evan turned to the kids and asked, "Do you think that Grampa Charles should have given Grampa George some of the nice things that he had since Grampa George didn't have as much? Wouldn't that have been more equal?"

The children immediately responded, all in agreement, that this would have been unreasonable and unfair to expect of Grampa Charles. They concluded that a person was entitled to the possessions he had acquired according to his own efforts.

"Well, the Little Red Hen," Ellen spoke up, "kept what she had worked for."

Emily smiled proudly at her youngest child. She and Evan had agreed that children can and should be taught to reason from a very young age and now they were seeing the results of their efforts.

"Evan and I went through some real hard times when we had to depend on the farm and what it could produce for the family," Emily went on, "living pretty much the same as Arthur Moore did."

"When I started working with my father on the farm," Evan interjected, "we started a small supplementary business of repairing farm machinery. My being a mechanical engineer along with my father's mechanical abilities enabled us to became quite good and our business grew. We both felt that this business might have potential, as well as it was right up our alley, and we both enjoyed it. One of our neighbors had built a small manufacturing facility down the road. They had a major fire and decided not to rebuild. After looking over the site, I felt that the Butler Building, which hadn't been compromised from the fire, had real possibilities to expand our repair business.

"Approaching my dad about this possibility, I was disappointed when he said it was a real good idea but he just didn't have the capital for such an expansion. Up until that time all the financing had come from my dad. I suggested we could get a loan which was absolutely against all previous Emerson value systems. I told him I thought we could pay it off within seven years, in view of how well farming and the repair business were doing, Dad suggested we get the figures together and see how they looked.

"Emily and I sat down that evening to see if there was any possibility of making this work. The figures really looked good. We had done real well. When we approached our neighbor, we were pleasantly surprised to have him accept our offer, and even more surprised when the bank readily gave us the backing we needed. The Emerson reputation stood us in good stead that time. We moved into the building slightly over budget, but not bad. Dad really loved this business. However, farming took a down turn, mostly caused by bad weather, affecting both means of income.

"I began to feel bad that I had talked my dad into this additional expense. He was good about it and said he had gone through similar times before. Emily, with her sunshine disposition, surely came through. She viewed everything we needed from the possibility that it could be derived from the farm. It was not unusual when I walked in one day and found her making soap. She was really good at it, even adding aroma to it. But, the first few attempts were a little heavy on the lye." Evan looked at Emily who giggled, remembering those first attempts at thrift.

Eddy said, "I remember that time and how we concentrated on cutting enough firewood so we wouldn't have to run the oil furnace so much."

"It was a challenging time," Evan concluded. "The guys working for us didn't realize how badly we were struggling. Every week they received their pay checks even if Dad and I had none."

"I remember Mom setting the playpen up in the shade and I had to watch Edith and Evelyn while she worked in the garden," Eddy continued. "Gramma Jane use to help, too."

"Yes, we really depended on that garden," Emily agreed. "But right on time," Emily said proudly, "the last payment was paid to the bank seven years later. That was a momentous moment."

"I remember having candles on a cake to celebrate," said Evelyn.

"Then the day came when I received a package addressed to me," Emily said. "I opened the box and found airplane tickets, hotel reservations and a check for expenses to Disney World. Gramma Jane had also included a coupon offering to take care of Ellen who wasn't even a year old. The card from Grampa Sam said I had earned my stripes and was now a true farm girl."

"That's all in the Disney World Scrapbook," Ellen said. "All the pictures of Gramma and Grampa and me were taken here at the farm. I took my first steps that week and they caught it in a picture just before I fell on my bottom. Gramma says I laughed as much as they did."

Alan looked over at Evan. "You do know that what you have built here is worth millions of dollars. I don't mean to intrude but Beverly and I had worked real hard in building our business not realizing the taxes that we or our children would be responsible for. Is all that you have here basically in your dad's name?"

"Yeah, we've been thinking about that," Evan said looking at Emily who nodded confirmation.

"You know it's not an easy subject, but if something happened to your dad you could lose a lot of your hard work," Alan went on.

Edith looked at Alan with confusion, "What do you mean?"

"Well, the inheritance tax really can wipe out half or more of what you have," Alan answered.

"That's not fair," Edith responded with hurt and anger.

"No, it's not. However the government views people like your folks and grandparents as those 'evil rich people,'" Alan replied.

"There are people with close association with the White House such as G.E. who make billions of dollars in profit but pay no taxes," Sarah joined in.

This time Evelyn protested, "But that's not fair!"

"The immoral thing is that in this country we openly speak of China as being a 'Crony, Capitalistic nation', when in truth the United States is also a 'Crony, Capitalistic nation,'" Alan said. "Tax laws are written in such a way that they can be exploited by Lobbyists and individuals with the right political connections."

"Something should be done," Evelyn responded with fervor.

"You're right, Evelyn," Alan agreed. "The tax laws should be revised without the Lobbyists pulling strings." He paused before causing a stir with his next comment: "Some think the only way that will happen is an overthrow of the government.'

Emily spoke into the strained silence, "That reminds me of something Evan and I were talking about the other day. We were reminiscing about our college days. We were in the same psychology class and one day brought up to the professor that human nature seems to need and want an adversary. We had discussed it between ourselves quite thoroughly and had concluded that it was an interesting part of human psychology."

"Yes," Evan broke in, "this is supported by the rivalries, sometimes even bitter, between sports teams; also by the fact that humans posture toward one another."

Emily went on to observe, "This human tendency can be used to polarize people."

"This seems to be happening in politics today," Eddy interrupted his mother. "Once people become polarized they readily believe anything that supports their faction, even lies."

Edith broke in, "Yes, they even use the expressions 'our side' or 'their side.'"

"I wonder," Evelyn questioned, "is the need for an adversary part of our DNA or part of our social environment?"

"Why do you ask, Evie?" Evan asked.

"Well, in the Middle East they have had warlords for millenniums. It seems to be natural – if they're not fighting an outside force they're fighting among themselves. Sometimes the hatred they level against their adversary is the result of truly inconsequential matters, it seems to me: the preference of one prophet over another. Each one convincing themselves that the opposing side is evil and villainous, they feel justified in unconscionable retribution against each other."

Emily nodded, "It seemed to your dad and me that the Liberal movement was becoming much too fanatical, almost as radical as these warlords, Evie. This is why we began to question the so-called Liberal movement. Some of the things being advocated denied reasonableness and truth. We've decided that we cannot afford to be polarized; neither can our country. The results could be tragic."

"You might think that the suggestion of an overthrow of the United States government denies reality, but another faction that appeared on the scene in the sixties supported just that," Alan said. "This faction was very adversarial and viewed the government and others opposing their agenda as enemies and villainous. They felt that the government of the United States was so villainous that it should be overthrown. The Weather Underground even resorted to bombings of the Capitol and the Pentagon."

Evan picked up the historical record: "The only FBI agent ever known to infiltrate this group, Larry Grathwohl, in an interview spoke about what he learned while associated with the Weather Underground. This group was made up of a large number of mostly college educated people, some from Columbia University and other well-known centers of learning. The main focus of this group was to overthrow the United States government. When he asked what would be the plan going forward, no one had really thought that through. The only proposals were that they expected that the Cubans, the North Vietnamese, the Chinese and the Russians would all want to occupy portions of the United States.

"Then he presented the possibility of a counter-revolutionary movement, those who refused to accept this agenda. Members of the Weather Underground proposed 'reeducation centers in the Southwest.' For those who refused to be 'reeducated'? They would be eliminated. When pressed what this meant the Weather Underground members 'estimated they would have to eliminate 25 million people in these reeducation centers.' Larry Grathwohl explained that 'eliminate' meant kill."

Evan paused for effect: "Kill 25 million Americans - right here in the United States - who refused to be reeducated into the Weather Underground agenda. The shameful thing is that their agenda claimed to be in support of freedom and democracy and equal rights. They followed the lead of mentally weak individuals who had no comprehensive plan except to overthrow the United States government."

"What do you mean by 'mentally weak'?" Sarah asked. "These were highly educated people."

"Yes, they were educated, but they lacked the ability to be comprehensive and think things through to the end, placing all the details of society into their proper places in their plans," Evan answered.

"You know what that sounds like to me," Sarah said with a smile. "You blow everything apart, and then you pick up the pieces and start from scratch, hoping that your next attempt will produce better results than the previous one did."

Eddy responded: "That's stupid. A lot of people would suffer needlessly."

"The Weathermen/Weather Underground no longer exists," Alan said. "However, some of its members have maintained a concerted effort in advocating the collapse of the United States government. One of these individuals was Saul Alinsky. He wrote the book *Rules for Radicals*. One of the rules was: 'Make your enemy live up to their own book of rules.'

"One of the favorable things coming out of the sixties was the environmental movement with a strong awareness of the earth's fragile environment. As a result from this awareness came major industrial adjustments. P. S. Norac writes about a river that was terribly polluted but has now regained its original pristine condition.

"However, the radicals commenced to beat the drum of the earth's ecology in order to advance their agenda against capitalism and industry. In the seventies they were the ones that claimed that we were entering into an ice age because of industry. Now they are saying that we are having global warming built on weaker science than what they even had in the seventies.

"If the government continues its plan to tax carbon dioxide it could easily bring about the desire of these radicals: collapsing the United States economy. I read P. S. Norac's book *LARRY* and questioned when it came to the Gulf oil spill whether the government's neglect was a product of inexperience and lack of ability or a direct attempt in support of these radicals."

"Sometimes Alan can be very Manchurian," Sarah said teasingly, looking at Alan.

"There's a lot of things out there that make you wonder," Alan said: "Trillions of dollars of debt and open disregard for the will of the people, to name just two. Also, there are plenty of individuals who feel the human race globally would be advantaged if we had a one-world government. Advocates of this belief openly say that the greatest obstruction to the accomplishment of this is the

United States. The successful transition to a one-world government would require a diminishing of the United States' position on the world scene. The frightening thing is that those seeking this are investing millions of dollars into politicians who seem to be sensitive to this end."

"Alan," Sarah said, "I don't know if these politicians really want to see the collapse of the United States."

"Well, their actions certainly seem to suggest that," Alan said, looking at his wife. "Just think. We just came out of Canada. The American dollar is now worth 10% less than the Canadian dollar. Do you remember that ever happening before? The United States currency has been the standard in which the world economy has been managed for many years. Now we have China saying that another currency other than the United States dollar should be the standard for world commerce. And we have a Federal Government that continues to print money in order to soften the impact of our increasing debt bringing down the value of the dollar even more."

"If the value of the dollar goes down," Evelyn said with a worried expression, "we're going to have to pay more for what we import . . . Right?"

Evan confirmed, "Yes, Evie, what is taking place now will impact you kids," he gestured to include the four young people, "for years to come."

"But that doesn't seem fair," Ellen protested.

"Well, dear, it isn't," her mom commiserated. "Hopefully the politicians will come to their senses before it's too late."

"If the dollar continues to deteriorate," Alan commented, "we will be spending more of our income for mere sustenance bringing us down to the level of many other countries in our quality of life. And on top of that the EPA is trying to enforce laws that will make energy more expensive . . ."

"Yeah," Eddy interrupted, "Dad and I were talking about that just yesterday." He glanced at his father who nodded. "We concluded that carbon dioxide isn't even an effective greenhouse gas."

"That's what concerns me," Alan responded. "These politicians are just not thinking things through. I wish people would do their research and have a comprehensive evaluation of what they are working toward. Every one of us needs to do our homework and not be polarized by any faction. If the United States loses its economic advantage, this would take away a source of much good in the world. Look at all the money the United States and its citizens contributed to helping other countries, whether, the tsunami in Indonesia, the earthquake in Haiti, AIDS in Africa, and on and on. If the United States were diminished, just imagine the power plays that would take place: If China prevails, would human rights be respected? If Jihad takes over, will women be respected? So far the United States, with all its faults, has been a positive force for the human race."

Ellen yawned and stretched before climbing into her father's lap and tucking her head against his shoulder. "I'm tired," she said sleepily.

"I know, sweetie," Alan said. "We've kept you up way beyond your bedtime. You kids have really impressed me. Evan and Emily, you should be proud of these young people. I somehow feel the future is going to be in good hands."

* * * The End * * *

Author's Commentary

We introduced Cousin Eddy in our commentary *Intellectual Power*. You might have noticed that he morphed on us. This demonstrates one of the important lessons to be gathered from *Cousin Eddy Takes on Greenhouse Gases - Part II*: Children should be taught how to reason and to be analytical. Eddy could easily have remained the Eddy of *Intellectual Power* if his father hadn't taken the time to help him reason.

Unfortunately we have highly intelligent individuals who through their growing up have not been taught to reason and put the composite parts of a problem into their proper places. Thus we have the statement of professors with grandiose teachings that take you into the clouds but they don't know how to touch the ground: make application.

RESPONSIBILITY

In the book *COMMON SENSE* by Glenn Beck, the author mentions Al Gore and the statement that he made to a group of young people. Those of us in our seventies, or approaching our seventh decade of life, are quick to understand the evil content in these words: that these youngsters were more qualified than their parents to make decisions.

By this statement I am not accusing Al Gore of being evil. But, the words of an ancient proverb come to mind: Do not be like the stupid one who does not know he is doing wrong. This also brings to mind the statement: You know people who don't know anything? He doesn't even suspect anything. That seems to be the way it is. However, those of our generation can testify to the historical facts about this evil.

Those of us who grew up in the forties and fifties were tutored by our parents to work hard and be responsible. Many times I felt my mother's nagging words: You're going to have to work in this world. To be honest, this value system is possibly a little too extreme, with our parents thinking that any play was a waste of time; there were much better things to do with one's time. As we matured, we appreciated the foundation and security this life gave us; though restrictive we were protected: the cage that keeps the canary in also keeps the cat out.

Those born slightly after us were not as inclined to come to these conclusions, although many have as they matured. In the sixties there was a movement called the New Morality which promised freedom from all restraints. Those of us from the older generations came to the conclusion that this was not a new morality but just the old immorality. However, many youngsters, excited by these potential freedoms, embraced this movement, feeling they could break the shackles of all responsibility and do whatever pleased them. Unfortunately, some of these young people sucked up these so called freedoms like a vacuum on steroids, resulting in a shift of our social structure.

Possibly the most glaring weakness of humanity is the lack of modesty, denying that we are finite and limited. With this nature we can understand immature people resisting restraint. Yet, examples of finite and limitations of our being exist all around us. As an example, if you were to walk down into the Grand Canyon you would naturally restrain yourself from getting too close to the edge. No one considers these restraints as a removal of one's freedom. It is just common sense. So it is with our social structure. It takes an educated awareness that will enable our children to be secure in their future.

Bill Ayers reflected the attitude of the New Morality movement by encouraging young people to resist and question all authority, including that of their parents: even going so far as to say, Kill your parents. This attitude remained as a subliminal message to all young people growing up. It was instrumental in creating many hardships in families.

Imagine for yourself the shift that took place.

From birth we are dependent on our parents. They are the ones that guide us and make sure that no physical harm comes to us. They instruct us not to touch hot stoves; after a few negative experiences we realize that this restriction, as well as others, is for our benefit. Our trust in them becomes quite absolute. I grew up with confidence in my parents. I was a middle-aged man, accomplished on my own, but still knew I could go to my dad for advice no matter what undertaking I took on; I was not alone.

In our study of the ancient Greeks, we learned that human beings have a tendency to exalt and try to establish superiority over their fellowman. Many of us can relate, however, that it was our parents who brought us down to earth, keeping us grounded in reality.

Then came the day when children were informed that their parents' abilities were questionable, their judgment not to be trusted. The subliminal message that their parents were stupid brought with it the message that they, the children, had to take charge: "He can't run his own life, I'll be damned if he'll run mine"; their security was violated. It was very perplexing for these youngsters as well as for many parents. I recall one friend saying: "We've been denied our right of parenting."

Now imagine some of these children growing up under these fractured guidelines; how their thought processes would develop. Those with a tendency to self-exalting and mania would have the most difficult time adjusting to this different world: no longer were there guidelines present to bring stability to their lives. To an immature, unstable mind, exalting and mania become addictive: the sensation is pleasant. Much to be avoided is the reality of life and a modest acceptance of our being. To sustain the euphoric sensation of exaltation many of these youngsters turned to drugs. Also recognized is the intense stimulation of mania in which many youngsters turn to the more mellowing drugs to stabilize their being: what a roller coaster ride the drug cycle becomes.

This was amplified for me one time sitting in a waiting room of a hospital. One of the wards using that waiting room was for individuals with drug dependence. A man entered, quite agitated. He walked to the counter and asked the nurse if so and so was there, obviously his son. The nurse confirmed that he was but told the man that his son did not want to see him. The son had overdosed and brought a great deal of stress to his family. The man was desperate: I don't know what to do. Why doesn't he see that it is killing him; it is killing us. The nurse advised him that it might be time to move on with his own life, basically telling him to abandon his son. His plaintive cry was, I can't do that. He is my son. Love should not hurt this bad. If this man hadn't been denied his right to parent would things have been different?

This only helps us appreciate that the basic building block of society is the family unit: father, mother, and children. Anything threatening this structure in any way has to be viewed as evil. Also, with the coming in of this mentality of pushing back all restraints, came a drug addicted society that did not accept the healthy sense of our being but chose to alter it. Take time to look at all the famous people that didn't know how to handle their celebrity: they chose the use of drugs to alter reality in order to cope with life.

Perhaps one of the most tragic ones is McKenzie Phillips. Her father denied all sense of responsibility and chose to shoot drugs with her. Every little girl deserves a father that truly cherishes her and would defend her even at the threat of his own life and would do all he could to prevent her from bringing harm to herself; a father who would gather her into his arms and comfort her with a scraped knee or a broken heart. Every little girl should be able to feel secure: Everything's OK. Daddy's here.

The painful truth is we have some men who are so demented and twisted that they would sexually abuse their own daughter. We become enraged when we hear of these tragedies and say to ourselves: that useless bag of dirt.

However, I think it would be easier to recapture the value of your life and adjust to a healthy adult life from child rape than from the introduction and addiction to drugs. How would we evaluate such a father?

In the entertainment world there is a high concentration of the use of drugs. The danger of these drugs is viewed and treated with amusement, lessening its threat. The product that they put forth often makes drugs appear as common, exciting, and sophisticated. There is very little concentration on the tragedies that drugs produce. These tragedies are merely viewed as the collateral damage of their way of life.

These very people are the same ones who protest the activity of our military when there are instances of collateral damage in war zones. Yet, our military applies great control and restraint to avoid this collateral damage even at the expense of its own safety. These in the entertainment community with their narrow social bandwidth apply very little restraint in lessening the collateral damage caused by their drug-influenced life style.

Can we have a society that will continue to exist if we don't also have the proper restraints? The cage that keeps the canary in also keeps the cat out.

Instead, we have individuals that excuse people from taking responsibilities such as Jeremiah Wright who tells his parishioners that they aren't to blame for their drug addiction or their affliction with AIDS, the government is.

The need to educate and train our children of their personal responsibilities cannot be overstated. You are going to have to work in this life. Life is not always going to be easy. The world does not meet you half way. Life is not always going to be fair.

In a world with such a high concentration of political correctness on issues of very little consequence, it would be hypocritical not to recognize the seriousness of saying that parents have questionable abilities.

At what point does the lack of restraint become licentious? How do we help our children cultivate a sense of virtue that empowers them with the proper restraint? Shakespeare wrote, Be true to yourself and you will then be false to no man. A good sense of virtue or a good conscience is not the possession of all people. Although I feel a tendency to it does exist in all humanity, it needs to be nurtured. In Plato's *Republic* the argument was set forth that this internal value system was merely a fear of retribution. This demonstrates that a good conscience is not understood by all men and, thus, even feared: people tend to be suspicious of and fear that which they do not understand. To a large portion of people, however, it is just common sense.

INTELLECTUAL POWER

In America we are on the leading edge of technology. We marvel, daily, at the many things that have developed and give credit to the intellect that accomplished these. We acknowledge that many of these things started out as mere theory, recognizing the path necessary to bring it from theory to application.

The common term has been frequently used: There is a thousand miles between theory and application. In order to reach the fulfillment of theory it takes a comprehensive mind, capable of accumulating all the factors and putting them in their proper places, with the ability to confront each obstruction with the same comprehension. Thus we understand the statement of a thousand miles.

These comprehensive minds are truly something to be acknowledged as well as the universities and colleges that have enhanced their abilities. Thus, great credit can be placed on the power of good education. As we deal with the members of these institutions of higher education, however, we quickly realize that there is a large difference between professors.

What has been said in amusement that defines some of these professors is: those who can do--do; those who can't do--teach; those who can't teach--teach others to teach. While this is stated mainly to be humorous, it does have some support in reality.

I think everybody has a Cousin Eddy, or knows of someone, who is scholastically brilliant but lacks the common sense of a fruit fly. He can quote Shakespeare; he can relate the ancient philosophies; we stand in awe of his abilities. However, we are surprised at his inability to make application. Eddy is not capable of traveling the thousand mile highway necessary to take something from theory to application; he can't even find the on ramp.

How exciting it is to travel with these professors of philosophy, sociology, etc., as they take us to fanciful clouds of thinking: Clouds adorned with much interesting and exciting reasoning. We travel with them and enjoy their excitement. We appreciate their scholastic abilities. But we do come to realize, they have yet to find the way to touch the ground.

Through the millenniums of human existence very few people have been able to accumulate the wisdom of old and apply it to contemporary living. Some of the exceptions that we note are George Washington, Thomas Jefferson, Benjamin Franklin, Alexander Hamilton, and the others who set up the framework of our Constitution. As we study these men, we can't help but be filled with admiration at their intellect and comprehension.

"We the people" have been sleeping. It is time for us to awaken and reflect back on the reasoning of these men and their comprehensive application. Why? Because the effort and work invested in establishing this country is being threatened.

ELITISTS

History shows that the elitist mentality is proven to be one of the worst evils that humanity has produced: the weak suffer what they must. The government that we have, with its saturation of elitists, is dangerous. While putting on the facade of wanting to take care of "we the people", the veneer is merely an attempt to gain more power. Kublai Khan, while demonstrating great benevolence, also had armies carrying on gross atrocities. Don't get sucked in by the veneer.

The direction in which democracy is now traveling is that of going to a high-bred feudal system with the increased burden of debt thrown on "we the people"; our financial freedoms will inherently be quite restrained and the elitists will continue to feed on the pork.

Trying to blind us from the facts, they manipulate the flow of information as did Kublai Khan, exposing the people only to their works of benevolence. As in any elitist society, the powerful do what they do and the weak endure what they must. The elitists will always manipulate things to maintain their advantage: George Orwell's *Animal Farm*: Some are more equal than others.

The statement that they cling to their religions and their guns intensifies the fears that we have. "We the people" cannot give up the empowerment that took thousands of years to come to fruition.

Elitism exposes itself in many ways. While we have leaders like Mahatma Gandhi who made a statement against elitism with a vow of poverty, we currently have ministers living in million dollar houses whose parishioners' entire yearly income could not pay the real estate taxes. These same so-called ministers preach the evil of capitalism to their congregations. It is clear to see the evil that is threatening our society is not Capitalism, not Socialism, not Communism: it is Elitism.

Communism, with its theory of absolute equality, could serve the people better if it held true to its intent. When Communism was established in Russia and China, its doctrine of absolute equality is and was violated and corrupted by a parasitic worm we know as elitism. Russia's social system was corrupted by those who felt that they deserved more entitlements than was their right: they were just more equal than others.

Today we have the same parasitic worm attacking our democracy. They take the nutrition intended for our democracy and lavish their friends from the earmarks they perceive to be unnoticed by us, "we the people". As we know, a parasite worm draws the nutrition away from its host until the host can no longer survive. At the death of its host it seeks another. Unless we get rid of the parasite, we will always be threatened.

Absolute social equality does have some value. But when brought forth by elitists we already know what the outcome will be: the powerful do what they do and the weak endure what they must. Because of the elitism that exists in Washington today, it would be unwise to move to a more socialized government which would require an expanded government and more opportunity for corruption. Seeing the product of corruption that elitism has brought to our government, we certainly appreciate this statement.

Take for example the property pimp that exists in our large cities. Millions and millions of dollars flow from our government into subsidized housing. The property pimp positions himself to grab as much of this money as possible. The managers of properties secure hundreds of thousands of dollars a year for themselves in their management schemes, supposedly justified by the profit they bring to their investors. Reality is, they neglect the properties and leave the poorest of our citizenry neglected.

This neglect goes unnoticed because they play the political game so that those in authority who should be checking their hand look the other way. It is easy to get away with this type of evil when you know that no one is going to be checking your hand. They feel completely entitled to this unethically received income: after all, some people are just more equal than others. The shameful thing is then they go to the poor people, whom they have robbed, and say it is the rich capitalists that have neglected them. This is a lie. So much of the money going for welfare for the poor is being consumed by this parasitic worm.

We cannot have people in government who view other humans as inferior and never take into consideration their own vulnerability. Each of us should think -- when we see a poor disadvantaged person -- by the change of just a few circumstances that could be me.

We don't apologize for repeating how fragile we feel democracy is and the need to sustain it by the value system that brought it into existence. One of the things that we have done is refer to Plato's *Republic*. The reason for this is to demonstrate how long it has taken for mankind to come to the position of expecting equality and equal rights.

Repeating some of the factors we gleaned out of Plato's *Republic*: The powerful do what they do and the weak endure what they must; an internal sense of virtue and value was only the result of a fear of retribution. However, the reasoning in Plato's *Republic*, itself, soon brought out that this reasoning was flawed and humanity did have within itself a virtuous nature that could be nurtured. It gives the example of the wife who would never even consider marital infidelity; it didn't even come into her mind.

The Republic brought out that the nature of the rulers should be benevolent and of the highest morality. It was discussed that in order to attain that level of benevolence the rulers should be eugenically selected in order to achieve the proper leadership. With this type of reasoning the elitist immediately identified themselves as fulfilling this role. As a result, it was deemed that rulership should come only from proper breeding. This can be seen even in our day in the case of Prince Charles who was not allowed to marry Camilla Parker Bowles to produce an heir to the throne of England as Camilla was not considered of the royal class.

For millenniums of time since Plato, the elitists have looked at the masses as a vulgar type of humanity from which nothing of any value could come. However, our democracy has demonstrated this to be a blatant mistruth. As an example, from a log cabin home came a man named Abraham Lincoln. The nobility of this man was unquestionable. Just think of the geniuses that fired up the Industrial Revolution and the common stock they came from: Eli Whitney, George Washington Carver, Daniel Massey, John Deere, and many others.

The elitists who live believing they are above the rim of humanity are often the ones that make the least contribution to society. Their contribution is many times not even relevant, to borrow a phrase from Dennis Miller.

Small government is the answer. The question is: without virtue and hard work would our democracy have developed?

WHERE WILL LIBERTY LIVE?

Frustrated from the lack of reasoning of the extremists, I searched for a tool that might demonstrate the type of dementia this seems to represent. These people's reasoning denies the reality that there are a lot of individuals in this world whose thinking and social structure cannot fully adjust to the values of democracy and equal rights. It is frustrating to see those on the extreme left align themselves with these factions and condone their violence. Those citizens of our nation that align themselves with the Jihadists could easily find that the snake they are playing with has a venomous bite.

In *Where Will Liberty Live?* we tell the story of three individuals and how they dealt with dementia. We hope you will not only be entertained but helped to see how important it is to rationally reason things out.

Where Will Liberty Live?

By

P. S. Norac

WHERE WILL LIBERTY LIVE?

Darrell and Darren listened as the minister praised their recently deceased brother-in-law, Tom. He had been a good man and had taken good care of their baby sister, probably better than they had dared hope. Their sister, Liberty, had always been a delicate child needing special care. After the comforters had all departed the three siblings gathered together to commiserate the loss they now shared: all of their mates were deceased.

It wasn't long before their reminiscing took them back to the days of their childhood. Their shared memories brought back the camaraderie they had enjoyed as children when the two brothers had learned to tame their own energy to enable Liberty to keep up with them; the neighbors would smile and call them the three musketeers. Everyone was aware how the two boys nurtured and cared for their little sister.

They were pleased to discover the bond was still there after the interim years when they had lived hundreds of miles apart.

"I drove by the old homestead the other day," Darren said. "It doesn't look too bad considering how long it's been empty. It's been for sale for quite awhile. It probably could be bought quite reasonably."

Without saying a word to each other, all three had mustered up the sentiment that they might like to go home. It's a strange thing that the place where you grow up always seems to be home.

Liberty said softly, "I'd like to see the old homestead."

"Me, too," said Darrell sympathetically. "It's only three hundred miles."

"Let's plan that," Darren joined in.

The plan was to drive up the next day, stay overnight at the old Inn in town, and drive out to the house on Monday.

Monday morning they contacted the realtor handling the sale and arranged to meet her at the house. They just had a need to see inside, but didn't want the neighbors to think they were up to mischief. As they drove into the yard a sense of sadness came over them: It had been so neglected. Their father had taken great pride in keeping the place up.

Megan Brown was waiting for them on the porch, the door opened behind her. She had arrived a few minutes early to air the old place out. As the three approached the steps their eyes were wide, taking in the details that had been so familiar to them in their youth. Even though the house had been neglected, there was that sense of comfort of coming home and an eagerness to reconnect to the haunts of their childhood.

Liberty turned to Darren, "Remember when you fell off the railing and broke your arm?"

"You really thought you were walking a high wire," Darrell laughed, remembering.

"Yeah," Darren grinned. "That put an end to my dreams of the circus."

One after another their memories flowed. Finally Liberty smiled at Megan's confused expression and explained this was where they had all grown up. Megan had another appointment to show some property on the other side of town and could see this was going to take some time as the three older people walked through their old homestead.

"I tell you what," she said to Liberty, "I have another appointment and I don't want to rush you. I'll give you the keys and you take all the time you want looking over the place. Just drop the keys at the office when you're through."

"Thank you," the three said in unison as Megan handed the keys to Liberty and walked to her car.

They wandered from room to room amazed that the basic structure was still as they remembered. The sentiment they had and the flood of memories confirmed the feeling that there is nothing like family. It was as if the years in between had vanished and they were once more the three musketeers.

Coming to the back door they went into the shed. All eyes turned to the northern corner. They looked at the floor that had been replaced where the two-seater had been. "Remember when Dad," they all said at once; Darrell and Darren waited for Liberty to finish their thought: "Put in the indoor plumbing." She laughed. "We really thought we had moved up in the world."

Moving from the shed into the barn they were pleased to see that sometime in the past fifty years someone had taken time to put in a concrete foundation. For its age the old barn stood well. Flashbacks of hide-and-seek, playing in the hayloft, or swinging from the rope swing their father had put up in the center of the peak brought more memories to share. The swing was no longer there but they looked up to see that the two iron hooks that had suspended the swing were. Darrell had been the only one with the determination to take the old swing up to a level of twenty feet. And who could walk into the barn without memories of Daisy Cow. She was a Jersey who gave the richest of milk. Oh, the butter that their mother had made. They had all been expected to take their turn at the old butter churn.

Their father had worked in the local sawmill. He was a skilled board sawyer, getting the optimum board feet of lumber out of each log. Both Darrell and Darren were proud that they had inherited that comprehensive, analytical ability that their father had applied to his profession, giving him the reputation for being one of the best in the area.

Walking out behind the barn they were disappointed to see that the land that had been dense with trees, stretching for miles in a child's imagination, had been cleared and turned into house lots. They had called their playground Sherwood Forest, albeit they were the three musketeers; as the game demanded Liberty played either the third musketeer or the fair maiden needing to be rescued.

As they returned to the house and entered the kitchen, Liberty called out to her brothers, "Don't forget to shut the door!!" mimicking their mother's oft repeated demand, recollecting that as children the occupation of the moment overshadowed these responsibilities.

Darren walked over to a wooden chair that had been left behind by the last inhabitants and turned it for Liberty to sit in. He and Darrell sat on the floor, their backs against the wall, legs stretched out in front of them, feet almost touching Liberty's. The close proximity displayed the fondness they felt for each other, each receiving comfort from the others' presence.

The memories and the conversation continued. Glancing at his watch, Darren exclaimed, "It's almost 2:00 o'clock! Megan will wonder what happened to us."

Liberty's face fell as she looked around the room. "I hate to leave," she said sadly.

"Me, too," Darren agreed. "There's no place like home."

"Are you feeling that, too?" Liberty asked, looking from one brother to the other.

Darrell said softly, "Yeah, I guess I feel that way. I really haven't felt like I have a home since Marcia died. Don't get me wrong, Jenny and Jeff have made me welcome; I have a nice apartment with them, but it just isn't the same, you know?"

Darren agreed, "I know what you mean. Since Anna passed, my house doesn't feel like home either. I guess this is the first time I've felt like I was home in a long time."

"I don't know what I'll do with Tom gone," Liberty said, her voice filled with emptiness.

"I'm going to buy this place," Darrell declared suddenly. Everyone knew he had the means.

Liberty and Darren looked at each other. They knew the reason that Jenny had insisted that her father move into the apartment at her place was because he had started showing signs of dementia and the doctor was worried about him being alone. Jenny had explained to her aunt and uncle that it would be easier to make the transition now while her father was capable of making the adjustment rather than wait until the situation was desperate. They had all agreed at the time.

Now, another solution seemed to be presenting itself. Although Darren and Liberty were taken back at Darrell's out-of-the-blue suggestion, now that it was in front of them they began considering that maybe it would be possible for the three of them to enjoy the autumn of their lives here in this place that they called home. Darrell's condition was in the very early stages and Darren and Liberty felt they would be able to be there for their brother as he needed them more. Darren thought it might even be better for Darrell, knowing they had a trust that only brothers share.

Within a year, Darren and Liberty had sold their homes, Darrell had purchased the homestead and the needed renovations had been completed. My, how the three of them enjoyed being home: There is no place like home.

As the weather turned colder, going into fall, they discovered that the old house had an infestation of rats. Apparently, during the summer the rats had been out in the fields foraging, but as the weather turned cold the rats followed their normal migration and came back into the house.

In spite of the traps, the rats had proved themselves quite cagey and their population, though diminished, was still far from livable. The situation became quite disturbing. Darrell seemed to be the one most upset. The day came when he and Darren were in the barn and looking up they saw a rat scurry across one of the beams.

"We've got to do something about that," Darren said, shaking his head.

Darrell spoke excitedly, "I guess we'll have to burn the whole place down!"

At first Darren thought he was joking until he glanced at the expression on his brother's face. He was dead serious. Darren started to try to convince Darrell this didn't make sense but Darrell insisted it was the only permanent solution. Finally Darren said, "If we do that where will Liberty live? You and I could live in a cabin in the woods, but Liberty is delicate. She needs to be taken care of."

Right then it was as if a dark shield had been removed from Darrell's eyes as he recalled his father's statement that he, Darrell, was responsible to take care of Liberty because she was weaker. He looked at his brother, his eyes flooded with tears, "Darren, I'm sorry but occasionally I have brain fog and I don't think clearly. I'm so sorry," he sobbed.

Darren reassured him, saying, "It's alright, Darrell. We're brothers. We'll work through this together."

Darrell realized that he had a friend he could trust to help carry his burden. He was not alone. From that day on often Darrell when speaking would look at his brother to confirm that his reasoning was in balance. The deep devotion they had shared in childhood had matured to support the emotional needs of both of them. My, it was good to be home with family.

Darren said, "I'll tell you what. This is what we're going to do. We're going to get a couple of rat terriers."

By that afternoon they had located two rat terriers, one a year old the other a year and a half old. The male they named Tiger and the female they called Tara. In a few days it was quite evident that the dogs were basically Darrell's dogs. The dogs seemed to sense that Darrell, with his mental condition, needed them. Darren and Liberty were part of their family, but the two dogs clearly felt that Darrell was special.

Within a few days, the new members of the household learned that they had a job to do, but for doing it they were well rewarded. When Darrell went out on the porch one morning he found two dead rats. Elated he called the two dogs and they rushed out of their doggie door. He praised them highly, then pushed open the door and led them into the kitchen. Opening the refrigerator he pulled out a hot dog, split it, and gave each one a half. The reward disappeared quickly and two little cropped tails wagged ferociously, begging for more. They soon learned that being a good rat terrier was rewarding. Darrell would bury the rats behind the barn.

One day ratting hadn't been too successful. One of the dogs dug up an old carcass and brought it up onto the porch evidently feeling that they would receive a reward. Seeing this Darrell called Darren and Liberty out. They all laughed that the dogs thought they could put one over on their humans. From then on Darrell developed the routine of incinerating the rats in the old barrel stove in the tool shed.

The two dogs had proved very successful and the rat problem nearly disappeared – with a strange rat wandering onto the property occasionally. It wasn't long before he was the next victim.

Darrell, Darren, and Liberty had gone out to do their shopping one morning. Returning home and entering the living room they found a large hole in the southern wall. The dogs had broken through the plaster and extracted a rat's nest located between the studs, leaving the carcasses of the baby rats all over the floor. Liberty was very upset and wanted to scold the dogs but Darren restrained her, saying they were just doing their job. Darrell gave them their reward.

The years passed and Darrell's health deteriorated. When he died the two dogs grieved as deeply as his siblings. Tiger, seeking comfort from Liberty, and Tara, seeking comfort from Darren, began sitting at their feet as they had sat beside Darrell. The comfort was two sided. As Liberty and Darren patted the small heads they remembered Darrell with fondness, contented that they had been there for their brother until the very end.

Liberty and Darren had just finished watching "Jeopardy" one spring afternoon. Darren turned to Liberty. "I've had a good life. The decision to move back here has been so rewarding. I think it was the best thing for Darrell." He reached down and patted Tara's head. "I think we did good, Liberty. But lately I've had a strange feeling that it's time to move on. I don't know what it is, I just have this feeling."

Liberty's eyes studied her brother. "That is odd, Darren." She patted Tiger's head as he curled in her lap. "I've had that feeling too."

The next morning Joshua Neeland, the mailman, walked up the steps to deliver the mail. Tiger and Tara were there to meet him. He reached in his pocket and gave them each a nugget of dog food. Uncustomarily they put the dog food down on the porch and looked up at Joshua. "What's the matter, guys?" That's strange he thought.

Pushing the thought to the back of his mind, he turned to go down the steps. Feeling a tug, he glanced down to find Tiger pulling at his pants cuff. Within a second Tara pulled at his other pants leg. "What is it, fellas? What are you trying to tell me?" He immediately felt worry.

Opening the door he called, "Liberty! Darren! Are you here?"

The two dogs ran into the hall and up a few steps of the stairs leading to the bedrooms. Pausing, they turned to see if he was following. Slowly he started up the steps. Coming to the first room he looked in and saw that Liberty was still in bed, apparently sleeping in. He knew he had to wake her just to assure himself she was alright. Unsuccessfully he tried to rouse her and then felt for her pulse. There was none. "Oh my god!" he said softly, rubbing his hand across his eyes.

He turned and slowly walked into the hall. Tara insisted that he follow her to the next room. Looking in the open door he saw Darren sitting in the chair by the window, also apparently asleep. But this time he approached with less hope. Finding no pulse on the old man he realized he had to call the police.

· · · ·

Darrell's great-grandchildren fell in love with Tiger and Tara and took them into their home. The two little dogs lived out the rest of their lives, coddled and loved.

* * * The End * * *

Author's Commentary

Our writings in *Cousin Eddy - Part II* also said if the United States government were diminished just imagine the power play that would take place: If China prevails would human rights be respected? If Jihad prevails would women be respected? Even with all its faults, the United States has been a force for good in the world.

Yes, our house, the United States, does have rats and if we were to allow it to be burned down, where will Liberty live?

TAX THE RICH

Barry had just turned 7 years old and was feeling very good. His grandfather had given him $20 for his birthday. He had never had this much money before in his life. He imagined it could buy him anything he wanted.

With a skip and a run he went next door where his best friend lived. He was eager to tell Marty about his riches. Marty's mom was getting ready to do some shopping and asked Barry if he would like to go along. When he said yes, she called Barry's mother and the three were on their way.

Arriving at the shopping center, Marty asked if he and Barry could go to the toy section. His mother gave permission, calling "You know what the rules are" as the two friends bolted off.

Marty was in the lead as they came to the toy aisles and turned to Barry as he pointed at a toy robot, "Can you afford this?" Barry assured him that he had plenty of money. He had Grampa's money.

They went from one toy to another planning together all the things Barry could buy with his money. Each time Barry exclaimed that he could afford to buy that with Grampa's money.

With their window shopping done, they went to find Marty's mother. On the trip home Barry chattered on and on about all the things he was going to get. Finally it was time to go home and Barry excitedly told his mother about all the things he was going to buy with Grampa's money.

His mother realized that Barry wasn't dealing with reality and feared that he would be disappointed and tried to explain not to get his hopes up too far. But Barry wouldn't listen; after all he had Grampa's money!

We now have an administration that acts like they have "Grampa's money". After all, they can tax the rich. When asked if they can afford any particular project the answer comes, "Sure, I can tax the rich."

In reality you can only tax the rich so much before you destroy the wealth that supplies the security that society needs.

WEALTH

After being shocked into realizing that something was wrong, we started to research in order to gain an understanding. We soon found that our new understanding, though "new" to us, had been around for decades. Many individuals had been trying to warn about the direction our country was going in.

Friedrich von Hayek (1899-1992) wrote the book, *The Road to Serfdom,* between 1940-1943, in which he "warned of the danger of tyranny that inevitably results from government control of economic decision-making through central planning." - Wikipedia.

Our research also led us to the writings of John Maynard Keynes. Keynes theorized that government spending could stimulate its economy and that the money spent would circulate and generate growth.

We find it interesting that the thinkers of our day believe that Hayek and Keynes are on opposite poles of the political spectrum. Listening to a debate, Hayek versus Keynes, I realized something I had been thinking for a long time: philosophical thinkers, while excelling in forming wonderful ideas, lack the mechanical ability to put the pieces in their proper places.

While Keynes's ideas of government spending as a stimulus has favorable credibility, how the money is spent is vital to success. The recent Stimulus Package failed to do this.

Many of the legislators do not have the comprehensive ability to understand how to best invest in our economy. They manifest a "just spend money" mentality.

The wealth generated by the economic growth during George W. Bush's presidency did not reach the working class of America. As the money flowed into the economy it merely ended up filling the reservoirs of the already wealthy; it did not flow downstream to the common man.

So it was with the Stimulus.

During this time period of growth of the Bush administration, we began hearing rumors of executives receiving bonuses that could be as much as twenty-five times or more that of the average family's income. When questioned, the answer would be: you had to do this to keep this quality of leadership. Although there are some individuals that have extraordinary abilities, this was basically an inflated view by an elitist society.

Then we had Enron's executives, who were receiving unreasonably high salaries and bonuses, proclaiming that they didn't know what was going on. What were they being paid for?

Henry Ford was unquestionably a mechanical genius, understanding how things worked. He knew that it was the workers of America and the money they spent that truly generated the country's wealth. As a result, he made the decision to increase his worker's pay from $2.50 a day to $5.00, doubling their income. He was strongly criticized by individuals who predicted that this would ruin his business. However, he knew he would eventually benefit. He became one of the world's wealthiest men.

Conclusion: Using the Keynesian philosophy we have to ensure that the monies invested are circulated through the common working man. His expenditures reach a broader diversification of our economy. Henry Ford knew that the wealth of a nation grew from the wealth of the common man.

Wealth does not appear in nature. It cannot be picked from a tree or harvested from a bush. It is strictly a product of humanity.

Wealth by itself is not evil; however, it has been used to empower people to do evil things. Wealth is basically a good thing. Since it is not alive, does not have any malice or intent, it does not consider justice or inequalities. It is just an "is" thing as inanimate objects are. It was from the strength of wealth that the Roman aqueducts were built, bringing benefits to all Romans from the highest to the lowest citizen.

In reality it advances society. In the hands of benevolent individuals it brings blessings to the less fortunate. A good example of this is the stories about Gilgamesh that some feel inspired Moses to write the Book of Job. Job is portrayed as a very wealthy man with an unquestionable caring and benevolent nature. But take time to reason: if Job said to himself, I am no more than one of these poor peasants; why should I have so much, and as a result gave away all his wealth, imagine the devastating affect this would have on the community. This one act of generosity would destroy his means of future benevolent acts that would, no doubt, have benefited the community in a more sustained manner. What we are establishing is that sustained wealth can be a stabilizing benefit to the community.

Aaron Thompson was a board sawyer living in a rural, heavily forested region of Wisconsin. When the opportunity to purchase a saw mill came up, he made the move and became a small business owner.

He knew that he was a skilled board sawyer, but he quickly learned there was much more to running a saw mill than just sawing logs. Now he was faced with the need to market and distribute his product. After due consideration, he trained his sons in the complexities of being a board sawyer and struck out to market and distribute his product. Surprisingly, his skill as a board sawyer was quickly overshadowed by his marketing and distributing skills. Soon, the mill was operating at high capacity, employing over 40 people.

Aaron had now cultivated a very high standard of living in the community. However, the employment of 40 plus people also benefited the community, bringing material advantage to many of the local store owners: gas stations, grocery stores and so on. Aaron was also very generous in supporting the many local charities. In fact, many of them began to depend on his generosity.

As is the nature of life, Aaron passed away. His sons now had to take over the marketing and distribution of the product as well as the physical side of operating the mill. They had become excellent board sawyers and ran the yard with efficiency; however, it was soon apparent they had not inherited their father's marketing ability. As a result the operation began going downhill. Within a few years the mill was closed and the employees were laid off, having a devastating effect on the community. Other businesses running on a very narrow margin of profit also had to go out of business.

A large majority of American workers are employed by similar small companies. If you take the time to drive around the United States you will see many empty buildings that were built for some business venture. This supports the fact that a lot of small businesses do not last: some for only a few months, some for a few years, some for decades and some for generations.

The wealth that was generated by Aaron's business no longer existed: the community suffered. It is very important that small businesses are enabled to sustain their wealth for as long as possible for the benefit of the communities. As with any business there will be ups and downs in which good businessmen save capital in order to survive the low times.

Our present tax structure is not conducive to sustaining small businesses. And yet, it allows loopholes for the large corporations to exploit. Burdening small businesses with extra taxes, whether income taxes or taxes on such things as carbon footprint or mandated employee health insurance, only discourages the entrepreneurs that America needs. Presently we have coal-fired plants that are closing because of EPA regulations based on a factor that doesn't even exist.

How can any administration say that it cares for the American people when it recklessly takes away their jobs?

THE PROPER STEWARDSHIP OF MONEY

Walter and Mary spent the first ten years of their marriage unsuccessfully trying to have a child. Finally Mary was able to carry to term and a blessing filled their life in a 7 lb 8 oz little girl named Nancy. Unquestionably, this little girl was the love of their life. There was nothing they wouldn't do for her.

When Nancy was 16 years old, Walter and Mary decided to buy a small Mom and Pop convenience store. The purchase wiped out their savings and they knew they would be struggling for awhile. Walter had taken interest in a certain product line that he thought would be a potential money maker. When he called the vendor to make a purchase, the vendor asked how he would be paying. Since they hadn't done business before, arrangements were agreed upon to pay C.O.D. until credit was established.

The morning of the delivery, Nancy bounced into the store. Her energy radiated like sunshine around her. How Walter loved his daughter. "Daddy, can I have money to buy a new skirt?" Nancy asked.

"I don't know, Nancy, money's pretty tight right now," Walter said, but the hesitation in his voice told her he was having a hard time saying no. "Well, how much is it going to cost?" he relented.

"Twenty dollars," was Nancy's response.

"Well, go to the cash register and take out what you need."

It was a busy day and Walter forgot about the episode. Two o'clock that afternoon the expected delivery arrived. The driver cheerfully set up the display where Walter had prepared for it. When it was all set up it looked good. Walter went to the register to get cash for the payment. To his embarrassment he didn't have enough. With a red face, Walter explained that he didn't know what had happened but he didn't have enough money to cover the bill. The driver said he would have to call in and see what his boss wanted to do.

Walter could tell from the one side of the conversation that he could hear that there was a quandary whether they should just take the product back or make arrangements. Finally, it was concluded that if Walter could come up with a third of the bill, they would leave half the product and readjust on the next delivery. Walter agreed.

After the driver had rearranged the display and left with half the product, Walter opened the cash register and started to check the receipts to find out how he could have miscalculated so badly. Walter was dismayed to find there was about $200 missing. What could have happened to $200 he thought? He started going back over the day, worried that someone must have stolen money from the register while he wasn't looking. Then he remembered the exchange with Nancy. But she'd only needed $20 for a skirt. Well, she might have some idea what had happened to the rest, he thought.

Just then the door opened and Nancy walked into the store in a new outfit. Walter's heart sank. He couldn't believe his little girl would do this. "How much money did you take this morning, Nancy?" he asked.

"Oh, I think about $200," she said innocently.

"$200? But you said a skirt cost $20," Walter exclaimed.

"It did," Nancy smiled as she twirled to show off the new skirt, "but you said take what I needed and I needed a new blouse and shoes and purse to go with it. Aren't they pretty?"

She glanced at her father and realized that something was not right. "Did I do something wrong, Daddy? I still have $50 left. Do you want it?"

Walter ran a hand over his face before explaining, "Yes, Nancy, I need that $50. I was short and couldn't pay for that new product delivery today."

Nancy's face dropped, she was hurt that she had disappointed her father.

"What did you spend $150 on?" Walter asked, trying to keep calm.

"Well," she hesitated. "They had a sale on manicures at the Mall." Walter looked at his daughter disbelievingly. "Then I needed a pedicure for my new sandals," she finished, apologetically.

Walter was ready to lose it, "A pedicure!"

Nancy's eyes watered, realizing how upset her father was.

Our government has acted with less responsibility than our teenage character Nancy. When it became evident that our economy was in deep trouble a $700,000,000,000.00 stimulus package was enacted. There were many ridiculous investments that had very little potential to create lasting jobs. It takes very little research to confirm this statement.

Considering the need to cut back on expenditures, Harry Reid was offended that his state of Nevada would suffer consequences if the January cowboy poetry festival had to be eliminated because of suggested cuts to National Endowment of the Arts which underwrites the festival. The expenditure for cowboy poetry had less real value than our character Nancy's need for a pedicure.

Americans are upset. They need a break from this reckless, juvenile mentality that is bankrupting our country from Washington. Using the same mentality: You said take what I needed; do we really *need* this type of expenditure?

HIRING THE RIGHT PEOPLE

As we mentioned, some of these politicians should be held criminally liable for their actions. The sad thing is that they lack the comprehension to even suspect they are doing wrong. We must apologize for being repetitious, but there are many intelligent, educated people who lack the ability to comprehend how all the pieces fit together. We want to assure you that we do not paint all politicians and academia with the same brush. Unfortunately many of these individuals have found their niche in our political system.

We at P. S. Norac have amended an old saying: those who can do, do, those who cannot do, teach, those who cannot teach, teach others to teach, and those who cannot teach others to teach, become politicians. The truth is there are many good qualified civic-minded politicians. But they are severely handicapped by these intellectual drones who cannot generate a comprehensive plan to contribute to our political system and merely serve as a rubber stamp for the power brokers of their party.

A good testimony of this is the health care bill which has recently been passed. It is so flawed that it blatantly demonstrates the lack of comprehension that the designers had. Proof in point: the many waivers that have had to be issued.

We do have comprehensive minds in this country and they need to be encouraged to become part of the answer to our political needs. We must reach out to them. As we look at the extraordinary accomplishments of these comprehensive minds, rather in commerce or industry, we are confident that with a country as economically powerful as ours there can be, with their contribution, a resolve to a great deal of our financial and health care problems.

We are familiar with the terms IQ: intelligence quotient anc EQ: emotional quotient. Before we hire our potential politicians we suggest that we inquire into their CQ: comprehension quotient. Hopefully there would be bipartisan groups volunteering their time to assist in developing a system to accomplish this.

The truth is we have allowed our politics to be driven partially by snake-oil salesman. We sincerely believe that it is time for us to become a little more sophisticated and use our intellect to investigate these matters. We cannot afford to have intellectual drones governing "we the people".

GETTING MONEY OUT OF POLITICS

From the beginning of our country, money's influence in politics has prevented democracy from living up to its full potential. Even though we claim to be a democracy it does not take much research to uncover the fact that the governing of our country has been done mainly by the power brokers. It was the power brokers that influenced the Indian Removal Act of 1830. Today there are wealthy lobbying firms whose very existence testifies to money's corrupting influence.

Many of our states and municipalities are teetering on the brink of financial failure, some having already declared bankruptcy, because of illegally constructed labor contracts.

Why do we say illegal? The basis of this reasoning is quite simple: The legislators, hired by the community, have the legal responsibility to negotiate for the safety and the security of the community. Review of these contracts reveals the blatant disregard of these legal responsibilities with which legislators have acted. In many cases these legislators should be held criminally responsible; some already have.

It is against the law to take possession of any illegally attained goods. It is also against the law to bribe elected officials. The aforementioned contracts can easily be seen as a product of bribery, since many of these labor unions openly contribute and campaign for these officials. Even though the money exchanged does not go directly into the official's pocket, he unquestionably benefits.

Labor unions contributing to political causes also negates the vote of their members who do not agree with that political agenda. An individual should feel comfortable that his money is not being spent contrary to his values. Monies collected as union dues should be distributed in benefiting the health and welfare of union members, not used to advance any political agenda.

"We the people" should demand that laws be written and passed prohibiting labor unions from contributing to any political cause, directly or indirectly: This is vital to getting money out of politics.

We have written that political parties are no more than elitists country clubs. Look at the history of major political parties: rampant with evil, injustice and corruption, one might come to the conclusion that they should be emasculated; their power stripped away — please forgive the Clint Eastwood moment. However, political parties do play a major role in the mechanical outworking of the political system creating strong community awareness.

Our personal viewpoint is that belonging to a political party is unpatriotic since it tends to create loyalty to the party and not the country. The large contributions to these political parties have empowered them and created the undesired power brokers that have corrupted our political system. Political candidates feel obligated to play the political game, staying in good standing with their party in order to receive funding for their campaigns.

Now consider, if individual citizens would accept the responsibility – as we have published previously: true freedom is not possible without responsibility -- to put in the effort to study the political agenda of each candidate in order to make informed decisions as to which candidates and what causes we want to support, we would then contribute most of our monies directly to the individual candidate or cause, limiting the amount of money going to the parties and reducing the influence of the power brokers. The result will be that elected officials will be less inclined to vote along strictly party lines, hopefully reducing the gridlock in politics and taking back democracy, giving more power to the individual citizen.

LARRY

On our website, www.psnorac.com, under the discussion *Barack Obama*, when questioned if I was going to vote for Barack Obama for President, I commented: "That would be a tragedy. Hire a teenager while he knows it all." However, as was true with many Americans, I felt proud when Barack Obama was elected President. It was evident that our country was becoming color blind. I had seen this in my children and in sports.

My hopes now became centered in a young man named Barack Obama. Did he have the intellect and the comprehension to move our country forward? To deny him the opportunity would be wrong and a failure to recognize that occasionally we do have individuals who see the entire picture and know where all the pieces fit, regardless of their experience.

When the Gulf oil disaster happened, knowing that there was over a month's time before the oil would come ashore, I felt confident a serious tragedy could be prevented. But when I saw that the government was acting as an impedance rather than as an enabler, I became frustrated, particularly when I viewed the activity of Governor Bobby Jindal. *LARRY* came into existence to tell the story of a president with the character displayed by Governor Jindal.

LARRY is written with the intent of entertainment, but it also makes a statement on many fine men who have comprehensive minds, putting things together and successfully overcoming problems.

LARRY

By

P. S. Norac

Inspired by

Governor Bobby Jindal

Dedicated to the memory of

My father, Paul, Sr.

Who refused to understand the words:

"I can't"

LARRY

A red-headed twelve-year-old boy kicked a can down the sidewalk. The tin can veered off the concrete and the lad calmly followed it, picked it up to place back on the sidewalk, and continued his routine. Coming to a trash container, he picked up the can and tossed it in.

Larry had moved into town a little over a month and a half ago. His single-mom mother was recently employed at a local factory assembly line. Larry had not made any friends yet. He really hadn't tried. He had left a friend, Andy, back in Cherryfield; they had been as close as brothers. The two had been a familiar sight, if only for their contrast: Larry was tall for his age, slim, red-headed with freckles; Andy was noticeably smaller, black haired, unquestionably Italian. Andy's father owned a motorcycle that had always interested Larry. Andy just took it for granted, whereas Larry's admiration flattered Andy's father, and he took every opportunity to give the gangly young boy a ride.

Although Larry missed Andy, he was not the type to dwell on sadness. He hadn't really put much effort into making friends here in Sykeston. He was sort of an independent young person and just accepted that he would find someone, sooner or later.

Larry carried a burden that no child should carry: his mother was an alcoholic and a weekend drunk. She could generally hold down a job but on the weekends she became a mean drunk. Fortunately, Larry's nature was quite strong which enabled him to endure the evil leveled at him.

After picking up an additional piece of trash and depositing it in the container, he walked on toward the tenement house where his mother had rented an apartment on the third floor. As he entered the first floor foyer, the familiar smell of cat urine reached his nostrils. The lower tenants were not bad people; they just were not very neat. He ran up the stairs to his apartment where he knew this type of olfactory offense would no longer assail him.

Larry had developed an obsession for cleanliness: the result of his mother's imposing on him at ten years of age the responsibility of keeping their apartment cleaned, in addition to doing the dishes and the laundry. Ten years was a very young age to expect this type of responsibility, but Larry had character strength that prevented this type of burden from crushing him.

This obsession developed primarily because his mother, when drunk, would find some inconsequential thing of which to accuse Larry. A crud the size of a pencil head became viewed as a great neglect on Larry's part in his mother's inebriated mind. Rather than being destroyed by the accusation, Larry took on the attitude of being beyond accusation. Once his mother, when sober, had commented what a good house cleaner he had become. This confirmed to him that he was getting the hang of this cleaning skill and even when in a drunken state she gave every indication to the contrary, his conscience was clear. He knew -- he knew how to clean.

Opening the door, Larry heard his mother's drunken complaint as he entered the apartment. "Why did you leave those dirty dishes in the sink?" He responded in self defense, "They weren't there when I left. You must have put them there."

"You lazy sonofabitch!" she screamed.

"That's not speaking too well of you," he let himself respond.

An empty bottle just missed his head and shattered in the sink. "I don't need this kind of sass!" his mother shouted. Without another word, Larry cleaned up the glass, did up the few dishes, and left the apartment.

It was beginning to be his Saturday routine, walking around the neighborhood, escaping the tirades of his drunken mother. In these walks he seemed to always gravitate to Jones Auto Parts & Repairs. Clarence Jones, a slim, wiry, black man, had come back from the Second World War with G.I. money. He had purchased ten acres of land on which he built an auto repair shop. Clarence liked motorcycles and always had a few cycles that he had bought to repair and sell hanging around the yard. The business had grown into a somewhat larger building and a fenced in scrap metal and auto junk yard on the ten acres.

Clarence's son Bobby was running the business now. In reality he was a much better businessman than his father. Clarence continued his involvement in the business but left the major responsibility to Bobby, thus the motorcycles and tinkering on them became somewhat of a hobby for the older gentleman.

In Larry's walks he always stopped to look at the motorcycles. He would walk around them, touching the handlebars, but respecting that they were someone else's property, he usually resisted doing any more. But today he mustered his courage and pulled himself up onto the seat of a shiny, new-appearing bike. When Bobby saw this strange red-headed boy on their bike he started forward to shoo him off, but Clarence held up a hand to indicate that he would take care of this. Calmly walking over to Larry, Clarence approached. "It's a nice bike, isn't it?"

Larry started guiltily, and moved to get off. "That's alright." Clarence motioned with his hand. "You can sit there awhile."

Comforted by this invitation, Larry relaxed back onto the seat. Clarence reached out his hand, "I'm Clarence Jones." Taking the extended hand awkwardly, Larry responded, "I'm Larry Sanborn."

"Say, Larry, I've got something I'd like to show you."

Curious, but with a touch of suspicion, Larry got off the bike and followed the older man. They walked toward the junk yard. Approaching the entrance, two big black and tan Rotties lashed out at Larry, stopping at the end of their chains just short of the startled young man.

"Don't worry about them, they're just doing their job," Clarence reassured.

Larry wasn't reassured and stepped away to give the two guard dogs a wide berth.

Clarence walked to the left, approached the fence and lifted a canvas to pull out a small motor bike. "I think you might enjoy this."

Not understanding, Larry mumbled, "Yeah, I guess."

The small bike was a Rupp, the first motorcycle of a lot of young people. It was no more than a Briggs and Stratton motor with a centrifugal clutch driving a small rear wheel. Lifting the gas cap, Clarence looked inside the tank. Satisfied, he replaced the cap. Taking a rope that was hanging on the handlebars he wrapped it around a spool attached to the flywheel of the small motor. He set the choke and gave the cord a pull. 'Put-put' it sputtered a couple of times and then stopped. He wrapped the cord around again, this time pushing the choke in about half way. The engine started. Clarence operated the throttle a few times, pushed the choke in and the little engine ran reasonably smooth.

Clarence demonstrated how the clutch worked and invited the young man to get on and give it a try, "Take it around the junk yard," he said. "Move the throttle slowly, son," and Larry did. The little bike commenced to move.

Larry navigated the junk yard to the best of his ability, returning to where Clarence stood. "Take it around again," Clarence grinned. The pleasure evident on Larry's face brought great enjoyment to the older man and their smiles told the story. Larry took another turn around the junk yard.

"What do you think of that?" Clarence asked when the young man pulled up beside him.

"It's great!" the young boy exclaimed.

"Well I tell you what. Do you think you'd like to ride that bike some more?"

"Oh, yeah!"

"Maybe we can make a deal. Maybe there's something you can do for me in exchange for riding that bike."

Larry was all ears.

"Is there anything you're good at doing?" Clarence asked.

Larry thought a moment. "Well, I'm good at cleaning."

That seemed a strange answer but Clarence did not have any great expectations. "I tell you what: here in the shop and in the office we don't do a very good job of keeping the toilets cleaned. Do you think that's something you could do?"

Knowing that he was really good at cleaning, Larry answered with confidence, "Oh, yeah!"

"Then you keep the toilets cleaned and after school you can come in and ride the bike around the yard while we're open."

Clarence led the way into the office and showed Larry the toilet which the office girls used. This facility was kept reasonably clean; the girls wouldn't stand for anything less, but did not measure up to Larry's standard of cleanliness. He could see right off that he was needed here. Next Clarence took Larry to the shop toilet. Opening the door Clarence stuck his head in and withdrew it saying, "Well, maybe we'll just have you do the one in the office."

"Oh, no, I can do this one, too," Larry protested.

Clarence shrugged, "If you think you can, son. I don't know what you can do with this one, but you're welcome to try." He looked into the eager face of the boy beside him. "When can you start?"

"Can I start today?" was the unexpected response.

A little taken back, Clarence hesitated, "Yeah, I guess so."

Larry said, "I'll have to go home and get my supplies."

Clarence tried not to show his surprise, but thought, "This little boy has supplies?"

Within a half hour Larry appeared with two buckets full of all sorts of cleaning supplies: steel wool pads, scouring powder, glass cleaner, brushes of every type.

Larry approached Clarence, "I'm going to start in the office toilet first, if that's OK."

"Go to it, son!"

Larry had been in there for quite awhile when Clarence thought he'd better see how the young boy was doing. When he opened the door and entered, he was surprised: The little boy did know how to clean! "How're you doing, Larry?"

"I'm doing good!" Larry was a natural optimist. "All I've got left is this corner over here. It's giving me a little bit of trouble." He nodded at a piece of tile which had a stain from a rusty steel bucket.

"That's a pretty bad stain," Clarence commiserated. "You might not be able to get that all out."

"Well, I really want to try," Larry looked up from the floor where he was scrubbing on his hands and knees. "I might have to let it go this time so I can get to the other toilet, but I'll work on it a little more each time I come."

Gathering his supplies he moved to the shop. At first he just stood inside the door of the bathroom, baffled as to where to begin. It really was a mess. Nevertheless he started in. The hours went by and Clarence came in to see how it was going. He was surprised to see that Larry had made quite a dent in the condition of the room.

"We're about to close for the day," Clarence said. "You'll have to work on this Monday."

"OK." Larry started gathering his supplies into the buckets. "After I get these walls cleaned, we really need to paint them," Larry said as he picked up the buckets and headed for the door.

Clarence grinned, and thought, "We?"

"See you Monday," Larry called cheerfully as he left the building. Clarence watched as Larry walked over to the fence and looked at the little Rupp before heading for home.

Monday came and the school day ended. Larry was thrilled and eager to take on the responsibility that he had left behind on Saturday. He gathered his supplies and was soon walking into Jones Auto Parts & Repairs. He explained to the office girls that he was there to clean the office toilet. The girls had already been impressed with the results of his Saturday effort and were pleased to meet the source of this accomplishment.

It didn't take Larry long to bring the bathroom up to his standards. Gathering his supplies he moved on to the shop toilet. After about half an hour, Clarence came in. "If you want to ride that Rupp today you'd better get to it. We'll be closing in about an hour."

Larry looked torn. He knew he had agreed to clean this room, but the driving force behind his ambition was really the opportunity to ride the Rupp. "Are you sure?" He looked at Clarence's big smile.

"I'm sure," Clarence said with pleasure. "You go ride that little bike."

Eventually both bathrooms were being kept up to Larry's expectations and the majority of his time after school was spent riding the little Rupp. The day came when Larry arrived to find a big sign on the shop toilet: WET PAINT. KEEP OUT. Clarence had taken the time to paint the walls and floor a shiny battleship gray. "You'll have to wait until the paint dries," Clarence told Larry. "You just clean the office one today and go ride your bike."

The next day after cleaning the office bathroom, Larry went to the shop to find a fresh layer of new paint and a brand new flush. He now felt that his cleaning measured up to the standard with which he was comfortable.

Larry had now developed a routine of spending most of his spare time at Jones Auto Parts & Repairs. As he would ride his Rupp around the junk yard the workers would ask him to do various errands: get them soft drinks, etc. The workers then put a basket on the back of the little Rupp and Larry was used as a gofer around the junk yard. He enjoyed it. Having a strong presence around the junk yard Larry became known in the community as Larry the Junk Yard Boy.

· · · · · ·

One day in one of the local stores, much against his nature, Larry started to leave without paying for a toy motorcycle that he had been holding and had an overwhelming desire to own. Before he got out the door, the store owner grabbed Larry by the shoulder and demanded, "What are you doing?"

Larry was mortified.

"Were you going to leave the store? You haven't paid for that!" The store owner tightened his grip as Larry tried to pull away. Directing Larry to the office in the rear of the store he called the local police. When the officer arrived he recognized Larry from the junk yard. He took the store owner to one side. Larry could not hear what they were discussing, but the store owner nodded and the officer came over to Larry.

"I'm going to have to take you down to the station," he announced. Larry swallowed hard and was one scared little boy. He'd never been in trouble before. He had always wanted to be a good boy.

At the station, the officer told him to sit on a bench near the entrance. As Larry watched with pounding heart and sweating palms, the officer walked over to speak with another policeman. They seemed to come to some agreement and the officer that had brought him to the station came back to Larry. "You just sit there for a while."

It seemed like an eternity passed before Larry looked up and saw Clarence coming in the door. Larry was relieved to see his friend, this man who had shown him so much kindness; and yet he was embarrassed and ashamed to have his friend know about what he had done.

Clarence spoke with the police officer before walking over to Larry. "What's this all about?"

The words began to tumble out of Larry, "Clarence, I'm sorry, I'm sorry. I've never done anything like this before. I've never done anything like this before. I'm so sorry."

"We'll have to talk about this when you come in tomorrow," Clarence said sternly. Larry could see the disappointment on his friends face. He hung his head and kept repeating, "I'm sorry. I'm sorry."

Clarence dropped Larry off at his home. Larry got out of the car still repeating, "I'm sorry. I'm sorry."

The next day after school Larry was reluctant to go to Jones Repair. But not being one to run away from responsibility, he knew he had to talk to Clarence and accept the results of his actions, even if it meant the end of their friendship.

Entering the shop he wanted to go to clean the toilets as if nothing had ever happened. But he knew that would not be acceptable. He looked for Clarence. Seeing him at the end of the office, Larry approached after Clarence nodded him to come over.

"This is serious, Larry. We can't have thieves around here. There are too many things around here that are valuable. That's why we have the two Rotties out there."

For a fleeting moment Larry remembered his introduction to the two guard dogs that he had since made peace with. In spite of the situation he had to suppress a smile and hoped that Clarence wouldn't think he was making light of the situation.

"What do you think we should do?"

"I'm really, really hoping that you can forgive me." Larry looked into the stern face of the man who seemed to tower above him. "I've never done anything like this before."

"It's not really up to me to forgive you. You did steal from that store. If we go down there and they can forgive you, then I feel I can forgive you, too." Clarence knew the store owner and had confidence that he was a good man who would go along with this teaching moment that they were confronted with.

Clarence parked in the store's parking lot. Larry hung back as they entered the store, but Clarence put his hand on his shoulder and gently urged him forward to where the store owner stood in the door of his office. Clarence spoke first. "This young man has something to say to you, John." In his distressed state, Larry did not pick up on the fact that Clarence had called the man by his first name.

John looked at Larry and exclaimed, "This guy is a thief!"

Larry did not know what to say. His efforts weren't going very well. He tried to speak, but his voice broke almost into a sob, "I can only say I'm sorry."

The store owner put on a good act and said gruffly: "Do you plan to keep on doing this?"

Hardly above a whisper, Larry said, "I will never do anything like that again."

"Are you sure?"

Larry almost felt it was futile to even ask, but finally managed: "Will you forgive me?"

The store owner looked at him sternly. Larry felt his whole life hanging on the consequences of the next words: "I'll forgive you."

Larry said, "Thank you!" gratefully.

Clarence put his hand reassuringly back on Larry's shoulder. "Let's go back to work."

. . . . . .

As the year progressed, Larry, besides his cleaning jobs, was occupied by doing various other little jobs around the junk yard. Larry, being good-natured, was able to give as well as take the jesting that went back and forth between the workers and became very well-liked by everyone who worked at Jones Auto Parts & Repair, from the office girls to the men in the yard to the guard dogs, Brutus and Major.

Going to Jones became the center of Larry's world. The most burdensome part of his life was Sunday when Jones was closed. On that day he was often subjected to his mother's drunken tirades. How grateful he was the day that Clarence told him that he had something for him. Clarence took out of his pocket a key to the gate of the junk yard. "Here's a key to the junk yard. On Sundays if you have nothing to do you may come and ride the Rupp. There are a lot of valuable things back there. You take good care of that key."

Larry did take good care of that key. Many times on a Sunday Larry opened the gate to be welcomed by two huge Rotties. There was an old camper van that had been junked out and Larry spent many hours on the bunk, reading comic books, doing his schoolwork, or just engaging in a boy's daydreams.

One day he heard a scratch on the van door. It was Brutus. Larry opened the door and Brutus came in as if it were the most natural thing to be invited into the camper. Larry didn't say anything but went back on the bunk. A few minutes later he felt Brutus climb up beside him and lay his large head on his lap. Both Larry and Brutus were comforted by this physical contact.

As the years went by many a Sunday was spent in that van. Major, ever vigilant, continued to make the rounds. The slightest bark on Major's part brought Brutus out of the camper to his side. However, when the disturbance was resolved Brutus returned to Larry while Major held down the fort. Major, while liking Larry, seemed to be committed to the responsibility of guarding the yard.

· · · · · ·

Betty and Carl lived a few towns over from Sykeston. Carl was an ex-con. He had spent time in jail for being a safe cracker; he felt he was pretty good at it. Now he had paid his debt to society and was out of jail. He would still use his craft when he felt so inclined or needed a little extra cash. He and Betty would travel to nearby towns to size up the businesses in those localities.

Driving into Sykeston, he saw Jones Auto Parts & Repairs and decided to take a look. Going into the establishment he maneuvered himself unobtrusively so that he could look into the office. Noticing the safe he concluded this would be easy picking. The old safe had been bought by Clarence many years ago and would not serve as much of a challenge for Carl. He hung around for a few minutes observing that the Saturday business was quite active. After making his analysis he returned to where Betty was sitting in their car. "I would say $10,000 to $15,000 there," he commented as he fitted himself behind the wheel. Putting the car in gear they drove casually out of the yard.

The next day, Sunday, Jones was closed. Early that morning Carl and Betty carefully maneuvered their car into the alley between the office and the junk yard fence. The bushes practically hid the car from the road.

Still using caution, Carl got out, opened the trunk, and removed a collapsible ladder. Placing the ladder against the side of the building he climbed up. Taking a linoleum knife out of his pocket he cut the soft sash about a half inch in from the glass. Running the knife parallel with the glass he made a cut on all four sides, approximately a half inch deep. Next he pried the wooden cut away from the sash, using a wood chisel, leaving the glass nearly perfectly exposed.

Cleaning away any debris that would hinder the glass from coming free of the sash, he placed a suction cup on the pane and slowly pulled the glass from the sash. Once he had a large enough access he took a small jumper wire and connected it to the security system, negating the alarm on that window. Cutting the foil from the glass, he pulled out the window pane and handed it down to Betty. He then levered himself through the window.

He stood for a moment, gathering his bearings. Kneeling, he commenced listening to the tumblers of the old safe. It took him three passes before the safe door released. Pleased with himself, he grinned as he estimated the contents of the safe at easily $15,000.

. . . . . .

Larry had been quite restless during the night. He felt eager to get away from the apartment to his retreat at Jones. Approaching the junk yard gate, he was met by just one Rottie, Brutus. Generally both Brutus and Major met him. Not thinking much of it, he opened the gate, locking it after himself; perhaps Major was just making his rounds. Now he could enjoy his Sunday, riding the Rupp, or relaxing in the camper with Brutus.

That would have to wait. Hearing a commotion he looked over to see Major scratching at the back of the building. He was really upset about something.

As Larry reached to open the door, Major charged in, nearly pushing the door off its hinges. Brutus was right behind. Major got to the office just as Carl was preparing to hoist himself through the window and make his escape. Major took one strong leap and his muzzle landed with a firm grip on Carl's buttocks. Carl swung the canvas bag full of money but could not make the dog let go. Major had a real hold on him. There was no way he could hoist himself and the eighty pound dog through the window.

Carl yelled to Betty, "Go get the gun." Betty did as she was told and approached the ladder to climb up and give it to Carl.

In the struggle, Major continued to intensify his grip until the flesh of Carl's buttocks tore free, leaving his underpants and Bermuda shorts hanging from Major's jaw and a stream of blood spurting from Carl's left buttock cheek. Sans clothes from the waist down, Carl hoisted himself through the window.

Brutus had taken on the chase and leaped up to the gaping hole where Carl had just disappeared. Seeing the big black canine face, Betty panicked, lifted the gun, and pulled the trigger. Blood spurted from Brutus's head and he fell back, a heap on the office floor. Larry ran to Brutus where he lay motionless. The satchel full of money was left behind in the struggle and lay beside the lifeless body of his friend. Lifting the satchel he knew he had to get to Clarence.

Going back through the junk yard gate, he took time to reset the padlock before running the two blocks to Bobby's house where he hoped he'd find Clarence. Pounding on the door, Larry burst out when Laura Kay opened the door: "I've got to see Clarence! They killed Brutus. I've got to see Clarence. They killed Brutus!"

The disturbance got everyone's attention and Clarence came to the door. Seeing how upset Larry was Clarence gathered the young boy into his arms. This was the first physical human comfort and reassurance that Larry had received for many years. All the anguishes of his life were invited to come out and he wailed in anguish: because of Brutus and because of all that he had endured. Clarence understood and signaled for everyone else to leave them alone.

When Clarence felt that Larry had recaptured his strength, he sighed and said, "Well, let's go to the shop and see what we need to do . . . you don't have to come if you don't want to."

"No, I do . . . I do," Larry said, gasping for breath.

Bobby, Clarence, and Larry drove the two blocks to the shop. Opening the office door, they were met by two Rotties.

The bullet had merely grazed Brutus's head, knocking him unconscious. He would have a bad head ache, for sure, but he was going to be alright. Tears of relief flooded Larry's eyes as he knelt and put his arms around the big dog. Major nuzzled in for a share of the reunion.

Assessing the events, Bobby picked up the phone and called the police. When the police arrived they started looking over the scene to establish as many facts as they could. Seeing the blood stained shorts the officer poked at the underpants with a pencil. In the folds of the fabric he discovered the plug of flesh that Major had managed to hang onto, about the size of a golf ball.

"That's going to need medical attention," the officer said with a grin at Major. Major wagged his tail and his panting jowls gave the impression of a smile. "Good boy," said the officer, ruffling the dog's head. Major seemed to be proud of himself, too. The officer then radioed in that all local hospitals should be on the watch for a severe dog bite fitting this description.

Carl had been reluctant to go to the hospital, knowing that it could be his undoing, but he reasoned that being Sunday no one would know about the attempted robbery until Monday. The way he figured it he had time to get his wound taken care of and be out of the area by then.

But this was not to be Carl's day. Not only had he not gotten away with the money, to his dismay he discovered that

202

the doctors had been alerted. They managed to stall him off until the officers came to arrest him. There had been a number of robberies with this MO, and the police hoped this would be the end of this crime spree.

· · · · · ·

The day came that Clarence knew was destined to come. Larry was not ready for it. Larry had been running the Rupp around the yard and had been thoroughly enjoying himself. Suddenly the little bike sputtered and came to a stop. Trying to start it a number of times, all Larry could get out of it was a sputter. Pushing the little bike back against the fence, he went to find Clarence. "The bike broke. It won't run," Larry announced.

"Well, I guess you are going to have to fix it," Clarence said matter-of-factly.

Larry had expected some help. "I can't fix it," he protested.

"You know it's funny. 'I can't' are words I don't understand," Clarence answered.

Larry was confused. To him it was quite simple. He began trying to explain what 'I can't' meant. No matter what he said Clarence kept saying he didn't understand.

Bobby, listening to the conversation, finally caught Larry's eye and motioned him over to the desk where he was doirg paperwork. He beckoned Larry to lean closer and said in a soft voice, "Tell him, 'I'll find a way.'"

Larry walked over to where Clarence stood, and repeated, "I'll find a way."

With a nod Clarence walked to his tool box, removed a few tools, and motioned Larry to follow. The two went out to the Rupp. Clarence handed him a tool and instructed him to take the spark plug out. After Larry removed it, Clarence said, "Take a look at the electrode and tell me what you see." Larry had no clue what to look for. Clarence took the spark plug and explained the various things to check.

"Does it look moist?" he asked. When Larry answered in the negative, Clarence responded, "That indicates there is ro fuel there and there's a good chance it is not fouling out. Now put your thumb over the spark plug hole."

Larry did as instructed. "Now take this wrench and turn the flywheel in the same direction as when you start it . . . Turn it slow." Larry started to turn it.

Clarence said, "What do you feel?"

"It's sucking my finger in," Larry said.

"Good! That means you have vacuum and if you have vacuum it means you should have compression; a strong indicator that we can get the engine running," Clarence said. "Now let's check the spark. Take the spark wire and hold it close to the block," Clarence showed Larry what he meant, "and I'll turn the engine over."

Clarence wrapped the cord around the spool and gave it a pull. The engine rolled over. Larry jumped back. The spark had gone through Larry; he had been holding the wire too close to the end. "You got spark, Larry?" Clarence said, laughing.

"Yeah," Larry said, sheepishly.

"Let's do it again but this time don't hold it so close to the end." They repeated the process and spark jumped off the end of the wire. "OK, Larry, have we got spark?"

"Yeah," Larry was catching on to Clarence's technique and asked, "What should we look for next?"

"Well, if I were doing it, I'd check if we were getting fuel," Clarence said. "Now close the pit cock on the fuel tank and take the fuel line off the carburetor."

Larry was not familiar with these terms: pit cock and carburetor. However, he did know where the fuel tank was. Moving his hands along the fuel tank and its component parts, his hand came across the pit cock. Clarence said, "Yes, that's the pit cock." Clarence reached in, grabbing the pit cock, explaining, "In this position the valve is open . . . in this position the valve is closed . . . Now what position is it in?"

Larry studied the part before responding. "It's closed," he answered.

"Now take this wrench and disconnect the fuel line."

Larry was catching on and observed the steel and rubber line to what he assumed was the carburetor. He took the wrench and disconnected the line.

"What are we going to do now?" Clarence asked.

"I suppose we're going to open the pit cock to see if fuel is coming through."

"You're catching on, Larry." Larry felt a wave of pride. When they opened the pit cock no real volume of fuel came through. Clarence asked, "What does that mean?"

"You don't suppose the fuel line is plugged?" Larry said.

"You are really catching on," Clarence said. "Have you got fuel in the tank?"

"Yes, the gauge is reading full," Larry responded.

"Well, let's see," Clarence thought out loud.

The fuel gauge was a worm screw type gauge; as the float moved up and down it would turn the worm screw giving an indication of the fuel level. Clarence closed his fist and hammered the fuel tank. Looking at the gauge and not being satisfied, he hit the fuel tank again. This time he told Larry to come over. "What does the gauge read, Larry?"

"Empty!" Larry exclaimed, puzzled. Clarence explained how the worm screw gauge worked and how it had developed a false reading. Larry put the fuel line assembly back together and put fuel in the tank. The little bike was now operational again. This was the beginning of Larry's developing an analytical, trouble-shooting mind.

Having observed what was taking place, Bobby approached Larry and said, "You might not believe this but what you just learned is one of the most important lessons you will learn in life. What do you think you learned?"

"How to fix the motorcycle," Larry shrugged.

"What did you learn not to say to yourself?" Bobby asked.

Larry, being good-natured, readily admitted that he should not say "I can't"

"What should you say?"

"I'll find a way," Larry said with a smile.

Bobby, looking at his father, said, "I am very grateful for having learned that lesson."

Clarence turned away to hide the sudden wetness that filled his eyes. Bobby had heard.

. . . . . .

Bobby had become known in the community for his analytical abilities. He had taken the business that his father had started and moved it in other directions. The "I'll find a way" mentality had served him well. Parting out and junking cars had put him in the scrap metal business.

He soon realized that some metals brought a very good price: copper brought $.75 a pound, and aluminum $.50 a pound. When some of the local mills closed down Bobby took advantage and made a quote on cleaning out the machinery. Basically, he quoted the price at the cost of the material, steel and otherwise. But the large electric motors, with their copper windings, made up the real gold mine.

A number of times Bobby would make a quote to remove the metal and find that there were machines he could resell. This required that they be removed, so he set himself up to do the rigging to accomplish this. In the course of years, Bobby became known as a genius when it came to rigging. (1) All because his father had taught him one simple statement: "I will find a way."

One of his more outstanding moves was a large machine that proved to be a real challenge to remove. The machine had been put in place when the building was initially built and through the years the building had been added onto, limiting the accessibility of removing it. Bobby came up with the solution of raising the machine straight up forty feet. By removing a section of wall, he was able to put it directly on a double-drop trailer.

In order to accomplish this Bobby literally built an elevator inside the building.

A number of years before, Sam had come to Bobby asking for a job. Sam had been a pipeline welder for ten years and had made some good money. When his parents started to age, he moved home to be nearby and bought a little house in the neighborhood. When he approached Bobby, Bobby said he couldn't afford to pay him the wages he was used to. Sam reassured him that he wasn't expecting that type of wages; he just wanted to be in the neighborhood to assist his parents. They reached an agreement and Sam began working for Bobby.

With Sam's fabricating and welding skills, the temporary elevator was put into operation. Bobby and Sam had worked out every detail that the lift would be safe: guy wires and anchors, etc.

Understanding Sam's skills can best be explained when examining the requirements of being a pipeline welder. A pipeline welder was only allowed four cut outs a year: this meant that when the weld was checked and found not to meet specifications the entire section of pipe had to be removed and replaced with a new section.

In the ten years that Sam had done pipeline welding he had remarkably had only one cutout. Even then he knew what had happened: he hadn't paid attention and had allowed his welding rod to pick up too much moisture. He knew when he was making the weld there was a problem, but he was hoping for the best. He could tell by the sound of the weld and how the flux was interacting. In fact, Sam got to rely on the sound of the weld so much that he could literally weld by ear.

Whenever Bobby was told or reminded how good he was at rigging he would say, "I've got a good crew." And this was true. Even Larry one time on the job walked up to Bobby and shared with him one of his concerns about moving this particular machine. Bobby had already addressed himself to these concerns but told Larry, "I'm glad you brought this to my attention." Bobby sincerely meant it. He appreciated that everyone on the site was aware of the responsibility and shared in it. His attitude encouraged this. Even though Bobby gave a lot of credit to the crew everyone knew that he was the brains behind the operation.

· · · · ·

As can be imagined, learning the attitude "I'll find a way" served Larry well, giving him an advantage for the rest of his life. Not only had Clarence taught him this vital lesson but he had involved him in his pet project: repairing motorcycles. Larry became so good at motorcycle repair that often people would bring their bikes to Clarence for Larry to work on.

Clarence was now in a position to give Larry a small salary which was considerably more than the average teen was able to command while in high school.

Larry grew into manhood under the tutelage of this benefactor; from a scrawny 12 year old kid to a 6' 4" broad shouldered teenager. Larry's involvement with Clarence filled the void of parenting that he never would have had.

One day Clarence looked at Larry's bright red hair. "I have to ask you, Larry, where did you get that red hair?" Larry straightened up from repairing a cycle to respond. "I got it from my grandfather, my mother tells me. Grampa died in the war and I never knew what happened to my grandmother. My mother was brought up in an orphanage and foster homes. My grandfather's name was Harry O'Neil."

A startled look crossed Clarence's face; his eyes opened wide; his jaw dropped. When he gathered his composure he commented, "I once knew a man named Harry O'Neil. There is only one man better to walk this earth and that is Jesus Christ."

Clarence had known Harry O'Neil in the war. He didn't like to talk about the experience, as was often the case with veterans who had returned from the battlefields. Clarence, along with others, had gone through what many would consider a crisis of faith.

· · · · · ·

Bobby and his family had planned a week-end outing in Chicago. Sunday they planned to attend services to hear a preacher they had heard good things about called Geremiah Rawng. Clarence had accepted the invitation to join them and the week-end was being enjoyed. On Sunday they sat in the auditorium, happily participating in the singing program that preceded the main attraction, Geremiah Rawng.

Geremiah Rawng was a very animated speaker and the crowd responded appreciatively. When the sermon turned from the Gospel teachings to that of hate, Clarence started to get uncomfortable. Glancing at Bobby and his wife he noted that they didn't seem to be as similarly affected. When the preacher's words turned to damning white people, Clarence's discomfort became more than he could ignore. Turning to Bobby he said with intensity, "I'm an American. I can't listen to this!" Standing, he left the auditorium. There was only a slight disturbance as a few in the near vicinity noticed the slim man heading for the door.

Bobby sat there for a moment. He wondered what had upset his father. Indicating to his wife that he was going to check on Clarence, he stood and left the auditorium as well. Circling the building toward the parking lot he spotted his father sitting on a bench. He sat down beside him. "Dad?" He had never seen his father this upset and he was fearful.

Shaking his head from side to side as if in disagreement, Clarence kept repeating, "I'm an American . . .

I'm an American." Clarence had always been articulate and expressed himself easily. This broken stammering added to Bobby's concern.

"Yes, Dad, you are an American. And a Patriot, too," Bobby said compassionately.

Clarence said vehemently, "You're damn right I am!!" He rarely used that vernacular. "I fought a war. Saw my friends die fighting that war so that this type of hatred would not exist!"

Clarence had found his voice: "I'm a black man, a black American, and proud of it. If not even a single black man had fought in that war the Americans would still have won; there is no defeating the spirit of America. However, the black soldiers made a dramatic contribution and I'm proud to have been part of that important factor.

"Now I'm supposed to sit there and listen to a man of my own race spewing hatred against white people who fought the same battle that I fought? The united effort that I participated in still generates pride in my soul. When I hear this so-called preacher spouting his hate and the potential divisiveness that this can create I fear that the spirit of America that defeated a hate-filled Nazi regime is under attack. To vilify any individual or group of individuals because of the color of their skin is evil; it is not American and I am an American.

"True there are inequalities, but these exist all over the world. We do need to address them, but hatred is not the answer. As far as I'm concerned it would be wrong for me to listen to this type of hateful speech. I am an American."

"You're right, Dad," Bobby said out of agreement more than out of loyalty to his beloved father. "I'm going to go get Lena and the girls. We'll head home."

Clarence reached to put his arm around Bobby. "When we get home there is something I need to tell you, Lena, and the girls. I want to wait until we get home, though."

Returning to the auditorium, Bobby sat down beside Lena. Leaning close he said, "We've got to go." Seeing the concern on Lena's face he reassured her, "Dad's alright. But, we've just got to go." Lena motioned to the girls and the family headed for the door. Once outside Bobby said softly, "Dad wants to tell us something when we get home." He held up his hand to ward off the questions he saw on the girls' faces. "He wants to wait until we get home. Let's respect that."

As the hours went by on the ride home, the intensity of the moment diminished, the atmosphere returning close to normal. They stopped for lunch at a little Mom and Pop diner. Though there was an air of soberness, things appeared to be quite natural. Bobby looked at Clarence across the table. His father seemed to be lost in thought. As he watched, a tear escaped from the corner of his father's eye. The tear seemed to recall Clarence from the past where his thoughts had been holding him. Wiping the tear away, he looked over at his son and smiled reassuringly.

Driving into the yard the family gathered their belongings and entered the house. Once things had settled down a little, Clarence held up his hand. "There is something I need to tell you. Let's go in the living room." He waited, following them in. Sitting down, they all turned to Clarence with anticipation. It seemed to take Clarence a long time to collect his thoughts. Finally he began:

"I am a black man and knowing what my ancestors have endured . . . the struggles, the weaknesses, the strengths . . . I am proud of what I am. I fought a war against an evil Nazi agenda that promoted that there was a superiority of race. Nazi's view of the Negro was so degraded that they would round up blacks and forcibly sterilize them. I had to fight this war. If the Nazis had won, the blacks would have been reduced to treatment worse than they were as southern slaves. This type of mentality remains evil in my way of thinking. I do not view black people to be superior, although I'm proud of the many accomplishments of people of my race. I do not consider white people to be superior, and I enjoy the contributions that they have given to advance humanity. I believe like the Founding Fathers said: 'All men are created equal.'

"There was one day on the battlefield in which we had come under a surprise attack. We had not anticipated it and were ill prepared to meet it. The battle intensified and we were taking serious casualties. The order came to retreat to a line approximately 1500 feet back to regroup and establish our defense.

"As I started to run toward the newly established line of defense, I felt a bullet shatter the bone in my left leg, just above my ankle. Falling down I began crawling toward a small knoll that would afford me some protection from the line of fire. I was nearly concealed behind the knoll when another soldier fell beside me. I thought that I should try to get to him to assist him when I realized that he wasn't injured but had fallen beside me to see how I was.

"He took off his helmet to wipe his brow. His was the reddest hair I had ever seen in my life. 'I'm Harry O'Neil,' he introduced himself.

"'I'm Clarence Jones. You better get going.' He looked at me. 'You better leave me here and get going,' I repeated.

"'I can't do that. You're an American.' Without another word he picked me up and threw me over his shoulder. He was a powerful man: my weight didn't seem to impede him at all. We were within 200 feet of the new line when I felt a bullet enter into the flesh of my arm. Harry fell down on top of me. I heard a volley of bullets providing cover for a group of soldiers who came to drag us behind the line. I felt a certain sense of security.

"The medics began to tend to me and I asked, 'How's Harry? How is Harry?'

"Finally one of the medics said, 'I'm sorry, friend. He didn't make it.' Apparently the bullet had gone through my arm and penetrated Harry's heart, causing instant death."

Clarence stopped. His next words were impeded by a series of sobs. He caught his breath and everyone in the room had tears in their eyes feeling Clarence's anguish. Taking a deep breath he said indignantly, "Now I'm being told by a black man that I should hate white men when a white man saved my life and a black man raped my sister. Harry O'Neil did not see a black man, he saw an American."

Laura Kay, who had always been Clarence's favorite, approached her grandfather with tears in her eyes and sat down beside him. "Grampa, I'm so sorry." Clarence reciprocated the kindness with a hug. Laura Kay looked so much like his wife had in her youth, which only added to the comfort. "Grampa, is this why you've taken such an interest in Larry?'

"Perhaps," Clarence said thoughtfully, "but I like to think that it's because I'm a good man." He was silent for a moment. "Larry's grandfather was named Harry O'Neil."

"Do you think they were the same man?" Laura Kay asked.

"I've been thinking that," Clarence admitted.

· · · · · ·

Clarence had been paying Larry a regular wage and it really represented a good income for a high school student. One day Clarence approached Larry, "I'd like to ask you a favor." Clarence knew the affection Larry held for him and he was not challenging that in any way or trying to take advantage. What he was about to suggest was something he wanted to share which he thought would be special.

"Sure. What?"

Clarence motioned for him to follow and they walked to the back of the warehouse. Clarence got on the forklift and moved a few pallets out of the way. Reaching over he pulled the canvas off an old Harley Davidson motorbike. "This is my bike; used to ride it when I was much younger. I think I broke a piston twenty years ago — might even be thirty — I'll have to think about that. This sure brings back memories," Clarence spoke softly remembering how it had felt to have Marianne's arms around his waist from behind him as they had cruised the highways and byways of their youth.

"What I'd like to do is work with you to bring this machine back to life."

Larry's love for these machines, particularly the older ones, generated a welcomed eagerness to do something like this. These old bikes were becoming sought after by bike enthusiasts.

They wheeled the machine out into the shop. The pleasure of revitalizing one of these old bikes was quickly engaged in. Larry's skill in repairing cycles was well known in the community and he found himself squeezing in time for the old machine.

Months turned into years and the old Harley Davidson kept advancing. Larry and Clarence used all the newest techniques: balancing the engine to insure its potential. Finally the old machine was ready to send to the paint shop for painting and detailing. Larry was eager to get the machine back. He asked Clarence if it was alright if he picked it up after school; Clarence was in full agreement.

Larry got to the paint shop and looked the bike over: It was love at first sight. This machine represented the passage of his life from a freckled face boy with a Rupp to a full grown motorcycle mechanic with a Harley, although it was not his. He was eager to bring it to Clarence, knowing that the older man would feel the same sensation. As Larry drove into the yard of Jones Auto Parts & Repairs the distinct sound of a Harley filled the premises and everyone came out to admire it.

Clarence was more than proud as he looked at the old machine. Everyone else had walked away having satisfied their curiosity, but Larry and Clarence still stood admiring. Clarence said mistily, "You'll never find a woman as pretty as this — except for Marianne. She was quite a Lady."

Larry smiled at the nostalgia. "I think we should call this old bike, Lady."

Clarence captured with the memories of the love and passion of his youth, agreed. "I think you're right, Larry." They took the bike back to the paint shop and had the name *LADY* scrolled along the fuel tank in bright golden letters.

The word had got out in the biking community about the restored Harley and people stopped by to have a look. Clarence had received many offers, but his answer was always the same: "It's not for sale." One man offered $15,000, and Larry felt his stomach turn in worry that Clarence would take him up on it. He was more than relieved to hear the same answer: "It's not for sale." Clarence and Larry both felt the bike was too valuable to sell, that it should remain in the family.

· · · · · ·

In Larry's senior year of high school Clarence approached him, "You know you are really good at this motorcycle repair business, Larry. I think there's a future in it for you. Now you're going to be leaving high school soon. I've got a storefront building downtown that I rent out. I've been thinking about converting it into a motorcycle shop. I think the two of us could make a go of it."

Larry was speechless, dumbfounded. This was just too much.

"I'll make you the same offer I made to Bobby when he was in high school," Clarence said. "You don't have to do this and you shouldn't feel obligated. I think every American should pay back to our country. I told Bobby to put in a four year stint in the military as a statement of patriotism. Then when he was done, if he wanted to, he could come back and take over the running of the business. As you know he's done a terrific job. But, I told him he was not obligated: if he found something else he would rather do I could manage. I'm making you this same offer, Larry. This would give you time to do some growing and gain a better perspective on life. If you want to, after your service, you can come back and we'll start that motorcycle shop. What do you say? Don't answer me today. Do some thinking on it."

Larry was a little uncomfortable: he knew he had to take on the responsibilities of an adult. He hadn't wanted to consider this yet; he just didn't feel ready. The day went by and this conversation kept repeating itself in his thoughts. He was comforted by the fact that it wasn't immediate and yet his graduation was coming up. The next day he approached Clarence that he had come to a decision. If the offer still held, he wanted to do exactly what Clarence had outlined.

When he turned eighteen, he went to the local Navy recruiter to enlist.

It seemed only days from the time he enlisted until he was putting on his cap and gown. The evening of the graduation came. Laura Kay gave the welcoming speech. She did such a good job. Bobby and Lena were so proud. Clarence shared their pride both in his granddaughter and in Larry. He invited Larry's mother to sit with his family. After the ceremony the entire group, the Joneses and the Sanborns, went out to celebrate at a local restaurant. As they were leaving the restaurant, Clarence said, "Come over to the shop tomorrow after church, Larry. I'd like to give you my graduation gift."

When Larry got to the shop the next day, the entire Jones family was waiting for him. He hadn't realized the affection the family had for him, generated through Clarence. Larry was made to wait in the show room where the motorbikes were on display. Bobby instructed Lucy Katherine, his younger daughter, to bring out Larry's present. She came out of the back room rolling the little Rupp which had been painted and detailed to the best that you could do with a Rupp. There was a big red bow around the handlebars. Larry truly appreciated it. It represented the time period he had traveled from childhood to maturity. He thanked Clarence appreciatively.

When everything was settled down and Clarence was certain that Larry thought this was his graduation present, Clarence grinned and said, "That's not the real gift, Larry." He nodded at Laura Kay who went into the back; Bobby followed his older daughter to assist her. They came forward, rolling . . .

Lady. Larry was so taken he began to weep. He never thought that anyone would care for him this much. But he knew he certainly loved a slim black man named Clarence.

The rest of the day was spent riding Lady. In his wildest dreams, he had never imagined such a thrill. He finally returned, bringing Lady back to Jones Repair. Rolling Lady into the shop he closed the doors and went around the building, checking all the security systems. As he was about to leave he turned toward the back of the building to take a last look at Lady. He had to reassure himself this was real. He started to walk away but felt compelled to turn and look again. My! How he liked that Lady.

He soon found himself climbing the stairs of the tenement house and entered the apartment. Expecting to see his mother in some drunken stupor, he saw her in her chair with the television on, passed out. He didn't pay much attention, this wasn't unusual. He went to the refrigerator to get a soft drink.

He looked again at his mother, but he felt there was something different. He noticed that there was a pad of paper on the table next to her chair. Even from where he stood he could see there was something written on it. As he approached and picked up the pad, he read: "Larry, I love you very much. But my job is done. At least I didn't leave you, as my mother left me when she ended her life, to grow up in an orphanage and foster homes. Here is the medal that my father, your grardfather, Harry O'Neil, was awarded in the war. You are so much like him. I know he would be proud of you."

. . . . . .

A month or two later Larry was on his way to boot camp.

Being in the Navy was easy for Larry. The discipline and required neatness didn't burden him. He was really enjoying this facet of his life. Plus, his inherited physical strength pushed him into the forefront. Larry realized that he stood out. He didn't know whether it was his red hair that made him different; certainly he had met only a few people in his life with hair the color that compared to his. He found himself a leader. He had not postured or pushed himself forward. It was just natural for him to take the lead. On the forced marches, Larry found himself concerned with the welfare of the others, realizing that their strength was being taxed more than his. His concern greatly enhanced the favorable feelings that people had for him. Others spontaneously followed Larry's lead.

His natural leadership strengths, enhanced by the strong mechanical and analytical abilities that he had received under the tutelage of a man named Clarence Jones, were soon recognized by his superiors. The opportunity to become a member of the Seabees was opened to him and Larry started receiving this special training.

He had just got settled into his new quarters and was walking to class the next day when he heard somebody excitedly calling his name. He was startled because he didn't think he knew anyone here. He turned just in time to have a beautiful Laura Kay hurtle herself into his arms.

"Oh, it is you Larry!" she exclaimed, hugging him tightly. Within seconds a handsome black man approached. Laura Kay disentangled herself and turned to introduce her husband, Jason Parkman. Both Laura Kay and Jason were in uniform. "Jason, this is Larry." It was evident that Larry had been part of some conversations between the two in the past.

Larry extended his hand, a big grin on his face. He had become very comfortable in making people feel at ease and initiating friendships. Jason felt Larry's genuineness and clasped his hand. "I've got to get off to class," Larry said glancing from Jason back to Laura Kay, "but I really want to catch up. Can we meet for dinner?"

Laura Kay enthusiastically said, "Oh, we have to!" She and Jason were being reassigned and were scheduled to leave the next afternoon. "Let's meet at Smitty's," the local watering hole that served a surprisingly good menu, "at seven."

"Got it," Larry said and took off to his class. Just before he entered the building he glanced back and saw Laura Kay still watching him. She waved and he opened the door to go inside.

At seven the three were already seated in a back booth at Smitty's. Laura Kay was eager to tell Larry everything that had happened to her since the last time they had seen each other. "I still remember when I rolled Lady out how taken back you were," she reminisced. Tears came to Larry's eyes as he reflected on that life confirming moment. He had always felt like a nothing, but now he had Lady, thanks to a slim black man named Clarence.

Laura Kay turned to Jason. "Did I tell you that Larry's grandfather saved my grandfather's life?" she asked excitedly.

"What!?" Larry exclaimed.

"Didn't you know?" Laura Kay met his confused stare.

"No!"

Laura Kay suddenly felt elated. It would be her privilege to tell Larry her grandfather's disclosure. She then repeated the battle scene as she remembered Clarence's telling it on that emotional day.

Larry listened intently. Then he said softly, "So this medal that my grandfather received in the war was awarded for saving your grandfather's life."

"I asked Grampa if he thought the Harry O'Neil that saved his life was the same man as your grandfather. He figured, with the name and the red hair and all," Laura Kay couldn't help but smile at Larry's red head, "it probably was, but he thought he should look into it. I don't think he ever has," Laura Kay concluded.

The rest of the evening was spent bringing each other up to date on their various lives. Larry, being male, abbreviated most of his story. Laura Kay was a little more verbal, with a few contributions from Jason. The evening proved a very pleasant experience and they parted late. The next day Laura Kay and Jason left for their new assignment and Larry immersed himself in his studies.

· · · · · ·

A year and a half passed. The phone rang and Larry answered. "Larry?" a female voice on the other end asked.

"Yes?" Larry responded, knowing the voice sounded familiar but not readily placing it.

"Oh, thank goodness, I finally found you. This is Laura Kay," came through Larry's phone. "Yesterday Grampa had a heart attack. It was bad. He's on life support. He knows he's dying," Laura Kay's voice stumbled. "He has only one request, Larry. He wants to see you. Please, can you come? You need to see him, Larry. Please?"

"I would do anything for him," Larry burst out.

"We're already at the hospital. I'll pick you up at the airport. Call me when you get in."

When Larry called the airlines to get a flight nothing seemed to work out to get him there in time. He came to the conclusion that Lady could get him there just as fast. Rolling Lady out of the secured storage facility he started her up. My, she sounded good. He knew she would not let him down. Within three hours of Laura Kay's call, he had gotten an emergency leave and was on his way.

The hours passed. Lady was running good and supported his fond memories of a man named Clarence Jones. He had to get there. He had to tell Clarence something. He had to get there in time.

Lady had been running a little over a hundred miles an hour for the past hour or so. The moon was bright. Larry kept repeating to himself, Lady is running so good. My, he loved that bike.

Out of the corner of his eye he spotted a state trooper as he topped a small hill. There was no question that the radar was operational. Looking in the mirror, Larry saw the blue and red lights begin to flash. Focusing on the road ahead he barely missed a raccoon out for his nightly forage and luckily did not lose control. Now, concentrating on his riding, he started down the next hill.

Larry could no longer see the flashing lights of the police car. At the bottom of the hill, he spotted an off ramp. Turning off his lights, he took the ramp. Going a distance down the secondary road, he pulled off and waited. Within seconds the flashing lights went by on the highway. Waiting another ten or fifteen minutes, he turned and got back on the road.

He had ridden about five miles when he passed two police cars parked on the side of the highway. Larry was now maintaining close to the speed limit. One of the police cruisers pulled out and followed him. When the lights came on, Larry pulled to the break down lane. The officer approached and spoke in a polite, conversational voice: "Say, I clocked a bike going a hundred and ten miles an hour a ways back, identical to this."

"Yeah," Larry said, "he sure blew by me."

The officer was not really fooled. "Well, I have to say, I've ridden these bikes, too. There aren't too many of them around. It's quite a coincidence to have two on the same highway at the same time."

"Yeah," Larry responded. "Isn't that something?"

The officer returned good naturedly, "But you got to remember that at those speeds they don't take you to the hospital, they scoop you up with a shovel."

Larry had always enjoyed speed, the sensation was addictive. He felt he had the right: if something were to happen most likely he would lose his life, but there was really no one to grieve. He was a loner; he had always been alone: even growing up he'd been a loner.

Now on this lonely road, with the moon shining bright, he started thinking things over: it might be nice someday to belong to a family. "In some ways, I guess I do. Clarence asked for me. I hope I make it in time," Larry pondered. "Laura Kay certainly made me feel good when we met last year. I know she'd miss me."

Maybe he should start taking better care of himself. For the rest of the trip he maintained between seventy and eighty miles an hour, a much more moderate speed.

The sun started coming up when Larry was only a few miles from Sykeston. Pulling in to Jones Auto Parts & Repairs, Larry approached the junk yard fence. He tried his key. They hadn't changed the lock. He began to push the gate open and two black Rotties rushed toward him. Larry jumped back and closed the gate from the outside. Their aggression was quite intense and there was no mistaking their displeasure at his presence.

Suddenly the intensity of their vocal objection lessened and Larry was able to get a word in. "Brutus. Brutus, it's me." Brutus came to an abrupt stop. "Brutus, you know it's me," Larry called. Finally Brutus pushed Major out of the way. Wagging his tail, he nuzzled his nose into the opening of the gate and Larry bent to pat the big black head. Major noticing the actions of his partner lessened his intensity and Larry spoke loudly, "Major." Recognizing the voice of an old friend

Major came forward to greet Larry. Larry opened the gate and rolled Lady inside.

If you could interpret the emotions of an animal you would say that Brutus was beside himself at seeing his old friend. He jumped up and then scooted away, his whole tail end wagging in delight, only to charge up to Larry again for contact with this man who had been his companion for many years. Larry was also pleased to see these two old friends. In reality they were two good old friends. He hadn't realized how valuable their friendship had been, and it warmed his heart as he bent to scratch their heads.

They had given him such a warm welcome he felt guilty leaving so soon, but he had to see Clarence. Crouching down he put his hands on their heads. "I've got to go for awhile, but I'll be back." They seemed to understand and stepped back. Going into the office, Larry picked up the phone to call Laura Kay.

When she answered, her first words were, "You must have really got some good connections to be here already."

"Yeah, the best," Larry said. "Pick me up at the shop."

"At the shop?" Laura Kay questioned. "You rode Lady, didn't you?"

"Yeah, I'll explain later. How's Clarence?"

"He seems to be holding on, waiting," was Laura Kay's response. "I'll be right over."

When Laura Kay arrived at the shop her face showed the stress that she was under and her eyes were red from weeping. Clarence had been a good grandfather; he was a good man. Not much conversation ensued on the way to the hospital.

As Larry got to the floor where Clarence's room was located there was a large group of people there in support of the family. Larry recognized most of them. They all made him tru y welcome.

Bobby approached, "He's been asking for you, Larry."

Motioning the others to step back, Bobby took Larry in to see his father and then quietly closed the door behind him as he rejoined the waiting group. Everyone seemed to sense the relationship that existed between the dying, old gentleman and this tall, red-headed young man.

As Larry approached the bedside, Clarence's old face lit up. "Larry, I had to see you. I so appreciate you've come," the old man spoke.

Larry sat down in the chair that was drawn up to the bed and put his hands over the thin black hands that lay on the coverlet. There was a moment of silence as he fought back the tears. He knew his old friend didn't have long.

"I couldn't have refused, Clarence. There is something I've wanted to tell you." The old man's eyes flickered shut, but he opened them with effort and looked into Larry's blue eyes. Larry squeezed the old hands gently. "I looked up the records. It *was* my grandfather who saved your life." He paused as he struggled to go on. "But the important thing to me is: he saved your life, but you *gave me* mine."

Clarence spoke and Larry had to lean close to catch the words: "You don't know how important that is to me. The reverse of that equation is that I lived but your grandmother and mother suffered. I never felt that was fair, but I can't rewrite the equations of life."

The old voice was silent and Larry didn't know if his friend was still with him. Then Clarence's lips moved again and Larry leaned closer. "The relationship that you and I have had has done a lot to overcome the guilt I've felt. I never knew I would have a red-headed son, but I do." Clarence smiled and closed his eyes, finally at peace.

Larry couldn't detect any breath but didn't want to admit it. He went to the door to motion to Bobby. Entering the room, Bobby knew his father was gone. His eyes filled with tears as he turned toward Larry who put his arms around the smaller man. They stood thus for a moment before Bobby pulled away and went to call a doctor.

The doctor confirmed that Clarence had passed on.

The funeral was massive. Everyone wanted to demonstrate their appreciation for Clarence. Black, white, and many other races were represented among the community members who gathered to pay tribute to the good man that Clarence had been.

After the funeral service, Bobby approached Larry. "Dad wanted to open a motorcycle shop with you when you got out of the Navy. The offer still holds," Bobby smiled, "it's just that you'll have a different partner."

Larry was touched. "I'll let you know, Bobby, but I don't know if it could ever be the same without Clarence."

"I understand. But I just want you to know, the offer still stands," Bobby said with sincerity.

. . . . . .

Benjamin Slaughter and Carole had been married for 38 years. Ben still ran his fourth generation family farm. He was a wealthy man, but few knew it. He and Carole had been high school sweethearts. He had attended the local Ag Tech College and she graduated with honors from the local Business College. She had displayed a great deal of potential in school, but her main ambition and dream was to marry Ben and begin their life together.

The summer after receiving their degrees, Ben and Carole were married. When his parents decided to quit farming, his sisters, although not having any desire to farm themselves, wanted the farm to stay in the family. They made generous offers to sell their shares to him and Carole and the young couple took over running the farm. Ben and Carole moved into the big farm house, renovating and putting their own signature on the rooms.

His mother and father built a small ranch house in a grove of ancient oak trees that grew beside the brook that ran through the farm. This water never dried up even in the driest seasons, providing water for the farm animals as well as any number of pets: dogs, cats, rabbits tamed to just this side of wild, and other wild creatures: deer, raccoons, a skunk now and then, in season. Nearby, the pond dug by his great grandfather gave sustenance and comfort to many local birds and those on their way through: going south in the fall and north come spring.

Carole also came from a farm family; however, she was the only child. Her parents felt that they could afford to sell the farm and take early retirement. Reasoning that Carole would inherit when they were gone, they decided not to wait but divided the proceeds with her and Ben, approximately $200,000 for each couple, and invested their half in their retirement. Being young at heart and healthy, they enjoyed traveling.

When Carole received this money she and Ben talked about the best way to use it. Carole had always been interested in real estate as an investment. Ben was a little reticent, he knew real estate could be risky, but after many hours of discussing the pros and cons, Ben was satisfied with Carole's intelligent approach and they decided to invest.

They hadn't been married quite two years when they were blessed with a beautiful baby daughter named Amy Coleen, born on Ben's birthday, July 5th. He always said, and Amy grew up believing, that she was the best birthday gift he ever got. Just over two years later their family grew to four when Rebekah Jolleen was born on Thanksgiving Day, November 26th. Everyone agreed that Rebekah's arrival made the day more worthy of thanks.

No one knew much about Carole's investment skills: she was viewed as just a farm wife and mom. Of all the things she was occupied in, motherhood was her first priority. Much as it sometimes irked Ben, he knew he slipped a little in her priorities with the birth of these two beautiful little girls. He didn't understand motherhood at its roots, but shared as much as he could in raising and guiding his and Carole's daughters, giving room for Carole's umbilical-cord-syndrome even after the girls were grown and on their own.

Carole had made some good investments and the initial money was now a multiple of worth. Ben suggested to Carole that maybe they could invest in some of the community businesses. Carole admitted that she wasn't as knowledgeable about business, but if Ben was up to it she certainly supported the idea.

Ben was a natural at reading people. He knew that in many businesses the real brainpower behind the business prospering was often two or three layers down from the top. These were the individuals whom Ben called *the people who touched the earth*, probably relating back to when he grew up on the farm: the people who carried on the physical responsibility of the business.

He also shared his father's observation: "There are just too damned many educated fools around." His father was very emphatic that an education did not guarantee aptitude. His father drove the point home when Benjamin brought home a D on his report card. His two sisters were both A-B students; his older sister, Amy, was a straight A student. Ben didn't see the sense in learning how to conjugate a verb; he was going to be a farmer not an English teacher. That semester he didn't put in much effort, thus the D in English.

His sisters started saying "D" stood for dumb. When his mother heard them treating their brother this way, things were corrected. In the family there was no putting another down: no diminishing another's character. The only thing that they were allowed to diminish and insult, provided they did it lovingly, was the dog. They had a dog that would respond to a variety of names -- Stupid, Ugly, Useless -- wagging its tail in appreciation of the attention.

Ben's father told him not to worry about the D. He knew Benjamin would do alright. His father said, when it comes to brainpower there's something you have to know: "Let me illustrate. You have two engines. One's a powerful 300 HP V8 engine. The other is a 30 HP 4 cylinder engine. Which do you think would get the most work done?"

Ben responded, "The 300 HP."

His father then went on, "Oh, there's a factor I forgot to mention: the 30 HP engine is connected to a low-gear-ratio drive train and the V8 is not even connected to a drive train. Now which one is going to get the most work done?"

Ben didn't even have to think about that one, he knew how machinery worked: "The little 30 HP."

"That's how it is with intelligence," Ben's father said. "There are a lot of intelligent people who aren't even connected to a drive train. It is the 30 HP engine that is connected to the drive train that will get the job done."

This lesson stayed with Ben all his life.

Another gem that Ben remembered from his father's words of wisdom was: A good manager when confronted with a problem finds a solution, a bad manager finds someone to blame. Thus Benjamin was taught the importance of finding a way.

As Ben and Carole's wealth grew they didn't change their way of living. They liked their friends and had no interest in moving into the so-called elitist community. Their attitude was similar to that which was reflected by the news commentator Tim Russets' father, Big Russ. Tim had told his father that he had been quite successful and having the means wanted to buy his father a new car. He told his father to choose anything, a Cadillac, a Mercedes, or a Lexus. So his father went out to shop and the car he selected was a Ford Crown Victoria. When Tim questioned why he chose a Ford when he could have chosen any car on the market, Big Russ's comment reflected the attitude that with anything else he wouldn't be comfortable with his friends.

So it was with Ben and Carole. They always managed to make their purchases slightly lower or in line with their friends'. No one knew how wealthy they were. They mostly bought used cars. On one occasion Ben did buy himself a new Cummins Diesel dually pickup. He ran the dually for 400,000 miles and it was junked out when one of the farm hands totaled it, sliding off an icy road one stormy winter night.

Carole was such a dedicated mother that her girls didn't know that she had another occupation until they were well along in grade school. However, Carole did need help and they had hired a housekeeper. On rare occasions, when Carole was tied up on some business venture, Mrs. Baker would be there when they came home from school.

Ben wanted the best for his girls. When Amy Colleen was approaching high school he sat the two girls down and told them that he and their mother had been very successful in making investments and that their parents would sponsor them to do anything they wanted. But he impressed on them *don't choose just a career, choose a life.* He told them it was time to start thinking about their future. He suggested they take a week to think about what they wanted to do. Then they would discuss their thoughts so they could start moving toward their goals responsibly.

At the end of the week he and Carole called the girls into the den. Ben told them he didn't want them to be pressured; this was just an exercise to get them thinking about their future. Both girls had spent a lot of time thinking about this assignment. Amy Colleen thought she might like to be a doctor: in reality she had the grades. Rebekah Jollene commented that she might like to run a business like her mother did. Carole was surprised. She hadn't realized that Rebekah had been seriously observing her mother and her mother rarely came up short of Rebekah's approval.

After discussing these prospective vocations, Ben said, "There is one occupation that I haven't heard mentioned that I thought I would. Would you like to have a guess?" He smiled at the confused faces turned toward him. "You, too, Carole, what do you think I'm referring to? It is a very special occupation."

All three girls started guessing, coming up with all types of ideas. Finally Ben asked if they were ready to give up. "Yes," they all chorused.

Ben smiled at Carole and said, "Motherhood!" Carole's eyes filled with tenderness as he went on: "It's very special; there is nothing like it. Just ask your mother. And if you girls chose to do just that I would give you my full support. I feel it is that valuable."

· · · · · ·

As time went on, Amy Colleen finished her four years of college and was on her way to medical school. Rebekah went to a local business college, in preparation for her plans. But she had also asked her mother if there was room for her in her mother's business. Carole was flattered and overjoyed that her daughter had taken such a keen interest in her life. But Rebekah also had another interest. She had fallen in love with Seth, a local boy who, like her dad, was planning to take over his family farm. She was following in her mother's footsteps.

Amy had just started in medical school when she met a young man who was pursuing the same vocation. One day Amy approached Mike who seemed to be upset about something. "You know the way the health care system is going," Mike said, "if it continues, we aren't going to make enough money to pay off our school loans." Mike didn't know that Amy's educational costs were well covered. "I've seriously been thinking I'd be better off if I convert my studies to a veterinary medical program."

Amy was quite surprised; she had really been impressed by his talents. But as they talked Mike displayed such enthusiasm for the thought of working with animals she could see this wasn't just a whim. He had given a lot of thought to this decision. She recalled her father's words: *choose a life not just a career.* She asked, "Do you think you'd prefer to work with animals rather than humans?"

Mike answered, "I really think I would. I love animals."

His words took Amy back to her own growing up: Living on a farm had allowed them to have all types of animals. She recalled her personal interaction with many of them, especially Trixie, a blue healer they had rescued. Trixie was so intelligent that the entire family was proud of her. She was not a pet; she became a member of the family.

She recalled the day a cousin had brought her little bench-leg beagle over to have a run on the farm. Trixie knew the boundaries, but Spoofy didn't. Amy looked out the window to see Trixie herding the smaller dog back toward the farm house where Trixie had determined she belonged. Spoofy had no choice: To avoid the nips when she veered away, she scrambled up the porch steps and Amy opened the door to let her in. Trixie followed. Satisfied with a job well done, Trixie flopped down beside the stove and took a nap, every so often opening an eye to make sure the visitor was staying put.

Discussing all the fond memories of the years Trixie had been a part of her life, Amy began to realize how much she missed the joy and fulfillment that working with the animals on the farm had given her.

"I really admire the service dogs," Mike exclaimed. "It sounds like Trixie would have made a good one. It is remarkable the things they are able to do." As Mike and Amy shared the progress they observed being made in this field, they caught each other's enthusiasm. Mike declared: "That's where I'd like to go."

Without thinking, Amy responded, "Me, too!"

Their relationship grew as they both turned their efforts to becoming veterinarians. After completing the necessary courses and receiving their Doctor of Veterinary Medicine degrees they both sat for the North American Veterinary Licensing Examination. Each proudly framed their license in preparation of hanging it in their own practice. Fulfilling the state's requirements was the last step needed to make that dream a reality.

Amy and Mike were married in a small ceremony at the farm on a sunny spring day. After a much needed honeymoon/vacation the young couple opened M & A Morin's Veterinary Clinic. With a little financial help from Amy's folks they were also able to follow their passion and set up a training center for service dogs.

Ben and Carole felt that their life was nearly perfect. Their daughters were both grown and married to young men that they approved heartily of and were pursuing their own dreams. In addition they had fulfilled the dream that comes on all parents, the gift of four beautiful grandchildren: three boys and a girl.

. . . . . .

Into this tranquil life came events that began to disturb Ben very much. He kept saying, "It cannot be sustained. This reckless spending of the federal government just cannot be sustained." He began looking into some of the expenditures of the $700 billion Stimulus Bill. "This is ridiculous," he said to Carole. "Look how this money is being spent. It is supposed to be creating jobs, but most of these projects don't and many that do are basically temporary. The money isn't even reaching the small business people. They're the ones who create jobs. Do you remember when we invested in Bobby Miller? He took that $20,000 investment and within five years had created four full-time jobs." Carole nodded, remembering.

Bobby Miller had been a millwright in one of the local mills. Years ago the mill had need for a large vertical lathe. But as time passed that need had diminished to the point where the lathe had sat idle for seven or eight years. The time came when they needed to put in some new machines in the machine shop and were questioning where the space could be found. Bobby suggested that they take the old vertical lathe out which had not been used for years. He made them the offer that he would pay for the rigging to remove it and pay scrap metal price for the lathe itself.

Bobby had inherited a farm which hadn't been functioning as a farm for decades, but the barn still stood reasonably straight. In the bottom of the barn he laid down a heavily reinforced concrete floor and installed the lathe there. As in many operations there is the unforeseen that has to be overcome. The large lathe had a three-phase electric motor attached to it: however there was no three-phase electric nearby. When Bobby studied the cost of bringing the needed power to their location, his wife determined that it would not be cost effective and that Bobby had made a bad decision.

Bobby wasn't the type to give up. He figured, if nothing else, he could buy a three-phase generator and power it off the power takeoff of one of his farm tractors. Bobby knew that if he could get the big lathe running he could get some of the work that was being sent out of state. Not many local companies had a vertical lathe of this dimension. So Bobby started moving forward: he had already lined up an electrician who would rewire the barn in order to accommodate the big lathe.

The electrician, Jerry Smith, had been doing industrial wiring for thirty years. (2) When Bobby told him his plan to run a three-phase generator off his tractor, Jerry asked, "Why would you do that?"

"It's too expensive to bring three-phase electricity way out here."

"You're probably right," Jerry agreed. After a moment's contemplation he said, "I've got a big split-phase motor that can be rewired as a phase generator. You can have it for $300. This will generate the three-phases you'll need to run your three-phase motor on your big lathe."

Bobby was thrilled. Working on the old lathe, Bobby discovered that the hour meter was still functioning. He calculated the hours and figured that it had only been used about 30% of its expected life cycle. He had really won out on this one.

Next he approached some of the companies who were sending their parts out of state to be turned and offered to do their work. They were very supportive and enthusiastic and began directing work his way. In a short while, Miller Turning became a reality. Carole assisted Bobby's wife in setting up a good set of books.

In five years' time the old lathe was working 24 hours around 5 days a week. Bobby also bought a truck and hired a truck driver to pick up the stock and deliver the finished product. As a result, four families were now benefiting from a $20,000 investment.

"Carole, look at this: we have tunnels for turtles. After the tunnel is built the job won't exist. And look at this: they're spending $300 million on obesity. Now the objective is that if they made good food available at small convenience stores, people would eat better and as a result we'd be addressing the obesity problem in the United States. This is ridiculous. If you go into the stores that are well-stocked with the best fruits and vegetables, you will still see people that are obese. The availability didn't change them and yet a third of a billion dollars is being thrown at this plan."

Ben continued with a few more examples but realized that he'd already made his point and Carole's expression was saying she agreed. In order to drive the point home, Ben concluded, "One industrial machine can operate for a decade providing jobs. Can't they figure out that's where to put their money?"

Within a few days Congress was trying to pass the health care bill. Ben had paid a great deal of attention to this bill and had gathered as much information as he could in order to understand it better. Not much information was being given out, but from what he gathered he concluded that this was a complicated endeavor which would require a considerable amount of time to put all the pieces together. A truly professional logistic mind would be needed, which, from the evidence, no one in Congress had.

He reflected on the illustration his father had given him about the powerful engine with no drive train and the small engine connected to a low-gear drive train. America had not been built on speed and convenience but its power had come from the lower geared drive train of common sense.

In the 60s when the Eisenhower interstate system was being developed, on nearly every job site you would see a B-model Mack truck. On some locations you might see hundreds of them, moving gravel to put in the road bed. If you talked to an old trucker about a B-model Mack the first comment usually was, "Oh, yeah, I remember those. The one I drove had a 5 by 4 twin stick." This meant that the truck had two transmissions, giving it an extreme lower gear: a B-model Mack, grossing a hundred thousand pounds, climbing an 8% grade with the engine running at full RPMs would only be able to advance itself by 2 miles an hour. The 230 HP engine was addressing all its power to a lower geared drive train. It wasn't fast but it got the job done.

This was the feeling that Ben had about health care. The evidence showed that it needed to have the proper amount of time devoted to it to gain the desired success. There are some things that you just have to drop into low gear.

Instead he noticed that they were rushing through legislation that didn't make any sense: we would be paying taxes on it before any of the benefits would be felt; when the comment was made that no one understood what was in the bill the response was to the effect, well, pass it and find out. Ben, as well as many other Americans, was upset about this.

The consensus was that Congress didn't know what it was doing.

When the subject came up, which was often, Ben said to Carole, as well as to everyone who would listen, "These people aren't professionals. Wait, let me correct that, they are professional *politicians* and apparently the only requirement for that is to know how to lie."

When he had a listening ear he expanded, "We need people that really know how to handle a multifaceted problem. We have them: in industry, in product distribution. Just look at the logistics of these large distribution operations. Their profit margin is marginal and yet they make billions of dollars. There is no waste; they can't afford it. If they ran their operations like our government is running our country they would fail. That's what scares me."

Despite everyone's concern, the health care bill was passed, by questionable means, with the majority of the country opposed to it.

Ben was really upset. Carole knew Ben and any time he was this upset he was determined that he had to do something. So it was that Ben moved from being an observer of politics to being an active participant. He had always voted as an Independent and maintained that neither party was any better than the other. He still felt that way.

. . . . . .

Ben got in touch with Louise Cantrell, a paralegal. Louise worked for a lawyer that Ben knew. Most people didn't realize that it was Louise's expertise that enhanced the lawyer's reputation for being thorough and winning his cases. Next he contacted Roger Bloomingstock, another paralegal. Ben outlined for them the project he was about to undertake that he felt needed their skills of research and ability to locate the right people.

He proposed that after the job was completed he would set them up in the business of their choice. This offer was to justify the fact that his project would make it necessary for them to leave their present employment which he acknowledged was no doubt very comfortable.

The future would prove that this was one of Ben's best decisions. The two were very successful in breaking down barriers and locating the individuals in the United States that Ben would need in his plan to correct the maladies that he had identified in the government.

As his plans began to unfold Ben made personal contact with these individuals to judge whether they would fit into his operation. In contacting them some were easily identified as not of the caliber he would need, being politically maladjusted, saying the fault is all the Democrats, or all the Republicans. Ben sought to get rid of partisan politics.

He also had Louise and Roger check into the backgrounds of all the politicians -- Senators, Representatives, and State Legislators -- to see if there was anyone in this group that he could utilize. He couldn't believe how corrupt politics was. However, with this overwhelming fact he was still able to find a few that looked promising. Ben then had Roger and Louise look into retired military people for mature, skilled individuals who could contribute to what he was trying to accomplish.

Finally Ben felt that he had enough people that were interested in following through on his ideas. He invited them to meet together to discuss the construction of a new political movement and a new government. Ben was thrilled at the harmony that was soon generated in this group. Their main drive was patriotism. Although egos did exist they were subdued by love of country.

At the second gathering, Ben, as the chairman, proposed that it was time to select the positions that each would individually fill. "I don't have to run for the presidency. My main motive is love of our country which is what has brought us all together. It's up to the group to choose who is the best qualified to be our leader. I propose we do this by secret ballot."

The result of the voting was nearly unanimous: Ben should run for President. The second in line was David Anderson. David had really brought some good information to the group and was a very powerful presence. Ben as well as others had voted for him. Many had been favorably impressed with the success of David's distribution company and marveled at the logistical mind that had put it together.

Although some people were aware of what was taking place it did not attract much media attention until it was announced that Ben Slaughter was going to be running for President as an Independent. The Democrats and Republicans quickly dismissed this announcement quoting the partisan individuals that Ben had contacted saying that they had not taken his proposal seriously.

They hadn't realized the strength of the individuals who were backing Ben; these were men and women of experience and quality. Within weeks the new political movement announced their candidates for President, Vice-president, and Cabinet. The public was invited to research these individuals. Their portfolios were posted on the internet.

It was said these were men and women of quality with high levels of life experience. The main attraction was they had never been politicians. These individuals were so dedicated to this cause that they refused any outside contributions and paid for the total cost of the campaign from within the group. They were very successful in getting their message out because it resonated in the hearts of the country's true patriots.

Some commentators were so impressed with this movement they coined the phrase Dream Team of Politics, which caught on. The biggest objection against the movement was, *These people have no political experience*, which brought the response, *Isn't that a relief!*

The candidates as well as the entire cabinet were very astute in approaching this new challenge. As they had with their business endeavors they made sure they were fully informed in order to be successful. When the country went to the polls in November, The Dream Team of Politics won the majority of the votes, even some of those who were diehard partisans.

· · · · · ·

The transition of power was accomplished smoothly. The Washington insiders could not understand what was taking place: The new administration declined the showy inauguration festivities of former presidencies. They were there to do the business of the country, not to entertain.

Many objected saying that the world was watching and expected a certain level of this tradition. Ben's answer was: "Future administrations can make their own decisions, but for this administration we want to set the example by cutting costs everywhere possible. Those who object do not understand the desperate situation that America is facing. We are now in the position to state that all expenditures must be absolutely necessary; let me emphasize *absolutely* necessary."

Ben Slaughter was not very popular with the Washington elite. They classified him as a farm boy who didn't understand anything. But to the voting public he was pretty well in tune. Probably for the first time in history cabinet members were chosen, not to repay political favors, but because they were the most qualified for these positions.

One of the first pieces of legislation of the Slaughter Administration was that every bill that came before Congress should be free of earmarks or any other attachments. Each item should be dealt with on its own merit. Many of the politicians gathered against this and it was heatedly debated, but Ben reached out to the public and explained how necessary this was, giving accurate figures of the billions of dollars that had been wasted by this long standing practice. He admonished the voters to write to their representatives in support of his proposals. The people were determined to take back America: The letters flooded the offices of their representatives.

Once again Ben approached Louise and Roger, thanking them for the job they had done so well. He did want to ask one more favor before they took on their own business careers: that they would stay with him for another four years to help uncover the corruption and waste that existed in the government. The two had enjoyed the entire political experience and were thrilled to accept Ben's offer. Ben knew the value of a good paralegal. They were the ones that could detect the slightest flaw in the best polished veneer of any cover-up. Roger and Louise excelled in this facet. Their tenacity was unrivaled. He was convinced they were two of the best.

The two had a very good working relationship. Louise would tease Roger that he was able to break a case wide open because of his intimidating size. He was a big 6' 4" muscular, black man. He never thought himself intimidating; he was just a nice guy. And he would return the tease by saying that Louise was so tiny, she was 5' 4" in heels she would always point out, that she could squeeze in without being noticed and break the case from the inside. True, physically they weren't compatible but mentally they were harmonic.

Ben hired 50 more paralegals and accountants to work with them. This honed their management skills for their future businesses. Washington became a very scary place: the political parasites read the writing on the wall and began exiting, knowing that there was no place to hide. Many congressmen and senators resigned hoping that their malfeasance would go undetected. Nevertheless Ben pursued any criminal actions that had been committed.

Probably what gave Ben the most advantage was that he didn't need to listen to the pleas of the partisan politicians. He had been elected by the people; he answered only to them. He also had the team of paralegals and accountants look into Fannie and Freddie, Countrywide and Acorn. It was a good thing that Ben was the president because David was not as hard-nosed as Ben.

Ben would regularly hold news conferences to have interaction with the press. When a question was asked in order to put Ben on the spot, he would answer it honestly, but then turn the tables by asking the reporter why he or she or the particular media source they represented had not covered some related point.

"Do you understand that your failure to cover this certainly gives a slant to your coverage?" Ben would ask.

"We didn't think it was important," would come the reply or something similar.

"Let's take it to the citizens," Ben would then propose. "If they respond to what we are saying and agree with you that it was not an important point, I'll apologize; but if it goes the other way, will you apologize?"

Ben chose points that were seriously credible when using this tactic, knowing that the public had already expressed concern. So it was that reporters attending the press conferences knew they had to do their homework or face humiliation. Too many of these humiliating incidents could signal the end of a reporter's promising career. Ben's exposure of media bias started to yield results and reporters returned to being reporters again.

A certain element of the press did not like Ben Slaughter, mainly because they feared him. One day on an open mike a female reporter was heard to comment, disparagingly, "He prefers spending time with coal miners."

The media picked this up and ran with it; at the next press conference Ben was prepared to address the matter. "Many of you heard that I prefer to spend time with coal miners. The truth is I would enjoy spending time with a coal miner and his family and the woman who nurtures his children. I find I do have affection for the people who touch the earth. That doesn't mean I dislike others, it's just that I feel this is where I came from and I respect these people." Ben paused, not able to suppress a slight, self-deprecating smile, "Though I must admit I get a little upset with the elitist of Washington when they think they're relevant."

There was no question; everyone knew there was open warfare on spending. Louise and Roger and their team exposed so much that it was shocking, far more than Ben had expected. So Ben continued moving forward.

A good example of the corruption that existed came to light when the Speaker of the House rented office space at a cost that was three times the going rate for rents in that area. Not surprising, the recipient of the rent was a campaign contributor. The mechanics of getting elected, and the pork that went out, offended Ben: he made sure that the citizens of America knew it by publishing all the revealed corruption on line.

. . . . . .

Carole and Ben were relaxing for a few minutes watching television when a News Bulletin flashed across the screen: OIL RIG EXPLODES IN THE GULF OF MEXICO. Ben, with concern, leaned toward the television to catch all the details. Ben had a natural inclination to want to know details and his interest elevated as he realized the potential for loss of life as well as the ecological danger this portended.

He reached for the phone and called Andy Clark, one of his aides. "Andy, have you seen what's going on in the Gulf?" Hearing the assent on the other end of the line, he directed, "Go down to the Gulf, get in touch with those in charge, get as much information as you can and keep me in touch. Also make contact with the men who were on that rig and get their assessment. Hopefully we get there before they have time to create a cover-up."

Then he dialed Roger. "Roger, I need you to find out if this oil well collapses do we have any provisions to contain an unrestrained flow of oil into the Gulf?"

"What oil well?" Roger responded in surprise.

"Turn on Channel 27. There's been an oil rig explosion in the Gulf!"

There were a few moments of silence before Ben heard Roger exclaim, "Oh, my God!" as he watched the flames fill his television screen. "Now, what is it you wanted me to do?"

Ben repeated his request. Roger was not the type to need his hand held and Ben knew that he would find the way to get the needed information.

As Carole and Ben continued to listen to the unfolding story they heard the sad announcement that there were 11 men not counted for. They turned to look at each other and saw their own dismay reflected in the other's face. They didn't have to verbalize: somebody's dad is not coming home; someone's husband is not coming home. They both had done enough living and been on the scene of like tragedies to understand the dismay and anguish this type of event created. Their hearts went out to these men and their families.

Before the day had ended Roger reported in to share his findings with Ben. As Roger began to give details to what he had found, Ben asked, "Is this enough equipment to contain an unrestrained leak?"

Roger was pleased with himself. He was prepared for these types of questions that he knew Ben would be asking. In line with his professionalism he began to relate all the factors and how they would develop.

Ben said, "In other words there has been no preparation for this type of tragedy."

"I'm afraid so," was Roger's response.

"We've been drilling in the Gulf for decades, and no one has taken time to address this potential problem?" Ben asked. He was silent for a moment. "I've got to think about this Could you get in touch with Louise and both of you meet me here in the morning?"

The door closed on Roger's tall figure; Ben spoke into the intercom: "Shirley, can you get me the Vice President on the line again? . . . Thanks."

"Hello, Dave, this thing in the Gulf has really got me concerned. Roger tells me there are no provisions to contain the oil if this well collapses. I don't know where this is going to go but we have to stay on top of it. Could you meet in the morning? Roger and Louise are going to be here . . . Thanks."

"Mr. President, Andy's on line 3," Shirley's voice came through the intercom.

Ben punched line 3. "Yeah, Andy, what have you got?"

"Have you heard? The oil rig did collapse and oil is shooting into the Gulf unrestrained. BP is trying to get the safety valve to shut off, but not having any success so far. They keep telling me they should have everything under control in 24 to 48 hours."

In the morning the four sat down in the Oval Office: the President, the Vice President, Louise, and Roger. Ben commenced to speak: "This thing in the Gulf has got me concerned. The fact that no one has ever addressed the potential of an unrestrained oil spill from one of these offshore wells has got me very puzzled. The knowledge of the potential ecological disaster that this could create is truly frightening. Now the way I'm viewing this, this oil is like a potential enemy threatening to invade our shoreline. It needs to be addressed with the same intensity that an invading army would demand.

"BP says they think they will have everything under control within 48 hours. However, my experience shows that guilty parties always try to put the best spin on things. Remember Sarah Palin says you can't trust the oil companies and she's had hands-on experience with them. Due to the fact that we've been drilling in the Gulf for decades and no preparations have been made to address an unrestrained spill is unconscionable. Just because this is the first time it has ever happened is no excuse. I think it is now time for the federal government to take action. This is something that needs to be expedited in case BP cannot get control of this leak. Rough estimates are that 30,000 to 62,000 barrels of oil are leaking into the Gulf every day."

On hearing this David immediately brought out his calculator. Logistics were not only his strength but also his habit. He punched out 62,000 times 42 and announced "That's 2.6 million gallons a day!"

"Yes," Ben confirmed.

"Isn't that approaching the Valdez spill?" Louise asked.

"No, not yet: The Valdez spill was as much as 750,000 barrels or 31 million gallons, as I recall," Roger answered.

David started punching keys again, "Well, if this spill isn't contained we'll reach that in about 12 days."

Ben began to speak, "The rough estimates are that the oil will reach the coast in approximately 30 to 40 days. That means that we have 20 to 30 days to assemble a force capable of confronting and pushing back this invading army. Although it is not a military exercise it will require tactical as well as technical expertise. David your logistic ability in my mind goes without question. So this operation will fall under your authority."

A smile of mutual acknowledgment crossed both men's faces.

"Louise, what I need of you and Roger is to find three E-3 Seabees."

Everyone looked at Ben with a puzzled expression. They all knew that his authority as President would entitle him to call in the highest ranking officer possible. Comprehending their puzzled looks, he explained: "I have confidence in people who do the physical work. These are the people who get the job done. They're not going to be concerned about their advancement."

He looked to Louise and Roger, "What I mean is that I want someone with proven physical experience, not some desk jockey that has politically advanced through the ranks. You understand what I mean? I don't want anyone whose greatest physical accomplishment is being potty trained."

His straight-faced statement caused everyone to look at each other to see if they had just heard the President of the United States make such a comment. Louise tried to hide her giggle with a cough. Roger cleared his throat with the same intent. But David took one look at Ben and laughed out loud. "Oh, these Midwestern farmers; I love their sense of humor."

Ben grinned.

· · · · · ·

Within four days of the oil well explosion, three Seabees sat in the Oval Office with the Vice President, Louise, and Roger. The President had been detained by other business.

When the President entered the office the three men in uniform stood at attention and saluted their Commander-in-Chief. Louise looked at David and Roger. Hesitantly the three stood up also, in support of this act of respect. Ben appropriately returned the salute. "At ease," he said looking around the group. "Please have a seat." He had already been briefed on the three military men before him.

Earl Jacobs grew up in Connecticut, son of a millwright in one of the local mills. It must be mentioned that when engineers come out with new designs it is the millwrights that make those designs work. Earl's father had always encouraged him in his natural mechanical aptitude. Earl was a family man with three teenage children, two girls and a boy. His wife, Ellen, was a military brat who adjusted well to Earl's military career.

Josh Crocker, from Mississippi, was three generations removed from slavery: his great grandparents had been slaves; his grandparents had been sharecroppers; his parents were farmers owning their own land. He was rightfully proud of his heritage. Growing up on the farm he and his brothers had learned the value of repairing their own farm equipment. The learning of engine rebuilding, welding, and fabricating, etc., had been a must in his growing up. With his wife, Sophia, he had two pre-teenaged sons.

Roger and Louise had questioned the third member of this group, Larry Sanborn. His credentials were stellar; the only question they had was that he wasn't married and knowing the value Ben Slaughter placed on a good marriage and the type of character that took, they wondered how Ben would receive him.

Ben began the conversation: "Gentlemen, and lady," he nodded to Louise, "you are the foundation of a team that has the assignment of holding back and containing a force that is threatening our shores. The objective of today, and I have set this day aside, is to do some brainstorming on how we can collectively gather a force that will contain this potential threat to our shores. As you know, an oil rig has collapsed and is now spewing oil into the Gulf of Mexico. Gentlemen, what do you think would be some of the information we need in order to move forward?"

"We should find out if this is the typical 8" size casement, what its length is, as well as its pressure," Josh spoke up. "That way we can have an accurate determination of how much volume is really leaking into the Gulf."

Larry was in tune with Josh and confirmed, "Yes, $E=IR$."

"That's right," Earl nodded.

Louise, Roger, David, and Ben were confused at these terms.

Josh looked at the four puzzled faces and commenced to explain: "$E=IR$ is merely a formula created from Ohm's law of electricity which can also be applied to hydraulics. If you know any two of the three factors you can mathematically come up with the third. In Ohm's formula "E" represents electrical force/voltage; in this instance "E" would represent the pressure at the bottom of the well casing. In Ohm's formula "R" represents resistance; in this case, "R" represents the size and length of the casing. In Ohm's formula "I" represents amperage; in this situation "I" represents the amount of oil coming out of the casing measured in barrels or gallons."

Ben and David nodded, getting the gist of what Josh was saying. Roger turned to give Louise a smile: "They're the experts," he shrugged; turning to Josh, "I'll take your word on this."

David commented, "The estimates are coming in that the leak is 30,000 to 62,000 barrels a day."

"The 62,000 is really on the high end of what I had calculated, assuming there is 2,000 feet of casing in the ground." Josh responded. "I was hoping to get a more accurate measurement. I would suggest until we do, using the 62,000 gallon figure will be safe considering that this includes natural gas, which will dissipate into the air, as well as crude oil."

"Well 62,000 gallons . . ." Larry paused, putting his thoughts together, "the old diaphragm mud sucker pumps that we use in installing our coffer dams can pump 4,000 to 5,000 gallons an hour." The group turned to the tall young man with the noticeably red hair.

Immediately David began punching keys on his calculator. "That would mean that around 27 of these pumps could keep up with the flow coming from the well -- if we were able to connect them directly."

"This is a beginning," the President interjected. "Now we know we can't connect directly to the flow, so we'll have to work out the logistics that will make this work."

Earl chimed in, "Well, how far out from the well does the oil reach before it comes to the surface? Has that been determined? We'll need to know where to start our perimeters of containment."

"That's a good point," Ben acknowledged the slightly balding, slim man from Connecticut. "But it's been 4 days already and I'm afraid that factor has already been compromised. The spill has already been affected by the water movement; we'll need to send planes out to determine how far it has reached. Louise, can I call on you to keep the notes and the minutes of this meeting so we can keep track?"

Louise lifted her notepad in response, "That's something I can do!" She had been a little uncomfortable with the technicalities that were being bandied about, but note keeping was something she could confidently do.

"So we'll need air support," Ben continued. "We'll need to know the coverage areas so we can determine how many units we'll require."

Roger spoke up, "What is the best way to get the oil out of the water?"

"The skimmer boats seem to be the best under these circumstances," David answered.

Ben turned to Louise, "Please make a note that we'll have to locate as many skimmer boats as available and have them in transit toward the Gulf as soon as possible." He paused as he looked around the group. "I know BP keeps saying they have this under control, but I don't think we can just sit still and take that chance. We need to have a backup plan in place. If this oil gets to shore it will ruin the lives of our Gulf coast neighbors, say nothing of the ecological disaster this will impose." Heads nodded in agreement.

Larry spoke up, "I've seen some simply made skimming devices using a diaphragm pump that I thought were quite effective." He went on to describe how the diaphragm pump does not lose its prime and thus would be less affected by choppy seas. "These skimmers could be put together in a fabricating shop in less than a week. We might have to build some of the support equipment: the flotation devices and the tanks for storage as well."

"I'm beginning to understand the bigger picture here." Ben summed up. "Due to the fact that the oil was not contained immediately it is now being dispersed into the entire Gulf which means the longer it is out there the more area we're going to have to cover to contain it. The number of skimmers is going to be critical to accomplish this in a timely manner."

"I'm seeing the bigger picture myself," David chipped in. "It appears to me we have two enemies: the oil and the vastness of the area needing to be covered. What is forming in my mind is the grid work of activity: one for locating the oil and another for retrieving it."

With this statement everyone in the group had more clarity where they were going.

"Because of the vastness of the area needing to be covered," Ben continued, "it's reasonable to conclude that it will be difficult maintaining the skimmer boats at maximum capacity. Even though 27 construction pumps can handle the volume, the logistics are starting to show that this is not the premier factor." He turned to Larry, "Your idea of building more skimmers is sounding very good to me. Louise, make a note that we need to locate a thousand or more fabricating shops capable of producing these quickly."

"That would mean a thousand of these potentially within a week," David mused out loud.

"You've got it, Dave," Ben responded. "Louise, we'll need some legalese written up that will free these shops of any liability if they have to put other contracts on hold to cover this project." Louise made a note.

Earl's thoughts moved to keeping the skimmers productive. "What I'm thinking is that if we establish a perimeter, possibly twenty miles out, made up of oil barges located about every fifty miles, this would enable the skimmers in general to need to travel less than 30 miles to empty their tanks. I estimate this would approximately double their productivity."

Louise hadn't had much to say. She questioned her contribution to the conversation. But because of the atmosphere in the group, there seemed to be no contention or posturing, she felt comfortable to ask, "When the barges are full where will they put the oil?"

All eyes turned to the small woman with approval. That would need to be addressed.

A number of ideas were floated by the group before Josh spoke up, "Well, with all the flat delta land in that area I don't think it would take too much time to bulldoze up a ten foot rim and create an eight hundred million gallon container site, similar to the ground containment around large oil and fuel tanks. I think this could be quite successful, by installing the proper liners."

"Yeah, that sounds great," Larry said. "We would have to install some type of docking facility enabling the oil to be pumped from the barges to the containment site."

"In my initial research I found we don't have a large enough supply of containment booms or oil absorbent material in the area," Roger commented. "If the oil does break through into the environmentally sensitive areas, the absorbent material will be needed for collecting the oil out of these areas."

"I think this is where we'll have to depend on volunteers," Ben said thoughtfully, "this could be quite an extensive project. Hopefully, the locals will want to do their share and come out in force."

Louise spoke up, "Will these individuals need to be trained in handling hazardous materials? Will they need protective garb?"

"Good point," Ben agreed.

"In the Seabees we do have some good hazmat training programs, right guys?" Larry looked at Earl and Josh for confirmation. "I think we could utilize their training staff."

Ben joined in: "If we could have them set up courses in the local high schools, we could invite the volunteers to take advantage of this training to minimize safety issues. As you brought out, Roger, we'll need to bring in more absorbent materials and containment booms, as well as whatever protective gear we'll need to provide for the volunteers. I think we should use these schools as the centers of operation for the distribution of these materials.

"Now this is just a rough draft," Ben concluded. "I know we'll need to adjust as we go along to expedite everything. My idea is as we locate the material around the country we'll have the loads brought in by tractor trailer. The driver will drop the trailer in the school's staging area." Turning to Earl, Ben continued, "Earl, you work with Louise in contacting the schools. I'll leave it to your discretion how many and what location. If you can also locate the barges needed to set up that perimeter you suggested, that would be appreciated also."

Earl and Louise acknowledged the assignment.

"Now Josh," Ben turned his attention to the young man, "that containment you mentioned sounds like a good idea. Hopefully we can utilize a location where minimal dredging will have to take place to accommodate the barges. I'll leave that to you. As you deal with the contractors needed for this, reassure them that we will be issuing waivers for any contracts that must be interrupted for this emergency."

Josh smiled with appreciation.

"Larry, you and Roger will have to set up a team to be sure we can get these skimmers built and put into operation in a minimal amount of time. I'm sure there will be obstacles along the way, but I know Roger well, and your credentials show that you'll find a way. I have confidence in the two of you."

Roger looked first at Ben. He was surprised at the pleasure Ben's words brought. They had worked together for a number of years, but it made Roger marvel to be praised by the President of the United States. His smile spoke his feelings. Standing, Roger walked over to where Larry stood with a fresh cup of coffee in his hand. Roger held out his hand and, transferring the coffee to his left hand, Larry grasped Roger's in a firm grip. "I'm ready when you are, partner," Roger said.

Larry looked eye to eye at the big man shaking his hand. "I've got your back, sir," he grinned.

David turned as Ben spoke his name. "David, I don't know whether to apologize or smile with gratitude that I have someone with such capabilities to head up this project."

Dave was flattered and answered, "I'll do my best, Ben."

Ben turned to the group, "The reason I have confidence in this group is that I know you'll take care of the details. There's an old poem, a variation of a quote from Ben Franklin I believe, you've no doubt heard, but if not I hope you'll appreciate it:

> For want of a nail the shoe was lost
> For want of a shoe the horse was lost
> For want of a horse the rider was lost
> For want of a rider the battle was lost
> For want of a battle the kingdom was lost
> And all for the want of a horseshoe nail

"I say this to impress that it is so often the details that can be the biggest threat to any plan."

. . . . . .

Within days tractor trailers with containment booms, absorbent materials, and hazmat apparatus were showing up at the selected high schools. Bulldozers were in place creating the containment site. Coffer dams were being put into place in order to build the docking facilities for the barges. Fabricating shops throughout the country were in the process of assembling skimmers. A fleet of planes and helicopters were actively locating the oil slicks, working in coordination with the available skimmers.

David had organized a fleet of planes and helicopters. They were deployed with flotation devices that could be dropped on the oil slick having a homing beacon that would enable the skimmers to locate these areas in a more timely fashion. The pilots would forward the coordinates of these oil slicks into a central computer base. David had gathered some of the professional computer programmers he had worked with in the past to write a program that would locate the closest available skimmer to these coordinates: thus the captains of the skimmers would be dispatched to these locations. This was especially effective for the more sizable oil slicks.

However, there were numerous fragments which had separated and remained a threat. For these David called for volunteers with boats capable of carrying a 1500 gallon tank on deck. The government also supplied the pumps that could effectively retrieve these small spills as well as the fuel for these volunteers. The volunteer vessels were dispatched in such a way that all areas of the immediate shoreline were covered, creating a defensive wall against the threat of oil coming ashore. Occasionally some of these small boats were sent further out to assist the skimmers. This gave the personnel of these smaller boats a sense of contribution, breaking the tedium of trying to locate these smaller, sometimes elusive, fragments of oil.

· · · · · ·

Most individuals do not appreciate or understand the character that makes up a good manager and the successful person who runs a small business. To these people it is not a job, it is an occupation. There is hardly a moment of their waking hours that their responsibilities are not foremost on their minds.

Ben was blessed or cursed with this type of personality. When he was responsible, he was absolutely responsible; his responsibilities were ever present. He knew that the people he cared about on the Gulf coast were depending on him. He could not let them down. Until he was confident that this oil spill was completely under control, this crisis occupied him.

As in other ventures of his life he would wake in the middle of the night, concerned about some detail or other. So it was one night Ben woke, turning on the light on his bedside table, he scribbled a few notes on the pad he kept there for just such occasions. Carole, wakened by the light, turned to look at him, her expression asking if he was alright. "Just making a note of something I want to take care of in the morning," he assured her, "go back to sleep."

The next day he called Earl, "You know the trailers we re dropping at these schools -- the ground might be soft and the landing gears might sink into the ground. Too, we'll need stairs so that the volunteers can get in and out of the trailers safely."

Earl assured, "Already taken care of. We put large planks in place for the landing gears, and sets of stairs have been built."

Ben drew in a deep breath of relief.

The following night Carole was wakened again as Ben turned on the light to scribble a few notes. In the morning Ben called Larry. "Larry, we've got all these additional skimmers and barges collected. My concern is do we have enough moorings for all the crafts to be secured if we were to be confronted with a major storm?"

"Yes, we've been increasing our moorings and right now we have more than enough," Larry proclaimed.

Ben felt reassured. These guys were on the job.

He had expressed his concerns to Carole. The following night as Ben slid under the blankets beside her, Carole leaned over to kiss his cheek. "I think you can sleep on a windy night, I think you've got all your bases covered."

This was in reference to a story they had heard years before which had stayed with them because of the catchy phase and what it meant.

Farmer Brown had a bad habit of procrastinating. His wife had been nagging him to get to town to hire help before all the good workers were spoken for. Finally he went to town to get her off his back.

All of the normal places were empty of prospective workers. There was just one man sitting at a back table. He approached the man to ask if he was looking for work. The reply was, "Yes, my name is John, and I am looking for work. Are you in need?"

Farmer Brown said, "Yes, what are your qualifications?"

John responded, "I can sleep on a windy night."

277

Farmer Brown looked puzzled. What a strange answer. No wonder no one had hired him. But John looked fit and since no one else was available, Farmer Brown agreed to give him a try. When he and John returned to the farm, he told Mrs. Brown of the experience. She looked at him as if to say, I told you so, meaning he should have gone earlier while there were still some good workers available.

However, as the days progressed, John proved to be an exceptional worker. Farmer Brown and Mrs. Brown puzzled over that strange comment: I can sleep on a windy night.

Then the day came when the sun was beating down on Farmer Brown and John as they worked in the field. It was unforgivingly hot. Not even the slightest movement of air could be felt. The day ended. Farmer Brown, Mrs. Brown, and John ate the evening meal. John left to retire for the night. Farmer Brown and his wife did the same.

Around 9:30 the wind began to blow. Within minutes it grew in intensity, waking Farmer Brown from a dead sleep. "I've got to go get John and make sure everything is secure," he exclaimed, excitedly, as he pulled on his pants over his pajamas and bent to lace his boots.

Mrs. Brown rolled out of bed and grabbed her robe and slippers, saying, "Maybe I'd better come help."

Farmer Brown approached the bedroom where John was sleeping. He pounded on the door. No response. He tried *the door and found it locked. He pounded on the door again; still no response. His wife appeared and Farmer Brown turned in exasperation, "That no good John. I can't seem to rouse him. Is this what he means, He can sleep on a windy night? That no good John. You try to wake him. I've got to go get things taken care of."*

Farmer Brown rushed outside and made his way to the chicken coop. He found it closed and secured; the shutters tight against the wind. He went on to the barn. The doors were closed and secured. Starting to make the rounds, he found every place secured and safe in the storm. Now he understood what John had meant: He could sleep on a windy night.

John was aware what a thermal high pressure was. When the sun went down it would naturally create high wind. The conditions of that day had been perfect for such a scenario. Being aware of that John had made sure that all was secure before going to bed. Farmer Brown hadn't. Now John slept peacefully, while Farmer Brown frantically ran around in the wind checking on all the places that John had secured. Yes, John was right. He could sleep on a windy night.

So it is that many people do not comprehend the dimension of truly motivated, responsible individuals.

· · · · · ·

Three weeks from the explosion the last skimmer was put in place and Ben Slaughter's team felt confident of success.

The oil was still approximately twenty miles from shore. Then the dreaded announcement came: a hurricane was forming that could threaten the Gulf Coast and all their efforts.

David had designed a program to address this contingency and preparation for the hurricane took center stage. All equipment was brought to shore and securely attached to the prepared moorings to ride out the storm. Fortunately Hurricane Beatrice topped out as only a Category 2+ storm. The oil moved closer to shore but still did not threaten the sensitive marshlands.

However, one of the barges broke free from its mooring and was pushed up against the rocks, resulting in a gash in one of the tanks that allowed oil to spill out. As the oil came ashore again David's preparation came into play. As computers automatically dialed the volunteers and told them what station to report to the following morning, a sense of community filled the local citizens as they willingly rushed to get their hazmat equipment and report to the organizers. Individuals not called also showed up demonstrating their sense of community and patriotism.

Within a few days all things appeared to be again under control. Ben called the team of six to the White House. He wanted to hear their personal experiences and they were eager to share them with him and each other. Each one's pride was manifest as they related the problems they had been able to overcome.

The conversation then turned to BP and its so far failed efforts to plug the leak. Larry said he had an idea he'd like to run by the group and see what they thought. He began to explain his idea of hooking onto the bottom of the well casing in order to have an anchor and leverage to plug the well.

"What we would need to do is send a rod into the casing, all the way through the bottom into the well. Once it passes through the bottom of the casing it releases into a 'T' anchoring it. At the top of the casing the rod would be threaded so that a plug could be screwed down into the casing. We could screw a plug tight into the casing pretty much like we would press a hub into a forklift's hard rubber wheel."

Earl commented, "I don't think you could get that type of pressure out of a screw press: you couldn't overcome the friction. The presses that are used to press the hub into a forklift tire are hydraulic, developing 50 to 100 tons of pressure." He paused before saying: "The design of the rod to release into a 'T' anchoring it to the bottom of the casing sounds very workable."

"Another thing we need to consider," Josh spoke up, "is that we have a considerable amount of natural gas being released coming up through that casing. It is possible that the casing is now chilled to hundreds of degrees below zero, making it very fragile, and too much pressure could cause it to fracture. Also the chilling has no doubt caused it to contract allowing it to loosen from the earth that it was pushed into. If we were to cap it without addressing this it could shoot out of the ocean floor like an extruded noodle."

Everyone looked at each other. A noodle didn't sound very threatening but it served to illustrate what could take place, and they all understood that the casing shooting out of the ocean floor could be very threatening. Without the casing, the oil bursting out of the ocean floor would be similar to a damn breaking allowing all the oil to gush into the ocean. This would be ecological Armageddon.

They batted around a number of different ideas. Finally Larry said, "It is evident we can't allow the casing to build up too much pressure. We'll need to find a way to raise the temperature and slowly constrict the flow."

"If the rod going down into the casing was hollow," Earl spoke up, "couldn't we force hot oil down into it with portholes that would allow the hot oil to release into the casing, mix with the oil and natural gas, warming it and thus warming the casing?" He looked around the group to see how this suggestion was received.

Heads began to nod as they assimilated the suggestion.

Continuing to work out the details, the group concluded that the solution would be a brass elbow that would fit down over the casing, allowing the oil to continue to flow, out now having the capability of controlling it by means of an additional valve. The rod would run through the 90 degree angle of the elbow, and being anchored to the bottom of the casing, would enable the elbow to be drawn down over the casing. The bore of the elbow would be such that as the casing and the elbow came to an ambient temperature, a seal would be created between the casing and the elbow, the elbow being brass and very malleable.

"We should send this idea to BP," Ben said, "and see if it's something they can work with."

The three Seabees immediately went to a mechanical draftsman and had the design drawn up. The next morning they were at the White House with the blueprints. David and the President guaranteed that the plan would get to the people at BP who were making the decisions.

Reluctantly BP conceded the credibility of the plan. Within a few days the apparatus had been fabricated and ready for installation.

. . . . . .

The country held its breath. Nothing had worked so far.

As with the other attempts, BP named the operation. When they questioned what it should be called someone asked who had designed this device? "A Seabee named Larry came up with the original idea," someone revealed.

"That's what we'll call it then, 'Operation Larry'," the head engineer proclaimed.

The news media ran with it and everywhere people were questioning if 'Operation Larry' would be any more successful than the previous attempts. Larry was hounded by the press.

Larry hadn't realized that he would be thrust onto the public stage and was uncomfortable that he would be credited with the design, knowing how much Earl and Josh had contributed as well. Wanting to set the record straight he approached Earl and Josh. Instead of finding any posturing on their part, he found them amused at all the media frenzy that was causing such discomfort to this generally good-natured guy.

Larry approached David to ask for a few days off to get away from the pressure of the press. Understanding the discomfort of the spotlight, David agreed that Larry needed some personal time. Hopefully the media would center its attention on the operation and not the designer; the success of the operation should be the focus.

With the backing of the Vice President, Larry was granted a special leave. He flew back to the naval base where Lady was in storage. Through stressful situations in his life, Larry had turned to Lady for comfort and solace. Riding the classic Harley also connected him to his mentor and dear friend, Clarence.

Although the soldiers on the base were quite respectful, the media notoriety was still evident. Larry couldn't wait to get on Lady and take a nice long ride. Gathering a few personal items, he stowed them in the saddle bag, rode through security and out to the open highway. With his helmet on he was pretty well disguised, but there was no disguising Lady; she was a classic.

As the miles passed under the tires, Larry could feel the tension lifting from his shoulders. With this event garnering worldwide attention, he wished he had Clarence to go to. Clarence had always been able to help him put things into perspective. Again, although being a loner and generally being content, he realized why people needed family. The only family he had ever known was Clarence.

Out of the blue he remembered the tender sisterly embrace that Laura Kay had bestowed on him when they had run into each other at the training academy. That embrace had been a statement that to her Larry was family.

Unbidden, Larry was suddenly aware how much he longed for family connection. He decided to call Laura Kay and see if he could come spend some time with her and Jason.

Laura Kay picked up the phone. "Hello, Laura Kay, this is Larry." She was startled. She never thought she'd be receiving a call from him. Momentarily she was speechless. In the time lapse Larry broke in, "This is Larry. Larry Sanborn."

Laura Kay found her voice. "Yes, I know who it is! Wow what a surprise to hear from you! You've made quite a name for yourself."

"I know, but it's not my fault!" Larry responded. "I'd like to ask a favor. Could I come down to Florida and spend some time with you and Jason? I need to get away."

Silence met his request. Suddenly Larry felt he had been too impulsive. He might have been mistaken about their last meeting.

"Larry," Laura Kay's voice came over the phone, "I wouldn't deny you anything. You're like a brother to me. . . but Jason and I are divorced." Laura Kay thought that Larry's request was based on the friendship that had been so evidently developing between the two men during the time they had spent together. "So Jason wouldn't be here..."

"I share the feeling . . . you are like a sister to me . . . I really want to see you not Jason."

Tears filled Laura Kay's eyes. The divorce had been very stressful and the brotherly tenderness she heard in Larry's voice loosened the tight grip she had been holding on her emotions. She realized she needed to see him as well. She swallowed the tears before she spoke. "That would be great. I could sure use some family." There was a pause. "I have a small house here with an extra bedroom. The bedroom *is* small . . .

I'm not sure but that your head and feet will touch both walls." Laura smiled, remembering how tall he was.

Larry heard the humor that replaced the sadness that had filled her voice when she had told him about the divorce. "Hey, I've slept diagonal in many beds. Remember I was stationed in Korea for awhile and they're not big people."

Laura Kay laughed as she imagined that scene.

"You are bringing Lady, aren't you?" Laura Kay asked. As Larry confirmed it, she said, "I have a small garage where you can put her inside."

Within moments Larry and Lady were on the highway heading for Florida. Lady was running so good it was similar to the sensation of heading home.

· · · · · ·

The sky was radiating all the glory of the sunset as Larry pulled in to the drive of 1701 Oak Street. He saw the small garage at the end of the drive. Rolling the door up, he pushed Lady inside and pulled the door down behind him. Putting the security pins in place he grabbed his knapsack and left by the small entrance door. Turning the lock, he closed it behind him. Hearing the latch fall into place he thought, "I hope she has a key for this."

The back door of the house opened and Laura Kay stood framed in the doorway for a moment. Walking across the breezeway she met him halfway. They stopped a few feet apart, just looking into each other's eyes. Both sensed the comfort of seeing a family loved one after a long time apart. She opened her arms, saying, "Welcome!" Without hesitation, Larry stepped forward and bent to give her an appreciative hug.

The evening went quickly in bringing each other up to date on what had happened since they last met. They hadn't realized how late it was until the clock on the mantle chimed twelve o'clock.

"I suppose you're tired," Laura Kay said, glancing at her watch.

Larry didn't disagree.

Laura Kay showed him the guest room, and true to her description, Larry thought he might have to sleep diagonal. But it had been a long trip and he could feel himself unwinding. He knew he wouldn't have any trouble falling asleep.

· · · · · ·

The smell of coffee woke Larry in the morning.

Laura Kay's military career had been rather mediocre, mostly doing paper work at one type of desk or another. However, Larry's military career had been quite active and he thrilled to share with her all that he experienced being stationed in various parts of the world. His pride in being a Seabee was evident.

Turning to Laura Kay, Larry said, "You know the Seabees are 'can do' people. That's pretty much the opposite of 'can't do' people. Your grandfather taught me how to be a 'can do' person." Larry grinned. "I have to admit it took a 12,000 volt shock to get me started."

Laura Kay looked startled. She knew her grandfather wouldn't do anything dangerous.

Larry acknowledged her startled look. "It was 12,000 volts, but it didn't have any amperage. I felt it but it didn't do any harm," and he proceeded to tell her the full experience. That brought back many memories, and the two kept trying to top the other in reminiscences of Clarence, as a friend and mentor and as a grandfather.

"Do you think we ought to get caught up on the news?" Laura Kay asked in a lull in the conversation. "Aren't you curious to see if 'Operation Larry' was successful?" She smiled as she used the media term.

Larry cringed at the expression, but shrugged, "Yeah, might as well find out."

A reporter was giving an update on 'Operation Larry' as Laura Kay clicked the remote to a cable news network. He reported that BP had been successful in overcoming the pressure of the oil coming out of the casing and feeding the rod into the casing. The reporter went on, "The next technical problem will be the rod going through the bottom of the casing and releasing itself into a 'T'. That will provide the anchor needed to lower the elbow."

Laura Kay looked at Larry questioningly. "Is that right, Larry?"

"He's got it right," Larry nodded.

"Now we'll return to our regular programming," the announcer said as other news of the day began to be reported.

Laura Kay and Larry spent the day running errands and occasionally getting updated on events in the Gulf coast.

The first notice was that the rod had released into a "T" and had firmly grabbed the bottom of the casing. The next was that the elbow was being screwed down onto the casing. Hot oil was now being pumped down and monitors started to show a rise in the temperature of the casing. BP had connected to the elbow and was bringing some of the oil up to the surface while monitoring the pressure. When the casing reached ambient, the engineers appeared on camera with smiles of success.

"All signs are positive. It sure looks like 'Larry' is working," the reporters were broadcasting.

While checking out at the grocery store, the clerk commented, "You look just like that Larry that's been on TV so often lately."

"I get that a lot," Larry said, grinning at Laura Kay. Pushing their shopping cart, they left the store.

They were loading the bags into the trunk of Laura Kay's car when she said softly, "You know you aren't going to be able to keep that mask on indefinitely."

"I know," Larry responded. "You got any suggestions?"

Arriving at the house they turned on the news. "Does anyone know where Larry Sanborn is?" was flashing across the screen. All anyone knew was that he had left the naval base days ago. No one yet had mentioned that he was riding a classic Harley.

"Well, you can stay here as long as needed," Laura Kay said, looking up at the tall red-haired man beside her. "I really enjoy having you here." Larry looked down into her bright brown eyes as she went on. "I've taken a month's leave to recover from the divorce. I still have three weeks left. We should be able to find something to do."

"You might not understand this . . ." Larry paused, "yet you might. When I'm under stress I find a good long ride on Lady very therapeutic. I'm not sure why but it seems to help clear my head." He looked down, gauging the look on Laura

Kay's face. "Would you like to take a nice long ride? We could go up to the Poconos. They're real nice this time of year."

Laura Kay looked up at Larry. The sensation of getting away for awhile was very inviting. She didn't answer right off and Larry shrugged, "It is something to do," he offered.

Answering, hesitantly, Laura Kay said, "I think it sounds great. But you know my mother didn't like motorcycles and I'm not sure if I do."

"Let's go for a day or so," Larry suggested. "If you're not comfortable we'll come back and get your car."

That sounded like a good compromise. Laura Kay responded, "That sounds like a plan. When should we leave?"

"I'm ready when you are. Let's pack light. We can always find a Laundromat." Larry turned toward the door. "Can you give me the key to the garage?"

"What key? I never lock it!"

Larry looked sheepish. "Well, it's locked now."

"Oh, you didn't!" Laura Kay began to laugh.

"I checked and all the windows were latched. I have a strong obsession about Lady's welfare," Larry admitted.

"I guess you do," Laura managed between giggles.

"It's a pretty simple lock. I'll probably be able to jimmy it." Larry started toward the door.

"Wait a minute." Laura Kay moved toward the closet in the hall. "There are a set of keys here that have been here since I moved in. I've never found where they go. They might be the keys to the garage."

She handed the keys to Larry and followed him out the back door. He inserted the key and the knob turned easily as the door swung open. He turned with a grin, "Guess we know where these keys go." He handed them back to Laura Kay.

She smiled. "Good thing I didn't throw them out," and went back to the house to pack.

. . . . . .

Laura Kay's arms circled Larry's waist, as he had suggested if she didn't feel secure. However, Lady had maintained a moderate speed, staying between 45 and 50, occasionally creeping up to 55. The sensation of speed on a motorcycle can be intoxicating to some but outright terrifying to others. This was the way Larry had planned, hoping that Laura Kay would enjoy the day. He was accustomed to much higher speeds himself.

Apparently Larry's plan worked. As the sun set and the stars began to appear, a feeling of euphoria and well-being settled on Laura Kay. "This is why people love motorcycles," she thought. "I wonder why Mama didn't."

As the full moon started to rise above the horizon, Larry pulled into a picnic area. They both got off to stretch. "What do you think?" Larry asked, seeing Laura Kay's face shining as she took off her helmet and shook her black curls free.

"I think I've got Grandma's blood," she said with feeling. "I just love it."

Larry was beside himself. He hadn't realized how important it was to hear these words.

Laura Kay couldn't help but feel his pleasure. "Was it the motorcycle," she wondered silently, "or was it this tall young man smiling down at her in the glow of the moon."

"I suppose we ought to find a place to shut down for the night." Larry said casually. "Let's see if we can find a motel nearby where we can get two rooms." He was well aware of Laura Kay's sense of propriety and didn't want to offend her by suggesting anything that might appear improper.

"We have a problem, Larry."

Larry was puzzled. He thought he'd solved that problem. "We do? What?"

"You're a wanted man. Everyone is looking for you." Laura Kay paused. "When we get to the motel I think I should sign us in. They're not looking for Laura Kay Parkman. You stay back on Lady; I think we'll be less noticeable that way."

Larry was uncomfortable with that. He was a caretaker and always had the sense that a man should take care of a woman. But he had to admit this was a good move so reluctantly he agreed. He had taken out a sizable amount of money to avoid using a credit card that would leave a paper trail. He pulled out his wallet and extracted four 50 dollar bills. "That should cover the cost."

Laura said, "My name is Laura Kay Parkman. What should I put you down as?"

He started to say Larry Sanborn without thinking, but then realized what Laura Kay was trying to do. "I guess my name is 'Sam Lawrence'," he said. "That's as good as any."

"Yeah," she playfully held out her hand, "Nice to meet you, Sam."

. . . . . .

Returning from the motel office, Laura Kay handed Larry a key as well as the receipts and the change. "Rooms 40 and 41." Glancing at the key she still held in her hand, she said, "I guess I've got 41."

They both got on Lady and proceeded to the rooms. As they separated Laura Kay mentioned, "Continental breakfast starts at 6:30. That's probably a little early . . . unless you want to get a good early start."

"No, let's wake up when we want to," Larry spoke from his door. "Sleep as long as you want. See you in the morning."

"Good night," Laura Kay said softly. "It's been a wonderful day." She closed the door before Larry could respond. He was smiling as his door shut.

Laura Kay slept with a contentment she hadn't had for a long time. Eight hours passed and she continued deep in the sleep that was purging the anguish that had settled upon her life in the last few months. When she finally awoke she couldn't believe how long she had slept and how freed of her burden she felt. Taking a quick shower, she dressed and went to look for Larry.

Opening the door she saw him sitting on a cast-iron love seat in the courtyard. He smiled as she approached. "My, she is beautiful," he thought. As she sat down beside him, they both felt a special awareness as her thigh brushed his. She didn't pull away and they both inwardly acknowledged that fact.

They turned toward each other as Laura Kay began to speak. "I haven't slept that well in a long time. Maybe motorcycle riding is therapeutic." Her exuberance reinforced the feeling that Larry had always had: Laura Kay was the most beautiful woman he had ever known. In school she had been so popular and he had felt so inadequate. But somehow things were different now. He felt he needed to express this to her.

"Do you know how Lady got her name?"

Laura Kay knew, but she wanted to hear Larry express it. She always loved stories about her grandmother because she had been told she was so much like her.

Larry told the story about Lady coming back from the detail shop. "Your grandfather said that there was no woman more beautiful than this classic Harley, except your grandmother, Marianne. He said Marianne was quite a Lady. That's how we decided to call the Harley 'Lady'. When Clarence said you looked just like your grandmother I had to agree. I thought it then and I think it now. You are the most beautiful woman I have ever known."

Laura Kay was a little embarrassed and felt the need to make light of Larry's declaration. Attempting to deflect the compliment, she said in a self-deprecating voice, "Oh, yeah: Swing and sway with Laura Kay."

In school this slogan had caught on, partially because it was a catchy phrase, but also because Laura Kay was very popular. Everything she did was done with intensity, including the way she walked, which made her skirt flare from side to side. Every so often someone would jealously say she did it on purpose: In reality she didn't.

When enough time had gone by and Laura Kay felt the fun had gone out of the slogan, she found a way to put an end to it. Wayne Steele gave out a wolf whistle one day as Laura Kay passed him. She stopped, spun around and walked up to him. Pointing her finger at his chest she told him that she had just about had enough; she didn't appreciate this kind of attention. Wayne was more than embarrassed being called to task by a friend of his family as well as one of the more popular girls in school.

When word got around about the tongue lashing, the slogan and the provocation it caused came to an end.

Larry, feeling that he had been defeated in his attempt to tell her how beautiful he thought she was, said clumsily, "No, no, not that. You are beautiful!"

Unsure and confused where this was coming from, Laura Kay hardly knew what to say. Before she realized it, she blurted out, "But, I'm black!"

"Oh, I hadn't noticed," Larry declared.

He stood and pulled her up beside him. "Let's go get breakfast." He smiled as they started to walk toward the lobby. "Oh, by the way, I'm white!"

Laura Kay put her arm through his and smiled up into his blue eyes. "Oh, I hadn't noticed."

* * * The End * * *

Author's Commentary

[1]   Genius

Describing Bobby as a genius is not a statement of IQ but that of aptitude. Aptitude is a combination of natural ability, pattern of logic, life experience, as well as efficient use of the senses. When it comes to the use of the senses, our character named Sam demonstrates this by being able to weld by sound, having fine-tuned this sense. Or an auto body man who can, by just running his fingers over a panel, detect a flaw that cannot be seen by the naked eye. Or the bulldozer operator who knows if he is setting a level grade by the pressure of the seat on his back. This is comparable to the pilot who flies by "the seat of his pants." These are life skills that even Einstein could possibly never have developed. Yet, the millions of examples of this are ignored, being viewed as merely common place. When we view the various skills that make up the composite known as the human race, we find no reason for any individual to exalt.

[2]   Wisdom Transplant

Jerry Smith is an example of the accumulation of wisdom developed by life experiences. There is no such thing as a wisdom transplant. The only way to gain wisdom is to live; using the opportunities you have to assimilate useable knowledge.

POOR RICHARD BUILDS A SUPERPOWER

One of the most influential individuals of our world is the man called Benjamin Franklin. For a long while he was disappointed in the religious clergy of his day; he felt they had not made enough investment in instructing social responsibility. One of the main themes that he promoted was industriousness with the intent of establishing personal security.

He eventually came up with the idea of presenting his values in a publication that he titled *Poor Richard's Almanack*. In this format he was able to promote his social philosophy by succinct proverbs; not surprisingly, it caught the imagination of the populace because it was fortified with common sense.

With his concentration on industriousness being one of the leading virtues, it is not surprising that the hard work of our forefathers brought forth the success that it did. In fact this high work-ethic does not exist in every culture. One of the difficulties that companies face in establishing plants in other countries is the lack of this work-ethic: these workers are completely confused by this concept.

Though Benjamin Franklin's intent was not in support of wealth and greed, it has become corrupted. His drive was mainly toward financial security. After designing and building his famous Franklin stove he was encouraged to patent it. His answer was: he didn't need to do that; he had enough money to be secure for the rest of his life and he wanted people to freely benefit from his invention. However, an individual discovered that it had not been patented and proceeded to apply for a patent; this was not Franklin's intent.

For nearly 200 years industriousness was the driving force of America. Then in the sixties, with the introduction of the so-called New Morality, came what was called the hippie movement. The fundamental doctrine, if it could be so termed, was that Americans were being enslaved by a commercial system that demanded an unreasonable level of work.

Having been brought up by a family highly motivated to work hard, I was ridiculed by an acquaintance for the amount of investment I made in work. He tried to convince me that I was enslaved to a false doctrine of a capitalistic society and that all my hard work gave me no particular advantage. Then he began to explain how he was able to exist with the minimal amount of investment in physical work.

Part of his technique was to keep his personal income at a level in which he could take advantage of all the social entitlements. Playing him along, I got him to describe all the details. He enthusiastically shared with me all the techniques that he had developed. I next asked if he really felt that we were enslaved, to which he answered emphatically, Yes. I asked, Do you think everyone should follow your example, to which he responded, Oh, Yes. Then he realized I had been playing him for a fool when I asked, Who would be there to pay for your entitlements? He was insulted. His next words were, You're stupid, and he walked away.

The entitlement programs that exist are expensive and seriously abused. In one community in which I lived the government came up with a Work or Walk Program, which basically said that you couldn't accept entitlements unless you were willing to work. When confronted with this, some chose to move to a community with less strict requirements.

However, the disdain that the hippie movement leveled against the commercial system has not gone away. It has migrated into a hatred for small business, big business, commerce, industry, etc. We have a stimulus bill with a very poor concentration of helping small business and small industry which is the machine that keeps our citizens employed. Instead we have stimulus money going to ridiculous projects such as tunnels for turtles.

The cap and trade legislation is merely an open statement of this hatred. Question: Global warming? Answer: Ice Age. Evidence shows that the climate of the earth has changed dramatically throughout its existence. Recent evidence shows that possibly Chicken Little, of "the sky is falling" fame, had a better argument than what is being presented today. How much carbon does it take to absorb one calorie of heat? In developing this formula, we could formulate a more truthful evaluation of carbon dioxide's impact on our atmosphere. The Global Warming alarmists tried to use tree rings to prove their theory, saying that the increased width of tree rings was caused by global warming. However, let's reason on this: 20% of tree fiber is carbon, proving that carbon is one of the vital nutrients of tree growth. Could it be that the increase of carbon in the atmosphere explains the wider tree rings?

Interestingly enough the hatred for industry, hard work, and capitalism also mirrors the hatred for capitalism that the fanatic Muslims have. Let's not forget: The attack on 9/11 was aga nst the World Trade Centers.

As I have written, humans have the tendency to go to ext emes. An ancient king once described all of his accomplishments--which were many. He proclaimed all these hard works to be nothing more than vanity and a striving after the wind. He said since there is no way to avoid the final years of life ending in death, nothing he had accomplished would exempt him of that destiny, proclaiming that a live dog was better off than a dead lion. Continuing to expose the futility of life, he concluded that we should enjoy our hard work: establishing that for some people hard work with its accomplishments is not burdensome but pleasurable. In a free world working hard should be an established right.

The other extreme can be seen by some Island dwellers that live in an area abundant with nutritious food. The demand for existence is met on a daily basis with a limited amount of physical work, merely picking the produce from a nearby tree or procuring meat from the abundant wild life.

An honest and just person cannot proclaim which manner of life is right. An individual should have the right to work as hard as he wants while another has the right to work as little as he needs, providing that he does not impose on somebody else: This is called freedom.

Ask yourself, from which of these two groups would you feel the advancement of society and its conveniences would come? If we lived in a society that throttled ambition, we wouldn't have the convenience of something as simple as a flush toilet.

Not only did Franklin put a high concentration on industriousness, he also placed great emphasis on a sense of virtue. He made statements that a democracy would not last unless its population had virtue. The importance of virtue is demonstrated in the success of our Democratic Republic when compared to our efforts in Iraq. Our problem in Iraq and Afghanistan is the governments that we have supported and empowered are found to be riddled with corruption. If these individuals had had a sense of virtue instilled in them, this corruption might not have taken control. We cannot make this statement with any real sense of superiority when we take time to review what is taking place in our own government. Without question, the virtue that our country was built on has nearly disappeared.

In order for us to maintain our democracy, we need to understand the importance of these building blocks that we have just discussed: industriousness and virtue. To appreciate the unique dimension of what took place in the 1700s, we have to understand all the factions and the history of these people who made up America.

We speak of Franklin and his emphasis on virtue and industriousness while appreciating that he had a close association with Quakers and understanding of their virtue and work ethics. Also to be appreciated was the influence of William Tyndale with his desire that every "boy that drives the plow" would be able to have the knowledge and the availability to read the Bible.

The main fact that we are trying to establish is this: the uniqueness of the United States democracy took thousands of years to develop. Thousands of years ago the ancient Babylonians made the statement, Let the educated be educated, but for the rest, let it be taboo. For millenniums the masses had been suppressed and oppressed. Tyndale had great opposition to his desire to translate the Bible into the common man's language thereby making it available to every man. Eventually he was betrayed and executed.

Establishing the Bible as being a part of the building block of the United States is not a statement of divinity but that of fact. Contained within the Bible are the social building blocks of freedom and equality. So, viewed as an intellectual source, it can be seen how the Bible took its place with other books of the day, such as Marcus Tullius Cicero's writings on Natural Law.

The ability to read was a highly sought possession. The knowledge gained from this motivation was recognized by people coming from Europe who marveled at the level of education Americans had: One individual even saying that you could travel to the remotest area and meet an individual living in a log cabin and marvel at his knowledge of the world and the social structure around him. Americans of this time thrived on being informed. How sad it is that we today have students in college who don't even know who Benjamin Franklin was.

With the sixties movement and its rebellion against all authority and social structure came the attack on these values. Today we have shock jocks making it their business to offend these values. While they exalt their freedom and their lack of restraint, they are actually destroying freedom by failing to realize that they are cutting off the branch that supports their life. Reason: take away virtue from our government and you have corruption; take away industriousness and you have decay. With the collapse of democracy comes the collapse of freedom.

We have individuals that create great disturbances over the potential extinction of a small fish. There should be the same or louder protest over the progressive extinction of virtue.

WATERBOARDING

What Would George Washington Say

No one can say for certain what George Washington would say about this controversial subject. However, peeking into history we can certainly evaluate how George Washington valued the individual's right to human dignity. Let's view some historical examples of how George Washington defended the right of human dignity:

On December 22, 1753 Major George Washington, only 21 years of age, was returning with his party from an unsuccessful attempt at Fort Le Boeuf, the French headquarters, to warn the French commandant, Jacques Le Gardeur de Saint-Pierre, to evacuate the Ohio Valley. He was accompanied by a prominent frontier guide named Christopher Gist, along with several men hired to assist with the horses and necessary equipment. The weather turned bitter and the men and horses could not go on, but Washington felt compelled to continue cross country on foot, anxious to deliver the French refusal to Governor Robert Dinwiddie. Gist volunteered to go with him. Enroute they secured the services of an Indian guide. After guiding the two men several miles through the woods, the guide suddenly turned on them and opened fire. The shots went wild and while the Indian was reloading, Washington and Gist were able to overpower him. Gist immediately wanted to kill him, but

Washington prevented this, letting the treacherous guide go free.

In spite of the possibility that this would increase danger to him if the guide collected others and returned, Washington demonstrated his respect for human dignity by holding to his personal values in the face of Gist's opposing stand.

In the spring of 1754, Washington received a call for help from the Seneca chief, Half King, who had been with him at Fort Le Boeuf the winter before. The French were threatening the Indians and Half King expressed confidence that Lieutenant Colonel Washington would be the one to help them defend themselves. On May 27th the French scouting party of about 50 was surrounded by Washington, Half King and a handful of Seneca braves. The early morning attack took the French completely by surprise and while the French commander lay dying the confused French soldiers surrendered. Half King, whose father had been cannibalized by Indian allies of the French, longed for retaliation against the French for allowing this indignity to his father. It required a great effort on the part of George Washington to prevent Half King from killing and scalping this French party who were innocent of the grievous act done to his father.

These foregoing examples illustrate Washington's attitude on retaliation as a young man. Twenty-two years later, in the midst of experiencing the long struggle toward

America's independence, do we find his values have been altered?

The Revolutionary War presented challenge after challenge to the now 43-year-old seasoned veteran. Historical records tell how the prisoners of war from both sides were treated. Neither side, the British or the Americans, had adequate facilities to handle the vast amount of prisoners who were captured. The Americans solved this challenge by either paroling them or exchanging them for prisoners captured by the British. However, the British commandeered any buildings necessary to house the American prisoners of war. The accommodations became so stretched to the limit that the British began using ships, now converted into prison ships, to house the overflow. Between eight and ten thousand Americans died in the stench of these prison ships. The terrible conditions and treatment received by the prisoners embittered them. Those able to escape or be exchanged rejoined the American forces with renewed hatred for the enemy.

Washington might have been enraged by this inhumanity, and possibly was. However, he maintained the instructions issued to Benedict Arnold in 1775: "Any other prisoners who may fall into your hands, you will treat with as much humanity and kindness as may be consistent with your own safety and the public interest." Later to Sir William Howe, in 1776, he stated: "It is not my wish that severity should be exercised towards any whom the fortune of war has thrown, or shall throw, into our hands. On the contrary, it is my desire that the utmost humanity should be shown them . . ."

In his 60's, now President of the newly established United States of America, George Washington still maintained his value system in reference to retaliation. In the year 1793, Edmond Charles Genet, a newly appointed French minister, not acting under the auspices of the French government, in defiance of America's policy of neutrality in relationship to the French and English conflict, enlisted volunteers from the American citizenry who were pro-French to join forces with the French against Britain. He was so successful that thousands in Philadelphia threatened to drag President Washington out into the streets, overthrow the government and join France in its fight against Great Britain.

Finally, through diplomatic channels, Genet was replaced by Joseph Fauchet, who in February, 1794, arrived in America with an official request that Genet be arrested and sent home to France for due punishment. Genet appealed to Washington for asylum. Still after more than 40 years of serving America with all its struggles Washington did not compromise his personal value system by seeking retaliation for all the pain and anguish Genet's actions had brought upon him, but granted Genet's plea, knowing that in France he would have been executed. Genet settled quietly in New York, marrying the daughter of New York Governor George Clinton, living out his life until 1834.

Benjamin Franklin has rightly been called The Father of American Philosophy. Please take time to reflect the value system that this represents as covered in *Poor Richard Builds a Superpower*. This being the case, George Washington could easily be called the Exemplar of American Values. This is reflected in the results of World War II when America did not choose retaliation but chose instead to help Japan and Germany rebuild, supporting them financially and physically.

Reviewing these facts it is evident that Waterboarding could easily be an offense to George Washington's value system. Our intent in our writings has been to encourage people to reason things out comprehensively, studying all the facts and applying them accurately. Our fear is that the country has become so polarized that individuals confronting any reasoning in opposition to their personal point of view would immediately reject it. In our view the polarizing of this country is as threatening to its existence as the trillions of dollars of debt that now exists and is perceived to threaten the very foundations of America going forward.

Now let's move forward with our discussion of George Washington's view of retaliation. Note what he said to the President of Congress within the structure of the American government in the year of 1777: "Retaliation is certainly just and sometimes necessary, even where attended with the severest penalties. But when the evils which may and must result from it exceed those intended to be redressed, prudence and policy require that it should be avoided."

Now let's take time to extract as much information from these statements as possible to enable us to comprehend what George Washington would possibly say. From the foregoing examples, retaliation was an offense to his value system. And yet in 1777 he observed: "retaliation is certainly just and sometimes necessary . . ." So, too, with Waterboarding, which reason could say would be an offense to his value system; however, through reasoning on the foregoing quote, we could conclude that George Washington could say that it was "just and sometimes necessary". However, understanding his character we know that he would recommend it to be used with the strongest of restraint.

Unquestionably, Waterboarding could be viewed as an evil. The question is: Is it in excess? Does its evil exceed the evil results of not using it? The United States Military has recently caught Osama Bin Laden as a result of information attained by Waterboarding; in his computers have been found plans to attack the railway system in America. If we had not caught this evil perpetrator, these plans could have reached their fulfillment. And with certainty they would have exceeded the evil of Waterboarding.

Is there a benchmark to be used to determine when the evil perpetrated by an individual negates his right to be treated with human dignity? Would the death of almost 3,000 people meet that benchmark?

In reviewing the preceding information we could reasonably feel that George Washington would reluctantly agree to Waterboarding only under the condition that it was done with prudence and the strongest desire to avoid it if at all possible. The fact that only three out of thousands of prisoners have been waterboarded makes the favorable statement to the prudence used in the circumstances we are now confronting. The individuals who put this practice into application by all evidence used this means for patriotic purposes and not sadistic pleasure. To try to criminalize these individuals is truly shameful and un-American. We feel that George Washington would defend them by saying it was certainly just and necessary.

Many of the facts presented in this discussion were gathered from the publication, *The Real George Washington*, Volume 3 of the American Classic Series published by National Center for Constitutional Studies.

WE THE PEOPLE

It is becoming a very scary America

Millenniums ago when democracy was being discussed, the objection was that it couldn't last because people would find a way to bankrupt the treasury. Trillions of dollars of debt is scary. Is our democracy nearing its end?

Benjamin Franklin wrote in his autobiography about a group of people who went down South with dreams of establishing a new colony. The colony failed, starvation was rampant, and many children were orphaned. Benjamin Franklin was instrumental in setting up an orphanage to take care of these children. He wrote that the reason this colony failed was because the people organizing this venture failed to take with them the people with the ability to do the physical work.

"We the people" of America are the workers. We are the people who built America. We built it. It belongs to us.

When our representatives judge us by the clothes we wear, it is evident that they fail to recognize that it is "we the people" who built America. Barbara Boxer, in describing some of the protesters who attended the Town Hall Meetings, designed to influence people to support the administration's health reform program, expressed surprise at how well dressed they were.

"We the people" are willing to admit that we are not well dressed when we come out of the coal mines and the only discernible feature of our faces is the whites of our eyes. But, we are the people who built America. We built it. It belongs to us.

"We the people" are willing to admit that we are not well dressed when we are up to our knees in mud repairing a burst water main. But we are the people who built America. We built it. It belongs to us.

"We the people" are willing to admit that we are not well dressed when we have a calf coming breached in one of our cows and we willingly assist, ending up with manure smeared from our neck down to our shoulder. But we are the people who built America. We built it. It belongs to us.

Today we are burdened with two political parties that are nothing more than elitist country clubs. They have been stealing from the American public for decades. They have opulent affairs with price tags that "we the people" would be embarrassed to be a part of. At these affairs they feed on "pork" from the tables of "we the people", happily lavishing favors on their friends. Why not? It doesn't cost them anything.

Throughout history people with elitist mentality have been nothing more than parasites on society. Take these elitists and expect them to carry on the responsibilities that we carry in our everyday lives; they would proclaim some gross injustice that they would be expected to do these menial tasks since they perceive they belong to a higher order of humanity.

Years ago I knew a man who was on welfare and had been out of work for a number of years. When a friend of mine mentioned that this man had found a job I was quite pleased; now he had an opportunity to move forward in his life. When I saw this man I mentioned how pleased I was that he had a job. His next words were, Well it wasn't really a job; it was terrible the things I was expected to do. He thought it was unjust, so he quit. However, I knew a number of people who had worked at that same establishment for decades, pleased that they had a job.

This elitist mentality shows up in all levels of society. But "we the people" are still the people who built America. We built it. It belongs to us.

ANARCHY DOES NOT WORK

Speaking from the experience of having lived through the social shift that began in the fifties, was ramped up in the sixties, and gained strong momentum in the seventies, and now finding ourselves in our seventh decade of living we feel qualified to say that anarchy doesn't work.

We know an individual now in his fifties who at one time adamantly believed in anarchy; allowing people to do whatever they wanted was the rule he lived by. The result of th's lifestyle produced two children, a daughter and a son, with a woman who was not his wife, and a wife and son who suffered from this dysfunctional lifestyle.

The son borne by his girlfriend is a truly likeable, caring and responsible individual. His daughter, although there was some doubt if he was her biological father he accepted responsibility for her, unfortunately, testifies to the lifestyle of her conception. It is a sad thing when we understand the suffering of this daughter. From this dysfunctional lifestyle she was not founded with any real values. She abused drugs that negated the birth control she was using resulting in three boys, one having mental challenges and one having serious health problems. How sad that a young woman would lack such restraint as to inflict these young children with such burdens.

The movement that started in the sixties, demanding absolute freedom to do as one pleased with no restraints, has created a dysfunctional world. We often repeat the saying: The cage that keeps the canary in also keeps the cat out.

Seeing the results of this dysfunctional lifestyle, this man today openly admits that anarchy does not work.

BELIEF SYSTEMS

Some individuals view god-fearing people as a threat to their desire to live without restraint, referring to them as "god people". This derogatory statement testifies to their stupidity. The fact is, if someone's belief system is threatened by another, it is evident that their confidence in their own belief system is quite weak.

We at P. S. Norac view all belief systems as being equal. We are presently working on a theme that will take us back in time to before the "Big Bang" that will help fortify this reasoning. Watch for the announcement on our website: www.psnorac.com.

Everyone's belief system should be treated with respect and dignity realizing that one's belief system is an integral part of a person's being.

It is said that the Dali Lama was asked about his belief system in an interview. The questioner asked, If I can prove your belief system wrong would you change? To which the Dali Lama answered, Yes, I would. Tell me how you are going to do that.

This comment helps us realize that belief systems in the non-physical cannot be argued from a physical viewpoint. And yet there are many testimonies from the non-physical that cannot be positively understood.

At this time we encourage you, the reader, to broaden out in your reasoning and expand your point of reference when it comes to religion and belief systems.

One man most recognized for his brilliance and intellectual power was Albert Einstein who testified that he believed in God. Clarifying the statement he said, Yes, Spinoza's God. Spinoza was a Pantheist, believing that God was everywhere. There are many forms of Pantheism. Many Native Americans believe in a form of Pantheism.

Once while in a small store on I-25 in Sheep Springs, New Mexico, I opened a conversation with two lovely young Navaho ladies. The conversation drifted to their native traditions. When I expressed how beautiful I thought their belief system was they enthusiastically opened up, confident that their belief system was not being ridiculed. In reality, their belief system is beautiful: When they talked about Mother Earth I could feel the depth of their emotions. Even though I did not share their beliefs I could appreciate the value of what they had. One young lady said that her boyfriend was very engaged in the old traditions.

What a shame that we as Americans have diminished the Native American belief system. They should be practicing their beliefs openly inviting all to share in the beauty of what they have.

This aids in our understanding of natives in the jungles of South America: When they cut down a tree to carve out a canoe, they take time to pray to the spirit of the tree. In all honesty, having no foundation to deny their belief system, we should treat them with dignity and respect. This shows an appreciation of their interpretation of Pantheism.

The coming together of the Founding Fathers was a special moment in the history of humanity. Their reasoning was broad enough to view humanity's weaknesses and strengths and construct a form of government that is truly remarkable.

Many of them considered themselves Deists and were reluctant to support the religious dogma of the day. Jefferson instructed all to question everything, including the existence of God. He was accused of being an Atheist. He strongly proclaimed himself to be a Christian but felt that the teachings of Jesus Christ had been compromised and corrupted.

As Deists these men searched the literature and information that was then available, going back millenniums. The impression is given that they felt the God of Nature channeled information to these ancient writers. One of the prominent writers that they gave credence to was Marcus Tullius Cicero. Cicero taught the components of Natural Law.

There are varying viewpoints of Natural Law. One is that the God of Nature is benevolent and is moving mankind toward a kinder, gentler society. The second is that the Law of Nature is structured by the survival of the fittest. These two concepts have existed for thousands of years as demonstrated in Plato's *Republic*.

These two contradicting forces have been the focus of many discussions for as long as mankind has been in existence. One of the thoughts created from Plato's *Republic* was that the powerful do what they do and the weak endure what they must. And yet credit was given to humanity and its inherent need for justice feeling that society should be just. For the millenniums these two conflicting views have ebbed and flowed through the history of man. History testifies that the dark side of humanity has had a stronger presence. It is amusing that the originators of *Star Wars* portray Darth Vader being seduced to the dark side of the force.

Jefferson testified to humanity's inherent nature for justice and right when he stated that Common Law existed long before Christianity was introduced to the Celtic lands. During the Age of Enlightenment, the reasoning that there was good in humanity contradicted the thought that the masses were vulgar, with little value. Believing that the masses were noble-minded, the American founders trusted that humanity was capable of self-government. However, in their writings they expressed some doubts that the populace would live up to its potential.

Even with their doubts they moved forward to establish a new government based on the premise that all men are created equal. They testified to the necessity of morality and virtue. They believed that religion would play a vital role in generating these qualities.

As this nation expanded its territory, communities were established. Often the first concerns to be addressed were a school and a church, often in the same building, where the members of these newly established communities would set time aside each Sunday to reflect on spiritual matters. Sometimes a lay-preacher, other times a preacher, would use the Bible's highly diversified content of history, story lines and admonitions to create a sermon. This weekly gathering was very effective in establishing the needed virtue within the community.

Surprisingly the teachings of the New Testament are strikingly similar to the benevolent nature of Natural Law. As an example, the scriptural book of James strongly enforces the equality of men. In Chapter 1 verses 9 – 10 James writes: "But let the lowly brother exult over his exaltation, and the rich one over his humiliation." (*FIVO*) The lowly one was encouraged that he was equal to the rich and the rich one was reminded that he wasn't any more than the poor, they were equal.

Scriptures like this generated a healthy view of our nation's diversity, encouraging a non-posturing society.

When Jesus was twelve years of age his parents "found him in the temple, sitting in the midst of the teachers and listening to them and questioning them." - Luke 2:46 (*FIVO*) We have often wondered, could Jesus have been questioning the teachers about the writings of Cicero or other ancient writers? Could these sources have influenced the foundation of his reasoning?

Christian writers also established strong virtues in their writings, emphasizing the value of restraint and highly criticizing individuals who did not manifest this virtue. 2 Peter 2:13 speaks of these as "wronging themselves as a reward for wrongdoing. They consider luxurious living in the daytime a pleasure. They are spots and blemishes, indulging with unrestrained delight in their deceptive teachings." (*FIVO*)

These words could easily have been written by a journalist of our day who recognized the destructive nature of a life with no restraint. People who demand the right to be indulgent should also be responsible for the consequences; it should not fall on the rest of society.

Thomas Jefferson said of religion: a person could believe whatever he wanted provided it didn't take money out of *his* pocket. This type of reasoning could also be applied to those persons who demand to do what they want: a person can do whatever he wants provided it doesn't have a negative impact on the rest of humanity.

However Jefferson also said, sometimes you have to protect people from themselves.

The Founding Fathers were very aware of the dramatic nature of what they were proposing and at times it was viewed as an experiment in humanity: could mankind measure up to this responsibility? It was very clear to them that it was the masses that would be responsible for maintaining this democracy. In fulfilling this responsibility they would have to put n the effort to be well informed and have a working value system as a foundation.

This value system has existed for decades in the United States as testified to by the expression "the greatest generation". Before my father passed away I said to him that the nobility of his generation was passing away; his response was, It is. This was a generation that fought the Second World War. It was their value system and the conviction that democracy was worth dying for that gave them the courage, conviction and strength to endure the horrors of the battlefield. In their minds there was something bigger than their own being. So it is today: the ideals of the Founding Fathers are bigger than any one being. Washington and the Founding Fathers were confident they were doing the right thing. Washington invested his entire life for this cause, putting his own personal interests aside.

From what we have already presented we would like to help you make the connection of the opposing forces that we have previously outlined as ebbing and flowing throughout human history: The benevolent side of nature versus what we at P. S. Norac interpret as the dark side of nature where the powerful do what they do and the weak endure what they must.

Hitler moved forward his idea of a superior race controlling all humanity. And this seemed only right to those that perceived themselves as composing that superior race since they viewed the masses as being vulgar and pitiable. Hitler wrote in *Mein Kampf* that these inferiors had no right to complain because of their natural subordinate position. Nietzsche wrote *The Will to Power*. Hitler was not introducing anything new. Authoritarian regimes have existed from history's beginning.

The question remained: Could a benevolent society appearing soft and weak in nature measure up to Hitler's threat? As our character of Clarence in our story *LARRY* so eloquently expressed it: There was no defeating the spirit of America.

We did not feel that the hatred that was generated in the sixties and seventies could possibly advance because it had such a lack of sound reasoning and intelligence. It was quite an awakening when we realized that it had. There is so much material in print available that should have stifled that mentality.

We at P. S. Norac do not exempt ourselves from the statement "we the people have failed to stay alert." We, too, had narrowed our vision to the small circle of life that we were living: Being involved in the technical field, for Paul, and motherhood, for Sandra, consumed our lives. However, we felt that there had been a serious social drift, and decided, since we had such a love of books, we would turn our occupation to the writing of stories to expose the loss of the value system that we treasured.

When we realized the danger that our democracy faced, our writing shifted to how this could possibly have happened without our notice. We began to understand that the Founding Fathers had put strong confidence in "we the people". They had trusted that we would take what they had given us and nourish and develop it into a finer plane of humanity.

Would the Founding Fathers be proud of how we have advanced what they had started? Or would they feel that we were neglecting this special gift they had given us? How would they see the threat that is facing our democracy today?

First, one of the basic elementary facts that should be of great concern to us is that for millenniums it has been said that democracy as a form of government would not last because the people would bankrupt the treasury. How would the Founding Fathers evaluate our ability to confront this threat? Are we up to the challenge?

Second, and possibly more important, is the danger that the populace would not take the needed responsibility of being the fourth branch of government, requiring them to be informed and educated. We have allowed our politicians to push us around and abuse us, operating our government for their own advantage. We have been negligent in thinking that we could just hire surrogates to take our place. But they have not governed as we desired. Now is the time for us to do the heavy lifting.

Further understanding the value system put in place, the need for a virtuous populace, can be understood by one simple fact: You cannot legislate morality. Morality requires an education of the heart, a good conscience: an oft repeated sermon theme that was advanced in America. (1 Peter 3:21 - *FIVO*) The men and women who took this admonition seriously cannot be denied the place they had in building America.

The Bible demonstrated two value systems: morality by legislation and morality by the motivation of the heart. Before the Law came to be each one did what was in accordance with his own heart.

Moses, the writer of the Pentateuch, the first five books of the Bible, established for the nation of Israel a set of extensive laws: some truly beneficial and necessary, others offensive and burdensome. The nation became consumed with the application of law. So consumed that they actually neglected the intent of the law, namely, justice. (Matthew 23:23, Mark 7:9-13 - *FIVO*)

It is very interesting that in our world today justice has been perverted, in some instances, because of technicality of law. The concentration on law and application of law has become more important than the intent of the law, justice.

JOHN PAYNE

John Payne, a self-employed electrician, operated his business from a small farm in Pennsylvania. He had a good business; he was well known for being professional and knowledgeable. Many local manufacturing plants depended on his advanced skills enabling him to provide a comfortable life for his family. He could have expanded his business but he chose to keep it a one-man operation.

He and his son Rick had a good relationship. John and Evelyn were dedicated parents wanting the best for their two daughters and son. They strongly believed in teaching their children the value system they had inherited from their parents.

John's father and mother had been married 67 years before their deaths within six months of each other. Evelyn's parents had a long marriage of 59 years when her father died; her mother was still alive. John wanted so badly for his children to have the joy, pleasure and security in marriage he had seen his parents and in-laws have, as well as what he enjoyed with Evelyn. To him there was no greater joy than the joy he shared with the wife of his youth. (Proverbs 5:18 – *FIVO*)

John started taking Rick, now 14, with him on some of his jobs to advance his work skills. Rick served as gofer, going back to the service truck to get whatever tool John needed to complete the job. One day on completing the job at a dimension mill, John went to find the foreman to get his work order signed. He was told that he was in the lunchroom.

Entering the lunch room behind his father, Rick's eyes widened at the sight of the pictures on the walls: images of naked women with very little left to the imagination. When he realized his father was looking at him he turned his eyes away, but when his father walked on his natural curiosity drifted back to make further examination.

John made short work of getting the signature and soon he and Rick were back in the service truck. He turned the ignition on but then paused a minute and turned it off. This was something he didn't feel should be ignored, This was a good time to explain to his son the proper view of the pictures they had just seen.

Turning to Rick he asked, "What did you think of those pictures?"

Rick was clearly flustered; not knowing what would be the right answer. He didn't want to disappoint his father, but he had to admit he had been pretty curious.

John took the pressure off by going on. "Let me share with you something Grampa shared with me. It has been a viewpoint that I've lived my life by. I feel the result of it has given me a pleasure and a security that can hardly be expressed by words. You have to attain it before you can understand it.

"Grampa and Gramma were not embarrassed by their sexuality; they didn't flaunt it but we kids always knew they had a comfortable sexual relationship. My dad said to me, 'You know, we Payne men have a pretty strong sex drive. At least I know I do and I expect you do too. But,' he said with a chuckle, 'you have to know how to reign in your horses. Otherwise you can ruin the opportunity of having the best thing life has to offer: a good marriage.'

"You see, son, sexuality is a special communion between a husband and wife. It is private and exclusive. It can take you into fanciful flights of intoxicating ecstasy. And other times it can be common place and comforting. Knowing that it's exclusive, couples are comfortable to express their sexuality freely with their mate. Each couple should feel free to participate in whatever sexual practices they find they are comfortable with. They should keep these practices private and not share these with others. It is like a secret that only you two know or a jewel you want to protect and don't want to share.

"Before Grampa died he and I talked about the world we are living in now. He expressed his concern with the volume of sexual stimulus that exists in our world and wondered if young people would ever be able to get the proper sense and control of their sexuality.

"Rick, you've heard reports of sexual predators on the news. They are viewed as being abusers. They abuse young children by introducing sexuality in such a twisted way that many are never able to cultivate the beautiful relationship that can exist between a husband and wife. So it is with the excess sexual stimulants that young people are bombarded with today. It was Grampa's conclusion that this was just another form of sexual abuse. Nothing was more offensive to him, and to me, than an adult that would look at a child as a sexual object, not having any restraint.

"Pornography is just one of the stimulants that must be evaluated and put in its proper place, whether it's photographs, or the explicit romance novels that are so popular today. Males are aroused by visual, that's why you'll see pictures like back there in the lunch room. There is nothing wrong with sexual arousal, son, it's a healthy part of life. But it shouldn't be the occupying dominant part of your life. That's why Grampa told me you have to know how to reign in your horses. That's why it's so important for men to learn restraint.

"Remember seeing on the news the Islamic women who were required to wear Burkas? What do you think about that?"

"I never could understand that," Rick responded, now more at ease with the conversation. "It seems oppressive. Why do they have to?"

"Well," John responded, "because of this strong visual stimulation men have they feel the women should be covered from head to toe when out in public so that other men won't be aroused."

"Why don't they train boys to reign in their horses, as Grampa said," Rick said. "Then as they grow up it will be normal to keep themselves restrained and see women as people and not sexual objects."

"You see, Rick, your mother and I and your grandparents on both sides cultivated a special relationship. There is so much more than just sexuality in a good marriage. One of the things I remember and cherish the most is the sharing.

"From the time a little girl realizes the destiny of motherhood she creates an anticipation and a wonderment of the process. Men can never experience this special gift. How wonderful it is when a wife shares this miracle with her husband.

"From the moment of conception, the glow on your wife's face when she tells you that she is going to have your baby. Suddenly you are pregnant with her. Your mother and I have had that kind of relationship. You've seen her poke me in the ribs when I say 'when *we* were pregnant'," John grinned.

Rick smiled, "I remember thinking how odd. But I know what you mean."

"The morning comes when your wife presses her pregnant belly against your back and you feel this little ripple of energy as the baby kicks. You realize what you are feeling and you turn to your wife; the smile of pleasure she gives you, sharing that moment, confirms the special love that is found in marriage.

"Your mother and I have had some hard times when we doubted that we would be able to solve the problems, but we always knew we were in it together, we could depend on each other. You see, Rick, your mother and I feel that marriage is that special and we hope that you and the girls will be able to find mates that will enable you to know first-hand what we have known.

"But, son," John reached over and tapped Rick on the head playfully, "that's way in the future." He started the truck and pulled out of the parking lot. "Just remember, you can talk to me any time you want to."

DOWNTOWN TOMMY BROWN

Tommy Brown had become a local small town hero. His ability on the basketball court was talked about all over town. He was famous for his consistent three-point scores. The nickname "Downtown Tommy Brown" became a frequently heard expression.

A local radio announcer had originated the slogan: In a broadcast from the press booth during one of Tommy's successful games, the co-announcer made the comment "that was from *way* downtown" as Tommy's ball swished through the net, The announcer caught on to the phrase and every time Tommy was handed the ball there was a moment of dead air as the announcer let anticipation build. When the ball sailed through the net, the radio audience would hear a resounding "Downtown Tommy Brown" as the cheers from the crowd echoed over the air waves.

Eventually, at future games, the crowd took up the slogan. Every time Tommy scored a three-pointer the auditorium echoed "Downtown Tommy Brown."

Not only was Tommy good from the three-point line but he was also good at taking the ball to the inside. At six-foot-six he was a good rebounder as well. The small town team went all the way to the State championship on Tommy's shoulders.

With only twelve seconds to go in the game, Tommy's team was down two points. The opposing team worked hard to prevent Tommy from getting into three-point territory. Their strategy was to allow a two-pointer and push the game into overtime.

Tommy threw the ball to one of his teammates who had an easy pass to the basket. However, the teammate quickly turned and threw the ball back to Tommy. The opposing team was caught off guard and Tommy was open from the three-point line.

Before anyone could blink, Tommy let the ball arc over the heads of the players scrambling on the court. From the public address system came a resounding: "Downtown Tommy Brown" and pandemonium erupted. The small town team had won the State championship, bringing the opposing team's three-year winning streak to an abrupt end.

*   *   *

At eighteen years of age, Tommy was elated with the accolades he was receiving. His mother worked hard to keep his feet on the ground, but secretly he thought she was just being a wet blanket. He had won a basketball scholarship with free tuition for the first two years. His folks, having a bit of experience, realized that although they were off the hook for the first two years, they might have to come up with the last two years tuition for Tommy to finish college. Tommy felt they were worrying needlessly, but, being a good-natured kid and out of respect for them, he went along with their wishes.

When they suggested a summer job, Tommy was very agreeable. They started investigating their options. One of the opportunities that presented itself was that maybe Tommy's uncle Tony could find a job for him at the company where he worked. This company sometimes hired college kids for the summer.

Tommy's mom called her brother. She and Tony had a good relationship and had shared all of Tommy's exploits on the basketball court. Tony had played high school basketball and really loved the game. When the slogan "Downtown Tommy Brown" became popular, he couldn't help sharing the pride he had for his nephew with his coworkers.

* * *

When Tony introduced him as "Downtown Tommy Brown" at the jobsite, Tommy was welcomed with a degree of affection. The workers usually called him Tommy, but every so often someone would call him "Downtown."

Tommy was not an experienced physical worker. The most physical work he had ever done in his life was mowing the lawn. He hadn't realized the intensity of physical effort that was expected on the job. He quickly made it known that he was going to be above this physical work because he was going to college and get an education. Tommy didn't realize how offensive his attitude was until his coworkers began displaying a little bit of annoyance in his presence.

The job that they were on had five different crews working on the site. Tony was the foreman and Danny was second in command of their crew. It wasn't unusual for Danny to direct Tommy to do something. He directed Tommy to go to the other crews and ask to borrow a 24" left-handed pipe wrench. He was sure that one of the crews would have this tool.

Tommy took off on this errand. When approaching members of the first crew he made his request. After checking their tool boxes, they told him they didn't have one but maybe one of the other crews would. Tommy sensed something strange when he noticed they all had big grins on their faces.

Finally he came to the last crew. George, a veteran in the business, said, "Well, let's take a look." Reaching into his tool box he took out two 24" pipe wrenches. He laid them on the bench, the open jaws facing each other. He then told Tommy to take the left-handed one. Tommy reached for the one on the left. George interrupted him saying, "That's not a left-handed pipe wrench." Tommy reached for the other. George asked, "What's the difference between the two?"

Tommy looked at both of them. "I don't know the difference," he admitted.

George smiled, "Son, you've been sent on a fool's errand. There is no such thing as a left-handed pipe wrench."

Tommy was hurt. He had spent the last few years admired by people. Now he was being made a fool of. When George saw the pain in the young man's face he decided he was going to get one up on Danny for instigating this game. George affectionately said, "Downtown, you take this wrench to Danny and you tell him that this is the left-handed pipe wrench he sent you to get. Now, no matter what he says, you say that it is a left-handed pipe wrench because George says it is."

Tommy caught on. When he got back to Danny he played the game by insisting that this was a left-handed pipe wrench. No matter how Danny protested that there was no such thing as a left-handed pipe wrench, Tommy said that George had assured him it was. After a few minutes, Tommy grinned good-naturedly, admitting that he knew there was no such thing as a left-handed pipe wrench.

Traveling home with his uncle Tony, Tommy listened as his uncle explained why the left-handed pipe wrench incident had occurred. Tommy had annoyed some of the workers by indicating that he wouldn't have to do this work for long because he was going to college. This was the men's way of putting Tommy in his place.

Tony said, "I'm sure your mother has tried to teach you the same things your grandfather taught us. He always said,

'Do not exalt anyone, especially yourself.' Basically we should view everyone as equals. The biggest factors differentiating people are circumstances and opportunities.

"Now, Tommy, you've just come out of a couple of years being exalted as 'Downtown Tommy Brown'. Let's consider if you had been one of those players who never got off the bench. Would there have ever been a 'Downtown Tommy Brown'? Yes, you did take advantage of the opportunity and were successful. I'm proud of you for that.

"Would Tom Brady have gained the recognition that he has if Drew Bledsoe hadn't been injured? I'm saying this so that you can understand that circumstances and opportunities play a very vital part in life. There is really no reason for anyone to exalt.

"Now, Tommy, think hard. I'm sure there were other players on your team who spent most of their time sitting on the bench. If called upon, possibly they might have accomplished what you did, except they never had the opportunity. Just realize that: it required the opportunity. No one knows what the others might have accomplished if given the opportunity."

"Yeah," Tommy said, "my best friend, Sam, could have been one of them. When we play one-on-one he almost always beats me — at least 40/60. But, you're right; he was never really given a chance. We both made the team. I ended up as a starter. Looking back, it might easily have been him.

"Part of the reason for my success with the three-point shot was what I learned from Sam. His father, like Dad, had played high school and college basketball. Dad's hopes for the NBA were cut short due to a knee injury. Sam's dad had hopes of the NBA, too, but he never made it because he got stuck on the bench.

"Sam's father told him that some individuals have natural abilities without having to train or practice but for the most of us we have to develop a technique that can be established with practice and training. He encouraged Sam to develop three or four special shots that he would be comfortable with; practice until it became automatic, he said. He told him that his shot had been shooting from the corner. Anytime he had a clear shot from the corner it was automatic.

"Sam had taken a great interest in the three-point shot. When we weren't playing against each other, I wasn't even aware of this until later, Sam was home practicing. He started out practicing the three-point shot immediately in front of the basket. When he felt comfortable that he had the time and the arc just right he moved to the left and then the right. He practiced hours on end. Once he had accomplished this flatfooted, he converted it into a jump shot.

"Next, he developed some maneuvers in order to shake free from any defender. With his back to the basket, he would fake right and left, slowly working himself toward the basket. At just the right position he would take a giant step over the three-point line, turn, jump and execute his three-point shot before any defender would have the opportunity to gain position on him.

"This is what I ended up practicing, too, and as you know, I did gain quite a bit of success with it.

"One day in a game, Sam executed the same maneuver he had shown me. But he missed. The coach was upset that Sam would even try this shot.

"Because we were best friends, I could see this hurt Sam deeply; he was really discouraged. He was only hoping to show that he deserved to have more playing time. The discouragement moved to a near depression. He had hoped to fulfill his father's dream of playing in the NBA.

"When his father realized how serious the situation was he took time to help Sam. At that time I didn't know exactly what his father had told him, but it certainly changed Sam's approach to life. Sam's attitude then became anything for the team effort. He would do anything, even foul out, if it would benefit the team.

"Sam and I had been real close and it bothered me he wasn't getting much playing time. One time when we were alone I expressed my feelings. He said, 'Don't think it doesn't bother me, but Dad showed me that in life you have to adjust to reality and learn to love what you have, not love what you don't have.' Then he told me some of the conversation he had with his father.

"His father had been concerned that Sam had taken on the attitude that many in the community had: that he was a victim because he was black. His father reassured him that there was racial injustice; however, making that a focus in your life can stifle your ability to advance. His father also pointed out that the coach was black, too, which pretty much negated that reasoning.

"However, they both shared the observation that Stanley Zwicker was getting plenty of playing time. Even though he was a good player, he wasn't exceptionally good. In both their judgments, Sam was the better player, and I had to agree. The interesting thing was that Stanley's father owned Zwicker Chevrolet Sales. They both thought that the new Chevy the coach drove, although probably not an outright gift, had possibly been a sweet deal.

"Sam brought to my attention that both my parents taught at the school and that might have given me an advantage. Then Sam reassured me that this didn't make him bitter; he was glad that at least one of us had the opportunity. I had to think that he was the better person. Sam's father, mother and grandparents, as I look back, certainly knew how to adjust to reality."

Tony said, "That's exactly what I'm saying, your grandparents and Sam's grandparents, in my opinion, are the nobility of America. These are the people that confronted the reality of life and adjusted to it, realizing that they would have to create their own path. Your grandfather use to say, 'Life is not always easy. You're going to have to work. Life does not meet you half way. If you burden yourself that life is unfair, you'll never take the first step.' This is the attitude that built America.

"You know, Tommy, here on the job it's a team effort. You can learn from Sam's example of being a team player: whatever it took to advance the team, Sam was willing to do. You were hired to do the grunt work here; you don't have the skills that the others have acquired from experience. So whenever you see something physical that needs to be done, address yourself to it. It's all in support of the team."

Tommy understood the counsel and took it to heart: before long the others began to notice. Tommy smiled when he began hearing his nickname being used more frequently on the jobsite. He began feeling that he was part of the team.

Friday was payday and Tommy and Tony were the last to pick up their paychecks. When the secretary handed Tony his, she said, "You make good money. My husband has a degree and he doesn't make what you do." The intimation was that Tony, without a degree, should feel fortunate to make this kind of money.

Tony, being jovial and good-natured, grinned and responded, "Well, send him down to the jobsite. We'll teach him how to do work that's worth something."

It probably took a day or two before Betsy realized that she had been put in her place by Tony's comment.

* * *

The job was coming to an end and Tony's company had finished well ahead of schedule. Everyone was proud of the team effort that had accomplished this in nearly record time. The company had developed the practice of giving bonuses in these situations. When everyone received his bonus, Tommy was surprised, since he wasn't one of the regulars, to see he received a bonus as well. Tony reassured him, "You worked hard. You deserve it."

The next day they were at a new jobsite. Tony and Tommy went into the office to get the blueprints and plans for the new job. As Tony looked over the job plan, he muttered, "Damn", noticing the Chief Engineer on this site was Joshua Ingles. He had worked with Ingles before and they had a testy relationship. On that previous job, Ingles had just become Chief Engineer when the previous Chief Engineer had retired.

Tony apologized for his comment, "I just get so tired of working with these educated fools. You see, Tommy, you have individuals who are very intelligent. Problem is, people tell them how intelligent they are so often they begin thinking their reasoning is *divine* and if anyone dares to question or challenge them they view these people as *heretics* or *apostates*. This happened on a previous job where I worked with Ingles.

"When I pointed out a serious flaw in his design he became very upset and viewed me as not having the qualifications to question him. The flaw was going to create a serious cost overrun if we moved forward according to his design. I took it to my boss and, fortunately, he believed that I knew what I was talking about. As a result, my concern got the attention that it demanded. Other engineers concluded that my concerns were justified and the corrections were made before it caused a great problem. However, Ingles took it personally and our relationship was tested for the rest of the job.

"As you know, I learned my skills from my father, your grandfather. He used to say that no one should think they were so smart that they shouldn't question their own reasoning. In fact he insisted that I question everything. It is easier to make corrections in your head or on paper before you get to the jobsite. It saves a lot of time and money."

Tommy understood this and would apply this reasoning to his life after graduating from college. As a result, he would earn the reputation of being a very competent and thorough engineer.

As they were talking, the door opened and Joshua Ingles walked in. Tony's face was easy to read: he wasn't sure how this meeting was going to go. But Ingles walked up to Tony, held his hand out, and as Tony reached out to shake his hand, Ingles commented, "I'm certainly glad you're on the job, Tony." Tony was really surprised. He had anticipated a continuation of the animosity.

Later he learned that Ingles had been on another job that had serious overruns because of engineering designs. When Ingles asked one of the old timers if he had been aware of these problems, the old timer acknowledged that he had been. When questioned why he hadn't come to Ingles with this, his comment was, "Well, you didn't ask. And besides, my wife needed a new car, so the extra work served me well." Ingles had almost lost his job because of these overruns. He was thankful to have Tony on this job, knowing that Tony would be honest with him.

This was the beginning of Tommy's understanding not to exalt. Every member on the team was vital for the team effort.

Tommy went to college and spent his summers working with his uncle. Each summer he was greeted warmly by the regulars. He really was a nice kid. Tommy's hopes of a basketball career ended pretty much the way his father's had with a knee injury. His education as an engineer, as well as the hands on experience he had received under his uncle's tutelage, contributed to his success.

* * *

Tommy had just finished a large job as Chief Engineer when he got a call from one of his college friends. Andy Monahan said he understood Tommy was between assignments. When Tommy acknowledged he was, Andy said he had a project that Tommy might be interested in; the pay was pretty good. Andy had received a grant to do some research in establishing a historical record of global temperature using the study of tree rings.

Initially, Tommy thought this might be something that would be interesting. He told Andy that he would think about it and get back to him the next day.

As Tommy started thinking about the project he began to realize there were too many variables in the growth of trees to be able to establish an accurate record of temperature using this data. He wasn't even sure there was any substantial correlation between temperature and tree growth.

He began to feel deja vu: This time he would know better than to go on a "fool's errand".

WHY AN ALARM

As we have written, we started this journey on our website because of our concern for our democracy. We were not political. Yet the facts that were being revealed compelled us to try to express our concerns in the hope that others would become aware of the danger as we had, enabling all to take proper action. Personally, we feel that belonging to a political party is not patriotic in that it restricts individual freedoms, constraining one within the parameters of the party.

We made the statement in *We the People* that the two existing political parties are no more than an elitist country club that has conducted itself for the benefit of the power brokers, who with their capital, have in effect been running our country at the expense of "we the people". This is something that needs to be addressed by "we the people".

However, something of greater concern, an even greater threat to our democracy has surfaced. For this reason we wrote the book *AN ALARM WENT OFF When I Heard 'G.D. America'*. At this time we would like to take the opportunity to share some of the foundation of our concern.

Growing up in the forties and fifties, we were disturbed by the activities of the "Weather Underground", a movement that appeared in the sixties that displayed contemptuous hatred, even expressing the desire to do anything within their power to bring harm to the United States government and its capitalism. From our observations back then, this movement had not developed strong roots as it seemed to have disappeared rather quickly. However, then in 2008, we heard the expression "G.D. America" which shocked us into investigating the roots of that statement. As we expressed in *AN ALARM WENT OFF*, apparently that hatred, born in the sixties, had grown like a toxic weed infecting some of our universities as well as some of our churches.

In 1971 Eric Hoffer, an American social writer who was awarded the Presidential Medal of Freedom in February, 1983, wrote in *First Things, Last Things*, page 71: "Nowhere at present is there such a measureless loathing of their country by educated people as in America." How much more applicable that statement is today?

Join with us as we piece together how this all evolved.

In the sixties there developed a rebellious nature that wove its way into the fabric of our social uniform: resentment toward all authority. The 1955 movie "Rebel Without a Cause" displayed how this attitude was developing even then. It became socially acceptable to openly express hatred toward the United States government.

Some of this hatred was supported by historical facts that exposed atrocities carried out by the United States government: i.e., The Indian Removal Act of 1830. History cannot be rewritten: The treatment of the Native Americans was shameful. Davy Crockett, elected as a congressman from

Tennessee in 1826 and 1828, opposed the Indian Removal Act. The power brokers of the day, the land speculators, were in full support of the government's actions. They successfully used their resources to defeat his reelection in 1830.

In the expansion of its territory to the west coast, the United States was not completely innocent, either.

However, regretfully, let's be honest: no country on the face of the earth has existed without some shameful events in their past: Germany, Russia, England, China, and on and on. Two wrongs do not make a right. As we have written, justice travels a crooked path and once achieved does not return to repair the fractured pieces of the past. Now, we as humans can only secure justice for ourselves in the present. To attempt otherwise will only inflict injustice on innocent people.

The hatred of the sixties has grown. Its strongest roots are in individuals who throughout history have displayed themselves as having a manic narcissistic intellect. They have a sense of living above the rim of humanity, feeling that the masses need to be held in check and under control, their control. The masses are pitiable and incapable of self management.

Let's look to some of our social writers and see how they express this fact.

T.S. Elliot, *The Cocktail Party*. Edited by London: Faber and Faber, 1974, page 111: "Half the harm that is done in this world is due to people who want to feel important. They don't mean to do harm—but the harm does not interest them. Or they do not see it, or they justify it because they are absorbed in the endless struggle to think well of themselves."

C.S. Lewis, *God in the Dock*, edited by Walter Hooper, 2002, page 292: "Of all tyrannies, a tyranny sincerely exercised for the good of its victims may be the most oppressive. It would be better to live under robber barons than under omnipotent moral busybodies. The robber baron's cruelty may sometime sleep, his cupidity may at some point be satiated; but those who torment us for our own good will torment us without end for they do so with the approval of their own conscience."

Eric Hoffer, *The Temper of Our Time*, 1967, page 83: "A ruling intelligentsia, whether in Europe, Asia or Africa, treats the masses as raw material to be experimented on, processed, and wasted at will."

There are people who have a need to feel important. In their manic narcissistic view "they begin thinking their reasoning is divine and if anyone dares to question or challenge them they view these people a heretics or apostates." *Downtown Tommy Brown*, P. S. Norac.

From the sixties, this hatred for the United States and its people has grown strong among the intellectual elite. Being socially accepted into this group requires a like contempt. There are highly educated people who have reached extraordinary accomplishments and we have no intent to diminish them or detract from their due acknowledgment when we use the term "educated fools". However, as expressed in *Intellectual Power*, there are highly educated persons who due to inadequate training or natural ability lack a comprehensive approach and yet fall among those who are described as having a need to feel important. The frightful thing is they act on this need, to the detriment of others, as expressed above by T.S. Elliot.

Let's examine what is taking place today.

The thing that truly disturbs P. S. Norac is the attempt to legislate restraints on carbon emissions: supposedly for the benefit of protecting the earth and humanity. This reflects C.S. Lewis's comment above "...tyranny sincerely exercised for the good of its victims..." Although there are thousands of scientists who have expressed that this legislation is based on flawed research and reason, tyrannically the government is still pursuing it. This has the potential of costing thousands of collars to each family. This falls in line with the reasoning of manic narcissistic people, denying all other intellect and input. However, P. S. Norac has demonstrated their reasoning falls more in line with that of an educated fool.

As an example, trying to fortify their theory that carbon dioxide as a greenhouse gas is causing global warming, they chose to use tree growth to establish a temperature history of Earth. Any comprehensive mind would deduce that there are too many variables to have success in doing this; yet these individuals in their manic state took off like a hyperventilating Odie dog, of Garfield fame, making this study, not seeing or understanding the facts. Not only are there too many variables, but carbon dioxide is a nutrient necessary in tree growth. To a comprehensive mind it is inconceivable that they did this.

The tragedy of this is that the economy and security of the entire world is being threatened by individuals with this mental deficiency.

Should we continue to allow these individuals to control and impact our economy? Since the American people are sensitive to the environment, these extremists have used the environment as a means to bring harm to the United States. We at P. S. Norac, as well as most Americans, appreciate the advancements that have been accomplished in environmental protection as well as the exposure to practices that have threatened the welfare of many of our citizens. But we shouldn't forget that efforts that are being brought forth by the extreme left with their contempt for the American people and the United States government are not being generated from a desire to secure the ecology but from a desire to further their hate and contempt.

As a result, we get more than half of our oil from foreign sources who make no secret of their contempt for us. This has put us at the mercy of other nations and has weakened our economy and threatened our security. Imagine if we were getting most of our oil here in the United States the trillions of dollars that would be circulating within our own economy instead of enriching some already rich oil sheik. However, these extremists are comfortable with this since it brings discomfort to the object of their loathing.

Let's take time to examine some of the framework of their reasoning.

Many on the extreme left feel that there should be a one-world government and that the United States is the biggest obstacle to accomplishing this. It can be easily demonstrated how incomprehensive their reasoning is. Although one-world government might be manifest destiny, it is only a weak mind lacking comprehension that would not understand that this is not the time. When the majority of the world has little concern for human rights, the weakening of the United States and other countries that have made such advancement in human rights would result in an unimaginable tragedy. If China or the Jihadists prevail, imagine the suffering.

The left are very narrow in their view of the world when it comes to fuel prices. They feel that since many European countries pay much more for a gallon of gas than the United States, Americans are recklessly gluttonous and should adjust to a more European style of consumption. The Secretary of Energy, Steven Chu, revealed that he concurred with this view in 2008 when saying: "Somehow we have to figure out how to boost the price of gasoline to the levels in Europe."

Our entire way of life and the freedom we have here in the United States is supported by having reasonable gas prices. We are not Europe. We are dramatically different. We have many rural communities that are supported by having reasonable costs in transportation. The population is too sparse to support mass transit. The incomprehensiveness of these individuals could be compared to trying to fit Shaquille O'Neal into a uniform designed for Danny DeVito.

The extreme left also feels that there should be a more global even distribution of wealth. A great example of this is the proposal of cap and trade in which everyone would be given a certain amount of carbon credits. In third world countries, where they would not consume enough fossil fuels to use all their carbon credits, they could sell their credits to the industrialized world with the result that the global wealth would be more evenly distributed. If you take time to view this you will easily understand that the reasoning was constructed by people lacking comprehension. It compares in value to trying to use trees to establish temperature history. Anyone can see that worldwide this could never be enforced. The power brokers would position themselves to make great gain and the poor would remain neglected.

Richard Sandor, the brainchild of the CCX (Chicago Climate Exchange), proposed that trillions of dollars could be made from this Exchange. With Barack Obama's coming from Chicago it is not surprising that we would hear the statement, in January, 2008: "Under my plan of a cap and trade system electricity rates would necessarily skyrocket."

Realize that this is all based on the *alleged* fact that carbon dioxide is the greenhouse gas mainly responsible for the *alleged* global warming.

Speaking of "hyperventilating Odie dogs", on April 24, 2012, the breaking headline news was: "Alert: 'Gaia' scientist James Lovelock [who in 2007 predicted Global Warming Doom: "Billions of us will die..."] reversed himself: I was 'alarmist' about climate change & so was Al Gore! 'The problem is we don't know what the climate is doing. We thought we knew 20 years ago.'" (Published on You Tube by The Alex Jones Channel)

Why an Alarm? An alarm must be sounded! It is not the Democrats. It is not the Republicans. It is the intellectually weak individuals who lack a true comprehension of reality in both parties. Of this group, those on the extreme left, with their ludicrous reasoning, i.e., that carbon dioxide is an effective greenhouse gas, have damaged and are threatening the security of all humanity.

The highly polarized individuals cannot be altered; that is not where our focus needs to be. But by bringing out these evident truths and exposing how ridiculous their reasoning is, Americans, as they always have, will adjust responsibly.

Democracy demands restraint and responsibility.

This information needs your help to be heard: Get the conversation rolling.

Thank you.